CIVILIZATION

OF

THE EASTERN IRANIANS

IN ANCIENT TIMES

CIVILIZATION

OF

THE EASTERN IRANIANS

IN ANCIENT TIMES

WITH

AN INTRODUCTION ON THE AVESTA RELIGION

BY

DR. WILHELM GEIGER

VOL. I

Published by

Gyan Publishing House
5, Ansari Road
Daryaganj, New Delhi-110002
Phone: 011-47034999, 9811692060
E-mail: books@gyanbooks.com

Distribution Network
gyanbooks.com
India, USA, Canada, UK, Australia

ISBN: 978-93-6280-384-9 (SET)
ISBN: 978-93-6280-627-7 (HB)
First Published, 1885-1886

2nd Impression 2024

Printed at: Gyan Press, Delhi.

**CIVILIZATION OF THE EASTERN IRANIANS IN
ANCIENT TIMES (VOL.I)**
Author: DR. WILHELM GEIGER

CIVILIZATION

OF

THE EASTERN IRĀNIANS

IN ANCIENT TIMES

WITH

AN INTRODUCTION ON THE AVESTA RELIGION

BY

DR. WILHELM GEIGER

AUTHOR OF 'A MANUAL OF THE AVESTA LANGUAGE,' 'AOGEMADAÊCHÂ,' ETC.

𝔗𝔯𝔞𝔫𝔰𝔩𝔞𝔱𝔢𝔡 𝔣𝔯𝔬𝔪 𝔱𝔥𝔢 𝔊𝔢𝔯𝔪𝔞𝔫

WITH A PREFACE, NOTES, AND A BIOGRAPHY OF THE AUTHOR

BY

DĀRĀB DASTUR PESHOTAN SANJĀNĀ, B.A.

MEMBER OF THE GERMAN ORIENTAL SOCIETY, AND OF THE BOMBAY BRANCH OF
THE ROYAL ASIATIC SOCIETY, SIR JAMSHEDJEE FELLOW (AVESTA AND PAHLAVÍ)
OF THE SIR JAMSHEDJEE JIJIBHAI ZARTHOSHTI MADRESSA

VOL. I.—ETHNOGRAPHY AND SOCIAL LIFE

LONDON: HENRY FROWDE
AMEN CORNER, E.C.
1885

CIVILIZATION

OF

THE EASTERN IRĀNIANS

IN ANCIENT TIMES.

TO THE MEMORY OF

THE LATE

SIR KĀVASJEE JEHĀNGIR READYMONEY, KT., C.S.I.

THIS TRANSLATION OF

DR. WM. GEIGER'S

CIVILIZATION OF THE EASTERN IRĀNIANS

IS MOST RESPECTFULLY INSCRIBED

BY HIS AERPAT

DĀRĀB DASTUR PESHOTAN SANJĀNĀ.

CONTENTS.

CHAPTER III.

MENTAL AND MORAL CULTURE.

CHAPTER IV.

ECONOMICAL LIFE.

TRANSLATOR'S PREFACE.

THIS History of the Civilization of the Eastern Irānians in ancient times is a translation of a German work, *Ostīrānische Kultur im Alterthum*, by Dr. Wilhelm Geiger, of Neustadt, a diligent investigator and judicious writer, whose extensive and detailed researches into the history and religion of the primitive Zoroastrians have become the subject of intense curiosity and interest among Oriental scholars in Europe. A pupil of Dr. Friedrich von Spiegel for more than nine years, Dr. Geiger seems to have succeeded, at least partially, by his unsparing efforts, in bringing Science and Tradition into mutual harmony and co-operation. And the following pages embody the most comprehensive results of his searching and indefatigable labours, during the last decade, towards ascertaining, from the genuine but scanty references in the Avesta[1] as now extant, the moral, social, economical, religious and (to a certain extent) political conditions of the early inhabitants of Eastern Irān, the first spontaneous adherents of the faith revealed by the philosophic poet, priest and prophet, SPITAMA ZARATHUSHTRA.

By those who, being familiar with German, are devoted to Irānian studies, the original work, which is unique in

[1] 'Within this awful volume lies
The mystery of mysteries.
Oh! happiest they of human race,
To whom our God has given grace,
To hear, to read, to watch, to pray,
To lift the latch and force the way;
But better had they ne'er been born,
Who read to doubt, or read to scorn.'—B.

Avesta literature and is composed after the plan of Dr. Zimmer's *Altindisches Leben*, is already known and appreciated; and the favourable attention paid to it by European scholars is a sufficient guarantee of the great value of its contents. It is needless here to point out what fresh seeds have been sown and what useful fruits are in store for the votaries of Eastern culture; however, it may be interesting to recount in brief the services which our young author has rendered to students of the Avesta by his close and careful investigations.

He has shown us that among the civilized nations of the early East, the history of the Avesta nation[1], apart from its ethnological importance, lucidly illustrates the fact, so long questioned, that several of the germs of what is best in Western civilization are to be detected in the doctrines and institutions of Irānian antiquity. It should not be supposed that I mean to assume any extensive borrowing on the part of Western nations; my main object has been to express my conviction that the mighty Genius, Zarathushtra Trismegistos, who succeeded in promulgating the Mazdayasnian Faith throughout the East, was without question one of the most ancient promulgators of those ideas which have contributed and will contribute for ever to the moral and material welfare of millions of God's creatures.

The author's picture of private life in the early Irānian home is of the greatest value and interest. In the honoured position assigned to the *Nmānō-pathni* 'the lady of the household' by the *Mazdayasnān* we may recognise the original of European chivalry; while in the political assemblage[2] of the *Nmānō-paiti* 'pater-familias,' *Vis-paiti* 'lord of a village,' *Zantu-paiti* 'president of a community or lord of a county,' and *Daghu-paiti* 'prince or ruler of a country,' with the *Zarathushtrotema* 'the spiritual and temporal sovereign' at their head, we may equally trace the germs

---

[1] The early Irānian people as represented in the Avesta.

[2] *Hanjamana*.

of the constitution of a modern monarchical kingdom in Europe.

Dr. Geiger's exposition of the Avesta doctrine of the Soul reveals a fresh point of historical interest. It clearly proves that the Avesta nation had already attained the utmost degree of knowledge regarding the Spirit which men have ever reached, and beyond which it has been found impossible for them to proceed, after millenniums of labour, unless some new method of acquiring spiritual knowledge can be discovered.

Furthermore, we see from the section on 'Morality' that the mission of Zarathushtra was of the highest moral significance. The Avesta lore does not merely enrich the world in respect to spiritual thoughts and religious tenets, but its principal aim is purely ethical, to inculcate upon mankind that '*Righteousness is the best virtue for man from his very birth!*'

A far more interesting mode of usefulness assigned by the author to the Avesta consists in the fact, that, but for its preservation and scientific elucidation, we should hardly have had any information regarding the Eastern regions of Irān; that we should never have been cognisant of the extremely important fact that Eastern Irān was not merely the most primitive home of the Zarathushtrians but also the birthplace of their civilization ; nay more, that Irān was 'the true national centre, whose importance in the general sum of the national history was decidedly superior to that of the West.'

Such are the ideas which naturally strike us while we survey the field of our author's research. However, it must be borne in mind that its extent cannot compare with the wide area over which Doctors E. W. West and Fr. von Spiegel have spent their lives in search of truths hidden beneath the dense forest of Eastern science. What these *pandits* of Pahlavi and Avesta research have achieved, is well known among those to whom their works serve for

daily reference; but I cannot here omit to mention that
in the absence of any memorial on the part of the modern
Parsi Community to perpetuate their literary services, their
elaborate works will ever remain as monuments marking
an important epoch in the history of Irānian literature.

With these preliminary remarks, I beg to submit a few
observations as regards the translation :—

In this book, which is intended to meet the wants of
the general English-reading public, and more particularly
of the literary portion of the Zoroastrian Community, my
purpose has been to render into clear and simple English,
as far as practicable, such of the chapters as are, in the
opinion of the author and the translator, of general interest.
Thus the Chapter and Section that are named the first,
are the third and twenty-third respectively in the German
original. The version of passages from the Avesta and
the Veda is strictly literal; while in the body of the work
a free rendering has been given wherever a literal translation would have made the language rather uncouth and
inelegant. Italics are used for Avesta words, verses, sen-
tences, or paragraphs, sometimes for Vedic and Pahlavi,
sometimes for meanings of Avesta words and proper
names, and usually for those words that are intended to
be emphasized. The transliteration of the Avesta alphabet
adopted for this volume is given on page xxi. All notes,
expressions of agreement with or dissent from the views
of the author, and quotations written by me are enclosed
in brackets [ ] to distinguish them from the original notes
by the author. It is also to be observed that the translator does not hold himself responsible for all the views
put forth by the German writer as regards his interpretation of the Avesta religion.—In the translation a few
italicized words are inserted in brackets, thereby sug-
gesting any other view believed to be more certain or
probable. In order not to perplex my Parsi readers, it
has often been considered proper not to translate the

Avesta proper names but only to adopt their transliteration; e. g. *Mazdayasna* for Mazda-worshipper, *yazata* for genii, &c. It is to be remembered that other works of the author as well as of other German scholars are quoted in italics under their original German titles or abbreviations.

The Introduction, containing a brief though impartial and scientific exposition of the Avesta religion, was written in German, at my request, by the author, who has also kindly perused my manuscript before it went to the press and expressed his opinion thereon. He has, likewise, given his consent to several alterations, additions, or omissions as compared with the original. To him my special and heart-felt thanks are due.

I must take this opportunity of acknowledging my deepest gratitude to my German teacher, Mr. G. Reifferscheid, of Messrs. B. and A. Hormaryee, for his kind and voluntary instruction, as well as for the prompt assistance he has rendered me in the course of my work.

I must not also conclude this Preface without tendering my warmest thanks to Dr. Alois Führer and Mr. Principal Wordsworth for the kind manner in which they consented to compare my translation with the German original, and gave their opinions regarding it.

DĀRĀB DASTUR PESHOTAN SANJĀNĀ.

BOMBAY, *January* 1, 1885.

BIOGRAPHICAL SKETCH.

DR. WILHELM GEIGER, son of an evangelical clergyman, was born at Nürnberg, Bavaria, on the 21st of July 1856. In 1861 he entered the Gymnasium of his native town, where he completed his primary education by the end of 1873. At the age of 17 he became a member of the University of Erlangen, where, during several sessions, he attended the lectures and other instructions of the famous Professor Friedrich von Spiegel, with whom he had the good fortune to form a close acquaintance and to whom he was deeply indebted for his ingenious and delightful initiation into Sanskrit, Avesta, Pahlavi and Persian studies. He next visited the Universities of Bonn and Berlin, where nothing possessed such attractions for him as the Avesta literature. 'The antiquity of the Avesta,' says Dr. Geiger in one of his letters, 'its language and contents, the purity and sublimity of its religious and moral ideas, excited in me the greatest love and interest for Irānian research.'

By his first edition and translation of the 'Pahlavi version of the Vendidād, Chapter I.' (*Die Pehleviversion des ersten Capitels des Vendidād herausgegeben, nebst dem Versuch einer ersten Uebersetzung und Erklärung*, Erlangen, 1877), he obtained the degree of Doctor of Philology in 1877, and was appointed in the same year *Privatdocent* (lecturer) of Oriental languages in the University of Erlangen.

In the year 1878 he published the Pazend, Old-Bactrian and Sanskrit Texts of 'Aogemadaēchā' (*Aogemadaēchā: ein Parsentractat in Pāzend, Altbaktrisch und Sanskrit, herausgegeben, übersetzt, erklärt und mit Glossar versehen*; Erlangen, 1878), of which, says the author, 'I found two MSS.

in the valuable collection of Dr. Martin Haug, while for the third one I am indebted to the kindness of the late Professor N. L. Westergaard of Copenhagen.'

Passing over his numerous essays published in the 'Journal of the German Oriental Society' (*Zeitschrift der deutschen morgenländischen Gesellschaft*) &c., I may mention as his next publication his complete German 'Manual of the Avesta Language, containing a grammar, selections for reading, and glossary' (*Handbuch der Avestasprache, Grammatik, Chrestomathie und Glossar;* Erlangen, 1879), in which the author has judiciously given the words corresponding to every Avesta word, in the traditional translation, to show their importance and accuracy.

In the 'Journal of the German Oriental Society' (Vol. XXXIV. pp. 415-427, Leipzig, 1880) he next published his translation of the Third Fargard of the Pahlavi-Vendidād. Since the autumn of the year 1881 he has resided in Neustadt as a professor in the Gymnasium.

From 1880 to 1882 Dr. Geiger was chiefly engaged in elaborating his comprehensive history of the 'Civilization of the Eastern Irānians' (*Ostiränische Kultur im Alterthum, mit einer Uebersichts-Karte von Ostirān;* Erlangen, published by Andreas Deichert, 1882), of which a translation, beginning with Chapter III. p. 167, has been given in this volume.

In the 'Transactions of the Royal Bavarian Academy' our author published last year his excellent Essay 'On the Father-land and Age of the Avesta and its Civilization' (*Ueber Vaterland und Zeitalter des Avesta und seiner Kultur,* 1884), in which he goes on to prove, courteously refuting the ideas or arguments of his predecessors, that the civilization of the Avesta people points only to Eastern Irān and belongs to a period long before the existence of the Median and Persian monarchies. He likewise puts forward several ingenious arguments in support of the view that Eastern Irān was the birth-place of the state of civilization represented in the Avesta, and sums up his theory as regards the age of the Avesta in the following words:

'We begin with a *documentum e silentio*: The Avesta must have been in existence in a pre-Achaemenian, most probably in a pre-Median epoch. For (1) *no mention is made in the Avesta of cities famous during the Median period, with the exception of Ragha,* the high antiquity of which is thereby proved. (2) *The Avesta speaks of none of those tribes or nations that were commonly known at a later period.* Neither does it allude to the Persians, nor to the Parthians, nor to the Medes, but merely to the Arians. (3) *The Avesta contains no historical statement* concerning the battles between the Medes and the Babylonians, the rise of the Persians, the prosperity and downfall of the Persian Empire under the Achaemenian Dynasty, the invasion of Alexander the Great which agitated and reorganized the whole of the Orient, the kingdoms originating from the decay of the Empire of Alexander, the dominion of the Arsacidae.'

D. D. P. S.

b

ABBREVIATIONS.

Afr. for Āfringān, ed. Westergaard; *AG.* for *Alte Geographie* ('Ancient Geography'); *AiL.* for *Altindisches Leben* ('Old Indian Life'); Av. for Avesta; *Av. tr.* for *Avesta, Livre Sacré du Zoroastrisme, traduit du Texte Zend* ('The Avesta, the Zoroastrian Scriptures, translated from the Zend Texts'); *Av. üb.* for *Avesta, die heiligen Schriften der Parsen aus dem Grundtexte übersetzt* ('The Avesta, the Sacred Writings of the Parsis, translated from the original Texts'); *Bdh.* for *Bundehesh* (Dr. West, 'Pahlavi Texts,' part I); Bh. for Behistun Inscriptions; bk. for book; B.R. for Böhtlingk and Roth, *Sanskrit Wörterbuch* ('Sanskrit Dictionary'); ch. for chapter; *Comm.* for *Commentar über das Avesta* ('Commentary on the Avesta'); Cf. or comp. for compare; *E.A.* for *Erānische Alterthumskunde* ('Eranian Antiquities'); ed. for edition; *Einl.* for *Einleitung zur Uebersetzung des Rig-veda* ('Introduction to the Translation of the Rig-veda'); Essays. for Essays on the Sacred Language, Writings, and Religion of the Parsis, by M. Haug, 2nd edition by Dr. West; Essays (Yule). for Essays on the Geography and History of the Regions on the Upper Waters of the Oxus, in Wood's *Journey to the Source of the River Oxus*; *Expéd. scient.* for *Expédition scientifique Française en Russie, en Sibérie et dans le Turkestān*; Gāthās (Haug). for *Die fünf Gāthās* ('The Five Gāthās'); *GdA.* for *Geschichte des Alterthums* ('History of Antiquity'); *H.a.G.* for *Handbuch der alten Geographie* ('Manual of Ancient Geography'); *Hdb.* (Geiger) for *Handbuch der Avestasprache, Grammatik, Chrestomathie und Glossar* ('Manual of the Avesta Language, Grammar, Chrestomathy, and Glossary'); *Hdb.* (Justi) for *Handbuch der Zendsprache* ('Manual of the Zend Language'); Herod. for Herodotus; *I.A.* for *Indische Alterthumskunde* ('Indian Antiquities'); *Journey* for *Journey to the Source of the River Oxus*; *K.Z.* for *Kuhn's Zeitschrift* ('Kuhn's Journal'); Lev. for Leviticus; Lex. for Lexicon; Mkh. for Minokhired, ed. Dr. West; Mod. P. for Modern Persian; n. for foot-note; *Nationalökonomik* for *Nationalökonomik des Ackerbaus* ('National Economy of Agriculture'); N.P. for New Persian; Od. for Odyssey; O. Ir. for Old Irānian; *OKA.* for *Ostiränische Kultur im Alterthum* ('Civilization of the Eastern Irānians in Ancient Times'); O.P. for

b 2

Old Persian; p. for page; Pers. for Persian; Phlv. for Pahlavi;
P.M. for *Petermanns Mittheilungen* ('Petermann's Contributions');
Reise (Shaw) for *Reise nach der Tartarei, Yārkand und Kāshghar*
('Visits to Tartary, Yārkand and Kāshghar'); *Reise* (Vambery)
for *Reise in Mittelasien* ('Travels in Central Asia'); *Ride* for *Ride
from Samarcant to Herāt*, by Ch. Marvin; rt. for root; *Russ. Rev.*
for *Russische Revue* ('Russian Review'); Rv. for Rig-veda; seq.
for sequentia; Sir. for Sirozah, ed. Westergaard; Skt. for Sanskrit;
s. v. for sub voce; Tr. for Translator; Trad. for Tradition; *Trad.
Lit.* for *Traditionelle Literatur der Parsen* ('Traditional Literature
of the Parsis'); Vd. or Vend., Vsp., Yṣ. and Yt. for Vendidād,
Visparad, Yasna and Yasht, ed. Westergaard; vol. for volume;
Voyages. for *Voyages en Perse, dans l'Afghanistān, le Béloutchistān et
le Turkistān*; Wtb. for *Wörterbuch* ('Dictionary'); *Z.St.* for *Zoroastrische Studien* ('Zoroastrian Studies'); *Zddmg.* for *Zeitschrift
der deutschen morgenländischen Gesellschaft* ('Journal of the German
Oriental Society'); *ZdGfE.* for *Zeitschrift der Gesellschaft für Erdkunde* ('Journal of the Geographical Society').

TRANSLITERATION OF THE AVESTA ALPHABET ADOPTED FOR THIS VOLUME.

GUTTURALS.— ᴀ a, ᴀᴀ ā, ꝯ k, kh, q, g, gh, h.

PALATALS.— i, ᴀᴇ, (ē), î, āí, ch, j, (ɛ e, ē).

DENTALS.— t, t, th, d, dh.

LABIALS.— u, ao, ū, āu, (ō,) p, f, b.

SEMIVOWELS.— or y, r, or v, w.

SIBILANTS.— s, sh, sh, z, zh.

NASALS.— m, n, or g̃, ã, ñ.

INTRODUCTION.

In my history of the Civilization of the Eastern Irānians in Ancient Times I have characterized their religion in a few pages, since it would have been impossible for me to devote to that subject an equally detailed description of other features in their civilized life, without enlarging too much the extent of my book. But it may not appear superfluous to preface the English translation of some interesting chapters on Ethnography and Private Life (*Ostīrānische Kultur*, pp. 167–422) with an exposition of the Avesta religion—a subject of special importance to my readers amongst the Parsees—adhering to the principles which have guided me in the elaboration of the entire work. I shall endeavour also to describe the religion as plainly and vividly as possible, not merely according to its contents (*doctrines*), but also according to its spirit, its tendency, and its history. I shall further confine myself as closely as possible to the statements of the Avesta, abstaining from all allusion to later authorities as far as practicable.

GENERAL REMARKS.

With the single exception of the Israelites, no nation of antiquity in the East has been able to attain to such purity and sublimity of religious thought as the Avesta nation. Nowhere do we meet with conceptions which approximate so closely to a pure monotheism, nowhere is the notion of the Deity so free from human adjuncts, nowhere is the purely spiritual part of religion worked out with such exactness and preciseness. If this in itself is sufficient to awaken universal interest, it must undoubtedly do so far more powerfully when we learn that this religion is not the result of a long unconscious development, but, on the contrary, rather the outcome of conscious speculation. The Avesta religion was founded in Eastern Irān, and its institution is connected with the name of Zarathushtra. Zarathushtra himself must have brought it already to perfection, as the legends of the Parsees indicate, on the soil of Media, whence he must have diffused it through the eastern provinces. Every founder of religion works with the aid of materials acquired from history. The Christian doctrine rests upon the basis of the old Judaic religion, Mahomet attempts to unite both Christianity and Judaism, while Zarathushtra grounds his work upon the old Arian religion of nature, which the Irānian nation shared with the Indian people.

Upon this fact of a common foundation are based all analogies between the Zoroastrian and the Brahmanical religions. It is not my task to enter here upon a discussion of their resemblances; I only remark that, according to my conviction, their similarity has been frequently exaggerated.

It is certain that Zarathushtra, conscious of its tendency, radically altered the existing materials. The form and tenor of the old religion were altered alike, to such an extent indeed, that scarcely anything has survived from the ancient faith except some names and certain primitive ideas. The last remnants of the symbolical conceptions of nature have been, scantily enough, preserved in certain *yazatas*[1], like *Mithra, Srausha, Anāhita*. But the characteristic and essential portion of the religion, that part in fact which gives it its true nature, is entirely a new creation.

In the place of the vague and irregular nature-worship, there appears a solid, compact, consistent system. The tenor of the new doctrine was essentially moral. The ethical conception of the Deity appears in the foreground, while the natural is withdrawn from view. In the earlier religion one deity stood on the same level as another.

---

[1] [Angels or spiritual Genii presiding over elements or elementary excellences as well as over physical, abstract, and ethical ideas. In the abstract, anything that is excellent and worthy of praise in the moral and material nature of the Universe and that glorifies the wisdom of the Deity is a *yazata*. *Translator's note*.]

Each was in his sphere the most influential; even more, according to the requirements of the moment each could be esteemed as the highest and the most powerful of all. This idea found no place in the new doctrine. The multitude of forces and powers was concentrated in a single deity, who stands far above all other supernatural beings—into

I. AHURA MAZDA.

AHURA MAZDA is the Ruler and King of the invisible, as well as of the visible world. It is He Himself Who has revealed His holy religion to Zarathushtra. In His being Ahura Mazda is a spirit. His most conspicuous attributes are *Asha*, 'Holiness,' and *Chisti*, 'Wisdom.' Even His name describes Him as the 'Wise' (*Mazda*), and as the 'Lord' (*Ahura*)[1]. Extremely characteristic is the very address which constantly recurs in the Vendidad:

Ahura · Mazda · mainyô · spēnishta · dātare · gaēthanām · astavaitinām · ashāum !

'Ahura Mazda the Most Blissful Spirit, Creator of the Corporeal World, Thou Holy!'

Or more briefly only:

Dātare · gaēthanām · astavaitinām · ashāum !

'Creator of the Corporeal World, Thou Holy!'

With this we may also further compare the first words of the Yasna:

Nivaēdhayēmi · hankārayēmi · dathushô · Ahurahē · Mazdāo · raēvatô · qarenağhatô · mazishtahēcha · vahishta-hēcha · sraēshtahēcha · khraozhdishtahēcha · khrathvishtahēcha · hukereptemahēcha · ashāt · apanôtemahēcha · hudhāomanô · vouru-rafnağhô · yô · nô · dadha · yô · tatasha · yô · tuthruyē · yô · mainyush · spentōtemô.
(Yasna I, 1.)

---

[1] ⟶)+(ư⟵ (Ahura) = Skt. *asura* from rt. *ah*, 'to be.' *Mazdāo* is very differently explained; but the idea of wisdom indisputably underlies the name.

'I declare it, and I venerate the Creator, Ahura Mazda, the Brilliant, Radiant, the Greatest, Best, Most Beautiful, Mightiest, Wisest, Best-formed, Most Exalted through Holiness, Giving Profusely, Granting Much Bliss, Who created us, Who prepares us, Who maintains us, the Most Blissful Spirit.'

In the above are given the principal attributes that constitute the nature of Ahura Mazda.

He is a Spirit. He is not anthropomorphous. Though He is represented as speaking, thinking, and acting, no passage of the Avesta authorizes us to assume that Ahura Mazda was thought to exist in any definite visible form. Surely His form could not be compared with that of the human body. The expression 'Best-formed,' *hukereptema-hę*, must not be pressed too far, and if, on the other hand, mention is made of 'the most beautiful body of Mazda,' *Sraęshtãm · at · tôi · kehrpem · kehrpãm · avaędayęmahi Mazdã Ahurā*[1], we must regard such language as symbolical. For the sun (*hvare*) is expressly spoken of as 'the body of Mazda[2],' and no one could well affirm that this designation should be understood literally. Light is indeed of the essence of Ahura; and hence the sun as the source of perceptible light renders Mazda, so to say, visible Himself.

So early as in the Gāthās Ahura Mazda is very frequently apostrophized as the Blissful Spirit[3]. Anthropomorphisms are exceedingly rare, rarer still perhaps than with the Jehovah of the ancient Jews. When Spentā Ārmati, the protectress of the earth and the genius of *submissive devotion*, is called the daughter of Mazda, it can scarcely be looked upon as a proof of anthropomorphism. It is merely a symbolical expression, which is intended to mean that all good on earth, as also piety of heart, originates from Ahura.

Let us only consider the passage itself:

*At · fravakhshyā · ağheu*sh · *ahyā · vahishtem ·
Ashāt · hachā · Mazdāo · vaędā · yē · ïm · dāt ·*

---

[1] Yasna LVIII, 8; XXXVI, 6.   [2] Yasht VI, 6.
[3] Yasht XVII, 2; Vendidad XIX, 6.

*Ptarēm · vaghēu*sh · *verezyantô · managhô ·*
*At · hôi · dugedā · hu*shk*yaothanā · ārmaiti*sh [1].

'Announce will I the best in this world,
Through Piety I know (Thee), O Mazda, Who created it,
Thee, the Father of the pious and zealously active Mind;
But His daughter is the *Well-behaving Humility.*'

The same can be said of the following passage :

*Pita · tẹ · yô · Ahurô · Mazdāo · yô · mazi*sht*ô · yazata nām · yô · vahi*sht*ô · yazatanām · māta · ārmaiti*sh *· spẹnta · brāta · tẹ · yô · vaghu*sh *· sraoshô · ashyô · rash-nu*shch*a · berezô* [2].

'Thy Father, O Ashi! is Ahura Mazda, the Greatest and Best amongst the Yazatas; thy mother is Spentā Ārmati, thy brother the good Srausha the Holy and Rashnu the Exalted.'

Mention is also made of spouses of Ahura Mazda. Here the names of the spouses show that we have again to deal with a metaphorical mode of expression. The figure is meant to symbolize their close union, their inseparable connection. Hence Ashi and Ārmati may be very appropriately designated in a poetical manner as the spouses of Mazda, while they are elsewhere called his daughters, by a somewhat different figure of speech. Besides the above, we meet with other abstract ideas, such as Blessing, Plenty, and Salvation (*ishem, āzûitîm, frasastîm* [3]), which are also the names of the wives of Ahura.

With particular emphasis fire, the importance of which in the *cultus* of the Mazdayasnān need not be pointed out, is invoked as the son of Ahura Mazda (*ātaremcha · Ahurahẹ · Mazdāo · puthrem* [4]). It is the holiest and purest element, that which diffuses light. As such it appears to be the earthly and visible image of the Deity, Who is Himself light and absolute purity. A conception just as deep under-

---

[1] Yasna XLV, 4.
[2] Ys. XXXVIII, 2.
[3] Yasht XVII, 16.
[4] Ys. II, 4.

lies the idea that the sun is the eye of Mazda[1]. This must not be understood too materially, for that would clash essentially with the spirit of the Avesta religion in general. Mazda has his throne above in Heaven, whence He looks with His radiant eye, the bright sun, down upon the earth. His look scares away the darkness, and the demons who lodge in darkness; He also penetrates into the souls of men, and perceives what is good and what is evil in them. Similarly, in the German proverb, 'The sun brings it to light,' the sun symbolizes the Divine Omniscience, which discovers every crime.

Ahura Mazda is a spirit. He is a superhuman and transcendent being. His attributes are therefore chiefly spiritual ones. He is the Wise, the Omniscient, the Holy or Pure, the Benign.

In the first Yasht, which is dedicated to Ahura Mazda, which describes His nature, His innumerable epithets are cited. Here He is called Wisdom (*Chisti*sh) simply, or the Wise one (*Chistivāo*[2]). He is named the Observer (*Spashta*[3]) Who sees all, the Infallible one (*Adhavi*[4]) Whom nobody can deceive and impose upon. So, too, as early as in the Gāthās:

Nōit · diwzhaidyāi · vīspā-hishas · Ahurō[5].

'Ahura is not to be deceived, Who has created all.'

*Yā · frasā · avīshyā · yā · vā · Mazdā · peresaitę · tayā ·
Yē · vā · kasēush · aęnaghō · ā · mazishtām · ayamaitę ·
bûjem ·
Tā · chashmēng · thwisrā · hārô · aibî · ashā · aibî · vaę-
nahî · vîspā*[6].

'The public counsels which take place,
O Mazda Ahura, and the secret ones,
Who imposest the highest penalty for a small one;

---

[1] Ys. I, 11 [*Hvarecha · kh*sha*ętahę · aurvataspahę · dôithrahę · Ahu-rahę · Mazdāo*].

[2] Also *Khratu*sh and *Khratumāo*, Yt. I, 7, 8; also *Zhnāta*, Yt. I, 12.   [3] Yt. I, 13; *Vispa-hishas*, Yt. I, 8.

[4] *Adhavi*, from the root *dab, dav*, Yt. I, 14.

[5] Ys. XLV, 4.   [6] Ys. XXXI, 13.

Upon all this Thou lookest as a warder with eyes radiant with holiness.'

Ahura Mazda is also identified with the Best Holiness, with *Asha-vahishta*[1]. 'Holy' and 'Pure' are His constant epithets. All is good in Him, as also only goodness issues from Him. And as the believers in Mazda shall imitate Him, so also they, as the 'pure' or 'holy,' are styled the *Ashavānō*.

But Mazda is also the *Benign*. He is called the Good-giver (*Hudhānu*sh or *Hudhāoman*[2]). He is not wholly in-accessible to men; the prayers of the pious ascend to Him, and are heard by Him. And there are as many visible earthly gifts for which He is implored, as there are spiritual ones, such as piety and good-mindedness.

> *Mazdāo · dadāt · Ahurô · haurvatô · ameretātaschā ·*
> *Bûrôish · ā · ashaqyāchā · qā-paithyāt · khshathrahyā ·*
>   *sarô ·*
> *Vaĝhēush · vazdvarē · manaĝho · yē · hôi · mainyû · shk-*
>   *yaothanāishchā · urvathô*[3].

'May Ahura Mazda grant well-being and long-life,
  Protection of profuse piety and of mastery over one's self,
  Power of the good-mind to him, who is devoted to Him in thought and deed.'

> *Hvô · zî · ashā · spentô · erekhtem · vîspôibyô ·*
> *Hârô · mainyû · ahûbish · urvathô · Mazdā*[4].

'Thou art in holiness the Blissful, Who turns away mischief,
  Of all beings, Thou, O Spirit Mazda!'

Though Mazda is thus a spirit, still he stands in close correlation to the world. He is *its Creator, its Preserver*, and *Ruler (Dātar, Pātar, Ise-khshathra).*

I have under the section 'The World' given the transla-tion of a sublime Hymn, which praises the omnipotence and

---

[1] Yt. I, 7, 12. [2] Yt. I, 15; Ys. I, 1.
[3] Ys. XXXI, 21; comp. also Ys. XXXIII, 10.
[4] Ys. XLIV, 2.

wisdom of the Creator [1]. I scarcely know of a passage of
the Avesta which can equal it in poetical beauty, though
the idea that the entire world, and what is in it, originates
from Mazda, and that He has bestowed upon man spiritual
graces, is also frequently expressed in other passages.
Hence the numerous appellatives, such as Bliss (*Spānô*)
simply, or the Blissful (*Spanağhvat, Sevishta*), the Creator
(*Dātare*), the Supporter or Preserver (*Thrātar, Pāyu*[2]).
Thus Ahura existed even from the beginning, before the
world came into existence, which He had called into being
by an act of His will, and thus He exists immutable and
unchangeable for all eternity.

*Yastā · maṇtā · pouruyô · raochēbish · rôithven · qāthrā ·
Hvô · khrathwā · dāmish · ashem · yā · dārayat · vahish-
tem · manô ·
Tā · Mazdā · mainyū · ukhshyô · yē · ā · nûremchît ·
Ahurā · hāmô ·
At · thwā · mēg̊hî · paourvîm · Mazdā · yazûm · stôi ·
managhā ·
Vag̊hēush · patarem · managhô · hyat · thwā · hēm · chash-
mainî · heṇgrabem ·
Haithîm · ashahyā · dāmîm · ag̊hēush · Ahurem · shkyao-
thanaęshû* [3].

'He who first conceived the thought: With stars may
    the effulgent space be clothed!
He through His insight created the Law (the system
    of the world) whereby He supports the pious;
Thou allowest it to thrive, O Spirit Mazda, Who art
    the same even now.
Thee chiefly I regard as Him Who must be praised in
    the mind by men.
Thee as the Father of the pious, for I perceived Thee
    with mine eyes
As the (true) Founder of the world's system, as the
    Lord (Commander) of the world through Thy energy.'

---

[1] Ys. XLIV, 3–5.   [2] Yt. I, 7, 8, 11.
              [3] Ys. XXXI, 7–8.

But not merely are the world and its order His work, it is also said of Him :

Yê·'dāt·manô·vahyô·Mazdā·ashyaschā·
*Hvo-daęnām·*shkyaothanāchā·*vachaĝhāchā*[1].

'Who created the good and holy mind,
And the doctrine, together with the prayers and the works of offering.'

Fire is again most particularly mentioned as the creation and gift of grace of Mazda :

At·thwā·mēṇghāi·takhmemchā·speṇtem·Mazdā·
Hyat·tā·sastā·yā·tû·hafshî·avāo.
Yāo·dāo·ashísh·dregvāitę·ashāunaęchā.
Thwahyā·garemā·āthrô·ashā-aojaĝhô[2].

'I will consider Thee, O Mazda, as the strong and the Blissful,
In order that by Thy hand, with which Thou createst help,
The benedictions (might be granted to me) which Thou gavest to the pious as also to the impious
Through the warmth of Thy Fire, the All-Powerful.'

And how Mazda rules over all from the beginning of the world to its end, is expressly described in the following stanza :

Speṇtem·at·thwā·Mazdā·mēĝhî·Ahurā·
*Yyat·thwā·aĝhēu*sh·*zāthôi·daresem·paourvîm·*
*Hyat·dāo·*shkyaothanā·*mîzdavān·yāchā·ukhdhā·*
Akêm·akāi·vaĝuhîm·ashîm·vaĝhavę·
Thwā·hunarā·dāmôish·urvaęsę·apēmę[3].

'I thought of Thee as the Blissful, O Mazda,
For I saw Thee as the First at the origin of the world,
For Thou didst create the works of offering, promising reward for them and prayers,
And evil for the vicious, but good blessing for the good,
Through Thy Glory at the dissolution of the world.'

This leads us finally to one power of Ahura Mazda not

---

[1] Ys. XLVIII, 4.   [2] Ys. XLIII, 4.   [3] Ys. XLIII, 5.

xxxii   CIVILIZATION OF THE EASTERN IRĀNIANS.

discussed above, which He exercises in conformity with
His Holiness and Justice, and by means of His Omniscience and Infallibility: He is the God, Who rewards
the good and punishes the bad, not only in this world
in which He sends blessing or misfortune to men, but
also at the end of this world, in the next one.

The idea of eternal retribution is so often expressed in the
Avesta, that it is not necessary to notice it here more particularly. In the section treating of 'Immortality' and the next
world, several such passages relating thereto will be found
translated.

We thus know that Ahura Mazda is a spiritual being.
He is *Wise*, *Holy*, *Just*, and *Benign*. He has created the
whole world, so far as it is itself good and faultless, but He
also supports and governs it. Before the beginning of the
world He existed, and will outlast it. He is the Champion of the Powers of Light against Evil, and will bring
victory at the end of the conflict.

In this sublime conception of the Avesta, Ahura Mazda
undoubtedly stands far above the deities of the Vedic Pan-
theon. As already mentioned, only the Jehovah of the
ancient Jews may be compared to Him. But however ob-
vious the similarity between the God of Israel and the God
of the Mazdayasna may be, still I reject entirely the assumption that the Avesta people have borrowed from the Jews.
Upon the Irānian soil a narrowly-confined nation has, independently and of itself, attained that high conception of
God, which, with the exception of the Jews, was never
attained by any Arian, Semitic, or Tūrānian tribe[1].

---

[1] ['Spitama Zarathushtra's conception of Ahuramazda as the
Supreme Being is perfectly identical with the notion of *Elohim*
(God) or *Jehovah* which we find in the books of the Old Testa-
ment. Ahuramazda is called by him "the Creator of the earthly
and spiritual life, the Lord of the whole universe, in whose hands
are all the creatures." He is the light and source of light; he is
the wisdom and intellect. He is in possession of all good things,
spiritual and worldly, such as the good mind, immortality, health,
the best truth, devotion and piety, and abundance of every earthly
good. All these gifts he grants to the righteous man, who is

Ahura Mazda does not stand alone. He is also the highest amongst all the spirits; thus He is surrounded by a body of genii or angels, who assist Him in His work, or to whom certain spheres of activity are assigned. The mightiest and most venerable amongst them are

II. THE AMESHA SPENTA.

There are six Amesha Spenta. Their name signifies 'the blissful immortal.' The most significant appellatives which they receive are *yavaę-ji*, 'living in eternity,' and *yavaę-su*, 'blessing in eternity.' Besides they are also called *hukhshathra, hudāo*, 'well-ruling, granting good,' or *hvare-hazaosha*, 'of one will with the sun[1].' The last name may indicate that it is their task to create light like the sun. Light however is the symbol of moral purity. The functions of the Amesha Spenta are also peculiar to the Zoroastrian system of religion. They have been compared with the Vedic Adityas, but without any valid reason. I do not see any cause why a founder of religion like Zarathushtra should not independently have arrived at the idea of joining with the Almighty a circle of angels or ministering spirits. The names of the Amesha Spenta are perfectly clear. They are abstract and indeed mostly ethical conceptions. They are called :

1. *Vohu-manō,* the good mind.
2. *Asha-vahishta,* the best holiness.
3. *Khshathra-varya,* the desirable sovereignty.
4. *Spentā-Ārmati,* humble sense.
5. *Harvatāt,* well-being, happiness, health.
6. *Amertāt,* long-life, immortality.

The abstract meaning is everywhere so clearly per-

upright in thoughts, words, and deeds. As the ruler of the whole universe, he not only rewards the good, but he is a punisher of the wicked at the same time (see Yas. XLIII, 5). All that is created, good or evil, fortune or misfortune, is his work (Yas. XLVIII, 4, and LI, 6).' *Vide* M. Haug, *Essays,* p. 302.—*Tr. note.*]

[1] Ys. XXXIX, 3: II, 2; Yt. X, 51; XIII, 92.

ceptible, that by that alone the distinct position of the Amesha Spenta is established, if contrasted with the genii of other religious systems. The double meaning is so marked, that we might really translate in a double way many verses of the Gāthās, in which the names of the Amesha Spenta occur, at one time in the abstract, and at another in the personal signification of their names.

In the Gāthās themselves, Ahura Mazda is frequently invoked together with the Amesha Spenta, particularly with Vohu-manō, Asha, Khshathra, and Ārmati.

*Yē · vāo · Ashā · ufyānṫ · manaschā · vohū · apaourvîm ·
Mazdāmchā · Ahurem · yaꝗibyô · khshathremchā · agzha-
onvamnem ·
Varedaitī · Ārmaiti̇sh · ā · môi · rafedhrāi · zaveñg · jasatā* [1].

'You both will I praise, Asha and Vohu-manō the incomparable,
And Mazda Ahura, and together with them the imperishable Khshathra,
And the blessing-dispensing Ārmati : come hither at my invocation!'

*Dāidî · ashā · tām · ashîm · vaḡhéush · āyaptā · manaḡhô ·
Dāidî · tû · ārmaitî · vishtāspāi · aꝗshem · maibyāchā ·
Dāostû · Mazdā · khshayāchā · yā · vē · māthrā · srevîmā ·
rādāo* [2].

'Grant, O Asha! this blessing, together with the gift of grace of Vôhu-manō ;
Grant Thou, O Ārmati! to Vishtāspa his wish and to me ;
Grant Thou, O Mazda! Thou Powerful, that we may proclaim your words as channels of grace!'

*Ahmāichā · Khshathrā · jasat · manaḡhā · vohû · ashāchā ·
At · kchrpem · utayûiti̇sh · dadāt · ārmaiti̇sh · ānmā* [3].

'But towards us He (Mazda) turned, together with Khshathra, Vohu-manō, and Asha ;
Strength created the body, but Ārmati gave prosperity.'

---

[1] Ys. XXVIII, 4.   [2] Ys. XXVIII, 8.   [3] Ys. XXX, 7.

From these examples we observe that Mazda and the first four Amesha Spenta are indeed the most ancient constituent parts of the Zoroastrian system, that these genii form, so to say, the basis upon which the whole structure rests. Or can it be a mere accident that just the most sensuous and the most humanly-conceived *yazatas*, Mithra and Anāhita, are scarcely mentioned in the Gāthās!

Let us now examine each individual Amesha Spenta. Each of them has a definite field of activity in the visible world also, while Ahura holds the supreme direction of all that exists. To Vohu-manō is entrusted the protection of herds; to Asha, that of fire; to Khshathra, that of metals; to Ārmati, the guardianship of the earth; lastly, to the genii, Harvatāt and Amertāt, the protection of waters and of plants. The intrinsic relation between the abstract signification of each individual name and the material functions, which the respective genius always discharges, may, I think, be further proved. Such proof I shall now endeavour to furnish.

That VOHU-MANŌ, *the good-mind*, is also the protector of herds, is explained from the social circumstances under which the Zoroastrian religion developed itself in the very oldest periods. At that time a great portion of the people still led a nomadic life. Others had established permanent settlements; they cultivated the fields, and attended to the rearing of cattle. Amongst the latter the new doctrine found access; *they* were the 'pious' and 'good-minded ones.' The life of a good mind was at the same time the life of peaceful herdsmen and peasants. We have passages in the Gāthās where we may translate Vohu-manō directly by 'herds:'

> *At · hî · ayāo · fravaretā · vāstrîm · aqyāi · fshuyaṇtem ·*
> *Ahurem · ashavanem · vaghēush · fshēnghî · managhô ·*
> *Noît · Mazdā · avāstryô · davāschinā · humaretôish ·*
> *bakhsh*tā[1].

'But she, the Cow, selected of those two the laborious countryman,

---

[1] Ys. XXXI, 10.

To be her pious lord, the protector of herds (or, of *the good-mind*) ;
But he who did not follow agriculture, O Mazda! did not participate in the good religion, though he attempted to deceive.'

The ambiguity of the Gāthā texts is thus actually increased, since we have now, for one single idea, the choice between a personal, an abstract, and a material translation.

That Vohu-manō was, however, not merely regarded as the guardian of herds, but of living beings in general, especially of men, may be perceived from the nineteenth Fargard of the Vendidād, where the word *vohu-manō* is to be rendered directly by 'man.'

Vohu-manō is the first amongst the Amesha Spenta. These are therefore spoken of as 'those who dwell together with Vohu-manō' (*Yōt · vaghēu*sh · *ā · managhó ·* sh*kyeinti* [1]). He plainly appears as their chief and spokesman, when he is in Paradise. As soon as a soul approaches, he rises from his 'golden throne,' addresses it, and shows it the place allotted to it [2].

ASHA-VAHISHTA, *the best piety or purity*, is at the same time the genius of fire. The reason of this lies in the fact that fire is the symbol of purity. Nowhere does the double nature of Asha more clearly appear than in the passage where Angra Manyu plaintively exclaims :

*Tāpayeiti · măm · asha · vahi*shta *· mănayen · ahę · yatha · ayaokh*shus*tem · raekô · mę · hacha · aghāo · zemat · vaghô · kerenaoiti · yō · măm · aęvô · jāmayęiti · yô · Spitâmô · Zarathu*sh*trô* [3].

'He burns me with the *Asha-vahishta* (the Holy Fire), like red-hot metal ; he best drives me from the earth, he, who alone makes me fly, is the son of Spitama, Zarathushtra.'

KHSHATHRA-VARYA, *the desirable sovereignty*, is a being not very clearly defined. To him is entrusted the care of metals. We trace the same idea in the Avesta itself,

---

[1] Ys. XXXIX, 3.   [2] Vendidad XIX, 32.   [3] Yt. XVII, 20.

when *khshathra-vairya* is plainly used for '*metal*[1]' or for '*a metallic instrument, knife*[2],' just as we have seen *vohu-manō* also denoting '*herds*,' and *asha-vahishta* '*fire*.' In what connection the ideal and material functions of Khshathra stand to each other, I cannot explain.

SPENTĀ ĀRMATI is of far more interest to us. This angel plays also in the Avesta a part dissimilar to and far more independent than those mentioned above. The name literally denotes '*moderate thinking*,'—the mind which always keeps itself within the bounds of what is right and good. By this is not only to be understood wisdom, but even more, *humility and quiet resignation to the will of God*[3].

Materially, Spentā Ārmati is the protectress of the earth. This part of her nature appears most clearly in the legend of Yima, according to which, when under that king, men, beasts, and fire (i. e. hearths) had multiplied themselves, and the earth had become too narrow for them, he uttered the following prayer :

Fritha · spenta · ārmaitę · fracha · shava · vīcha · nemaghacha · barethrę · pasvāmcha · staoranāmcha · mashyānāmcha · Aat · yimō · imām · zām · vīshāvayat · aęva · thrishva · ahmāt · masyękīm · yatha · para · ahmāt · as[4].

'Beloved Spentā Ārmati, extend and widen thyself, thou *mother of cattle and of men*.' 'Thus he (Yima) caused the earth to extend, whereby it became one-third larger than it was before.'

It is evident that Yima here addresses himself to Ārmati,

---

[1] Vend. XVI, 6, *ayaghaęnem · vā · srum · vā · nītema · khshathra-vairya.*

[2] Yt. X, 125 ; Vd. IX, 9.

[3] This appears clearly from the mere name of the demon *Tarō-maiti* (formally and materially an opponent of *Ārmati*), evidently 'arrogance.' And the verbs '*tarem-man*' and '*arem-man*,' in Ys. XLV, 11, have opposite meanings. I believe that *Ārmati*, as it follows hence, is contracted from '*arem-maiti*.'

[4] Vend. II, 10, 11. Also Ys. XVI, 10, where *Ārmati* denotes '*maęthana*,' 'a dwelling-place,' might be referred to for comparison.

as the genius of the earth.   As such Ārmati alone can be distinguished by the epithet ' *bearer* ' or ' *mother* .'   In quite the same way it is said of the earth itself: ' Together with other women we praise this Earth, who bears and nourishes us[1].'   Here the Earth is undoubtedly viewed as a person, and the author might as well have said ' *Spenṭām Ārmaitīm* ' as ' *imām sām.* '   Along with this idea an explanation is also at the same time given as to how humility could be made to be the protection of the earth.   This comes from regarding the earth chiefly as the humble, suffering one, which bears all, nourishes all, and sustains all.

Moreover Ārmati is the only figure amongst the Amesha Spenta that may be traced as a personal deity to the Arian (Indo-Irānian) epoch.   In the Rig-veda, Ārmati is found to be *devotion* or *genius of devotion*, and it is characteristic that just here in the Vedas also, as very often in the Avesta, we cannot with certainty separate the abstract from the personal signification.   By the Indian commentator Sâyana, Ārmati (Skt. *aramati*) is regarded as *Wisdom*, but, strange to say, he also defines the same word twice as ' the Earth[2].'

HARVATĀT and AMERTĀT[3] form an inseparable pair. Their names signify ' *invulnerability, good-preservation, health,* ' and ' *undying long-life, immortality.* '   They rule over the water and over plants.   The Avesta does not, however, indicate this directly; but we have for it the testimony of Neriosengh, which does not contradict in any way the brief indications contained in it (the Avesta).   In the Avesta, also, water and plants are always coupled together[4].

---

[1]   Ys. XXXVIII, 1. *imām · āat · sām · genābīsh · hathrā · yasamaidę.* In the designations that follow, the ' *genāo* ' is on another occasion specially called ' *ārmaitīsh.* '

[2]   Grassman, *Wörterbuch* sub voce ; Spiegel, *Erānische Alterthumskunde*, vol. ii, p. 38.

[3]   Comp. Darmesteter, *Haurvatāt et Ameretāt*, in the *Bibliothèque de l'école des Hautes Etudes*, xxiii, 1875.

[4]   Yt. XV, 16 ; XIX, 32.   Comp. Yt. XIII, 93, 94, where water and plants (*āpō · urvarāoscha ·*) begin to increase with Zarathushtra's birth.

The following invocation to these two genii is characteristic :

*Haurvatātem · ameshem · speṇtcm · yazamaidę · yāiryăm ·
hushitim · yazamaidę · saredha · ashavana · ashahę ·
ratavô · yaz ... Amcretātem ·'ameshem · speṇtem ·
yaz ... fshaoni · vāthwa · yaz ... aspinācha · yavînô ·
yaz ... gaokerenem · sûrem · Mazdadhātem · yaz ...*[1]

'We praise Harvatāt, the Amesha Spenta; we praise
the yearly good dwelling, and the years, the holy
masters of holiness. We praise Amertāt, the
Amesha Spenta; we praise the fields and herds; we
praise the tree *Gaokerna*, the strong one, which
Mazda created.'

Here Harvatāt rules over habitations, for every permanent dwelling-place, particularly in the arid district of
Eastern Irān, is dependent upon the presence of sufficient
water. Amertāt rules over the fields and herds, since he
causes the plants to germinate, and over the tree Gaokerna,
which is itself the king of plants, and which gives immortality.

The connection between the abstract and the material
meaning is not so clear in the case of any other Amesha
Spenta as in that of Harvatāt and Amertāt. Harvatāt,
'*health*,' is therefore the master of water, for the waters are
considered as dispensing health.

*Yayata · dunma · yayata · frā-āpem ...... yaskahę ·
apana*sh*tahę · mahrkahe · apana*sh*tahę*[2].— *Yô · vô .
āpô · vaģuh*ísh *· yazāitę · ahurāni*sh *· Ahurahę ....
ahmāi ...... tanvô · dravatûtem ......*[3]

'Come, ye clouds, with your waters ...... to drive
away sickness, to drive away death.'—'Whosoever
offers to you, you good waters, you daughters of
Ahura ...... on him you bestow ...... health of
body' ......

Something similar we learn of the plants. At the request
of Thrita, Ahura Mazda causes the wholesome plants ......

---

[1] Sirozah II, 6, 7.

[2] Vend. XXI, 2.   [3] Ys. LXVIII, 10, 11.

to sprout, 'in order to dispel sickness and death[1].' It is especially the Haoma plant which is commended as salutary: it keeps away death, and confers health of body and a long duration of the vital power[2]. In conclusion, we may call attention to the White Haoma, the enjoyment of which confers immortality.

In *one* word : water and plants bestow health and long life, happiness and immortality. Hence the conceptions of '*health*' and '*immortality*,' which are exalted into personal genii. Harvatāt and Amertāt are their commanders, and form, like the latter, an inseparable couple.

III. THE ELEMENTS AND ELEMENTARY YAZATAS.

We have already recognized in Asha-vahishta an Amesha Spenta of fire, and in Harvatāt an Amesha Spenta of water. Both these elements play an important part in the Avesta. But it is difficult to distinguish in individual instances, whether we should accept the personal or the material signification, whether we are on the domain of religion or on that of the *cultus*.

What a wide space the *cultus* of fire occupies amongst Zoroastrians need not be mentioned. I have myself discussed it in the section on 'Prayers and Household Customs.' For my part I can hardly doubt that fire was conceived also as a *yazata*, but where the element alone is meant and where the *yazata* cannot be determined without difficulty; the lack of tangible materiality of shape in these *yazatas*, the constant clinging to the mere idea by which the entire Avesta is distinguished, appears here more manifestly prominent than anywhere else.

Fire is conceived as half personal and half material when at night it awakens a man from sleep and impels him to

---

[1] Vend. XX, 3 [*paitishtā!ēē · yaskahe · paitishtatēē · mahrkahę*].

[2] [*Baęshasya, duraosha—dravatātem · tanvō, dareghō-jītīm · ush-tānahę.* Ys. IX, 6, 2, 4, 19.]

add fuel, so that it may not die out. The correct tendance of fire is accompanied simultaneously by a blessing[1].

The same sort of double meaning is met with when, with the several invocations at the beginning of the Yasna-ceremony, it is said: 'We invite *thee*, O Fire, thou son of Ahura Mazda!'[2] Here the fire is undoubtedly intended to represent a *yasata*, but at the same time the priest, as is already manifest from the direct manner of address, has in view the holy fire, which burns before him upon the altar.

When it is said that the Fire and Vohu-mano stood up against Angra Manyu in order to check the injuries he was inflicting, Asha-vahishta may be directly meant by the Fire[3].

Fire appears most thoroughly personified in the passage where it is named together with Vohu-manô and Asha-vahishta as an opponent of Dahāka:

Yahmi · paiti · pareqāithę · spęntascha · mainyush · agrascha · aętahmi · paiti · at · aqaretę · adhāt · ashtę · fragharechayat · āsishtę · kataraschit. Spęntô · mainyush · ashtem · fragharechayat · vohucha · manô · ashemcha · vahishtem · ātaremcha · Ahurahę · Masdão · puthrem · agrô-mainyush · ashtem · fragharechayat · akemcha · manô · aęshmemcha · khravîdrûm · ashîmcha · dahākem · spityuremcha · yimo-kerentem. Adhāt · frasha · hăm-rāzayata · ātarsh · Masdão · Ahurahę · uiti · avatha · maghânô · aętat · qarenô · hangerefshānę · yat ·

---

[1] ['Arise, thou master of the house! put on thy garments, wash thy hands, long for some wood for me, bring it unto me, kindle the clean wood over me, with both thy well-washed hands.' After this address, the Fire blesses the man, who brings him dry wood with a righteous heart, in the following words: 'May herds of oxen follow thee, and of heroic sons in plenty: may thy mind develop through action, may thy soul develop through energy: all the (days and) nights that thou livest, mayest thou live in the delight of thy soul.' Vend. XVIII, 19, 27; Ys. LXII.—*Tr. note.*]

[2] *Nivaędhayęmi · hąnkārayęmi · āthrô · Ahurahę · Masdâo · puthra.* Ys. I, 12; II, 12; III, 14; IV, 17.

[3] [*Yat · hitarat · agro · mainyush · dahêm · ashahę · vaghêush · antare · pairi-avâlem · vohucha · manô · ātarshcha.*] Yt. XIII, 77.

*aqaretem. Āat · hę · paskāt · fradvarat · azhish · thri-
zafāo · duzhdaęnô · uta · zakhshathrem · daomnô.
Inja · avat · handaęsayaǧuha · ātarsh · Mazdâo · Ahurahę ·
yęzi · aętat · nyāsāoǧhę · yat · aqaretem · frā · thwām ·
paiti · apātha · nôit · apaya · uzraochayāi · zām · paiti ·
Ahuradhātām · thrāthrāi · ashahę · gaęthanām*[1].

'For the heavenly radiance fought the Blissful, and the
Destructive Spirit for the imperishable. Then both of
them sent forth their speediest messengers. The Blissful Spirit sent out as messengers Vohu-manō and
Asha-vahishta, and Fire, the son of Ahura Mazda. But
the Evil Spirit sent forth as messengers Akem-manō,
and Aeshma with bloody lances, and Azi Dahāka, and
Spityura who sawed to pieces Yima. Then flamed
up the Fire of Ahura Mazda, thinking, "I will seize
for myself the heavenly splendour," but behind him
ran the three-headed evil dragon striving for his
destruction.

*Ho there! let me see thou Fire of Ahura Mazda; if
thou withholdest it from me, then will I not let thee
shine in future upon the earth, which Mazda created
for the protection of pious men.'*

Now the Fire lets the heavenly radiance slip from his
hands. Dahāka takes possession of it, but the Fire compels the Demon to surrender again the heavenly splendour,
which is secured in the sea Voru-Kasha.

Here Fire is introduced as thinking, speaking and acting :
it is a personal *yazata*. But in most cases we have to do
only with the mere element itself. Thus, for instance, when
the fire is divided into different classes. So too the *hvareno*,
'the heavenly radiance,' is very likely an attribute of the
Deity, but not a deity itself. On the other hand we can
fairly conceive Naryo-saǧha as a *yazata* of fire.

NARYO-SAǦHA is the messenger of Ahura Mazda[2], just
as the Vedic Indians designate the fire-god, *Agni*, as the

---

[1] Yt. XIX, 46–48.
[2] Vend. XIX, 34 : *ashto · Mazdāo · Ahurahę* ; or perhaps *astô* (?)
'the embodying of Mazda.'

'messenger' of gods[1]. Indeed the Deity sends down the fire from heaven, as lightning or sun-fire, to the earth, while on the other hand the fire burning upon the altar carries upwards the prayers and gifts of men to God.

Naryo-sa̅gha together with Srausha is the companion of Mithra[2]. He bears a club, by which the flash of lightning is probably to be understood. In the Brahmanical hymns also the genii fighting in the brunt of the battle are armed with clubs. It is for once allowable, in the present case, to introduce Vedic incidents for comparison, for even the name of Naryo-sa̅gha is found under the almost literally similar form *Narasamsa*, as an appellative of the fire-god Agni.

Apām-napāt forms the transition from the *fire-yazatas* to the *water-yazatas*. The name signifies '*son of the waters*,' and must have originally designated the flame of lightning, so far as it dwells in the clouds and is born of the clouds. For that reason Apām-napāt is invoked with Naryo-sa̅gha, who is however undoubtedly a fire-yazata, but often also with the waters to which he stands in close relation[3].

In the Vedic hymns also Apām-napāt is mentioned. This deity was thus invoked by the Arians even before Zarathushtra established his new doctrine. There too he is the fire of lightning dwelling in the clouds. Here the virgin waters foster and nourish him, until he bursts forth out of the clouds in bright-shining lustre. In quite a similar way is Apām-napāt pictured in the Avesta:

Berezantem · ahurem · khshathrîm · khshaetem · apām-
napātem · aurvat-aspem · yazamaidê · arshānem ·
zavanôsûm · yô · nerêush · dadha · yô · nerêush · tatasha ·
yô · upâpo · yazatô · srut-gaoshôtemô · asti · yazemnô[4].

'The great lord, the king-like, bright Apām-napāt with his war-steeds, we praise, the *hero* who blesses invo-

---

[1] *Dûta*, Rig-veda I, 44, 2; I, 72, 7, and frequently elsewhere.

[2] Yt. X, 52. Along with Srausha we also find the name of Naryo-sa̅gha in Ys. LVII, 3.

[3] Ys. LXXI, 23; Ys. I, 5; II, 5, &c. Even the epithet 'shining' (*khshaeta*) characterizes Apām-napāt as a fire-yazata.

[4] Yt. XIX, 52.

cation, who made men, who formed men, who, the yazata of the waters, listens most propitiously when he is invoked.'

Here we observe that Apãm-napāt, according to the Zoroastrian idea, participates in the work of the creation; the formation of men is specially ascribed to him. This also corresponds again with the Vedic conceptions of Apãm-napāt, of whom it is said : 'The son of the waters, in the strength of his deity, benignly created all the creatures[1].'

Even when it is said,

> *Apãm-napāose · tāo · āpô · Spitama · Zarathushtra · ağuhę · astavaitę · shôithrô-bakhtāo · vîbakhshaiti · vātascha · yô · darshish · awzh-dātemcha · qarenō · ashaonãmcha · fravashayô*[2],

> 'Apãm-napāt spreads the waters given to the fields, O son of Spitama ! Zarathushtra ! upon the corporeal world, and Vāta (*the wind*) the strong one,'

I do not consider Apãm-napāt to be a *water-yazata.* This may only mean that with the flashing of lightning (Apãm-napāt) and the roar of the stormy-wind (Vāta) the fertilizing rain pours down upon the earth.

If now we proceed to speak of the waters themselves, we again stand more upon the ground of *cultus* than upon that of religion.   The importance of water for life and culture in Eastern Irān, I have frequently enough and pointedly alluded to in the course of my ' History of Civilization.'   It is therefore conceivable that this element stood in high veneration. But also in invocations such as the following,

> *Nivaędhayęmi · hankārayęmi · aiwyô · vağuhibyô · vîs-panãmcha · apãm · Mazdadhātanãm · vispanãmcha · urvaranãm · Mazdadhātanãm*[3],

> 'We announce it, and invite the good waters, all waters which Mazda created, and all the plants which Mazda created,'

---

[1] Rig-Veda II, 35, 2.   [2] Yt. VIII, 34.
                    [3] Ys. I, 12.

water is only meant as an element. To the dignity of
a *yazata* it is not exalted.

The proper *water-yazata* is ARDVI-SŪRA ANĀHITA.
The veneration of this female *yazata* is a special property
of the Irānian religion, and has its history. For I believe
that Ardvi-sūra was originally the name of a large river,
the Oxus. This appears very clearly in certain descriptions
and eulogies of the Avesta :

> (*Ardvīm · sûrām · anāhitām · yazamaidę) · yā · asti ·
> avavaiti · masô · yatha · vīspāo · imāo · āpô · yāo ·
> zemā · paiti · fratachaṇti · yā · amavaiti · fratachaiti ·
> hukairyût · hacha · berezaghat · avi · zrayô · vouru-
> kashem · yaozenti · vīspę · karanô · zrayā · vouru-
> kashayā · ā · vīspô · maidhyô · yaozaiti · yat · hīsh ·
> avi · fratachaiti · yat · hīsh · avi · frazhgaraiti ·
> ardvī · sūra · anāhita · yęghę · hazağrem · vairyanãm ·
> hazağrem · apaghzhāranãm · kaschitcha · aęshãm ·
> vairyanãm · kaschitcha · aęshûm · apaghzhāranãm ·
> chathwāresatem · ayare-baranãm · hvaspāi · nairę ·
> baremnāi[1].

' (The Ardvi-sūra Anāhita we praise), which is as large
as all other waters that flow over the earth, which
powerfully streams down from the *Mount Hukarya*
into the sea *Voru-kasha*. All the shores are covered
with waves, all the middle heaves up in the sea *Voru-
kasha*, when into it streams down, when into it flows,
the Ardvi-sūra Anāhita. That has a thousand arms
and a thousand canals ; and each of these arms and
each of these canals is as long as forty days' journey
for a well-mounted man.'

We have here undoubtedly the picture of a mighty river
of great volume, with many tributary streams and branches.
But if we look to the original dwellings of the Avesta
people, as they appear from the geographical indications of
the text, there is no doubt that ' Ardvi-sūra ' can mean only
the Oxus ; for which on the opposite supposition we would
have no designation at all. At the same time the name

---

[1] Yt. V, 3, 4 ; Ys. LXV, 3, 4.

Ardvi-sūra Anāhita does not merely designate the stream by itself, but also the *yazata* to whom the stream is dedicated, and who rules over it. Hence these words can be put into her mouth :

> *Mana · raya · qarenaḡhacha · pasvascha · staorācha . upairi · zām · vîcharenti · mashyācha · bizaṇgra · nipayemi · vîspa · vohû · Mazdadhāta (asha-chithra) · mānayen · ahẹ · yatha · pasûm · pasu-vastrem*[1].

'Through my riches and my splendour, sheep and cattle wander on the earth, and two-legged men. I protect for them all the good things which Mazda created, just as a fold shelters (or as the fleece protects) the flock.'

From the *yazata* of the largest and holiest stream to the *yazata* of water in general there is indeed only a small step.

Ardvi-sūra Anāhita is one of those *yazatas* in the Avesta who were most completely moulded into a tangible personality. As a female *yazata*, Anāhita is also especially the guardian of the female sex. Her work in that respect is described in the following passage :

> *Yā · vîspanām · arshnām · khshudrāo · yaozhdadhāiti · yā · vîspanām · hāirishinām · zāthāi · garewān · yaozhdadhāiti · yā · vîspanām · hāirishîsh · huzāmitō · dadhāiti · yā · vispanām . hāirishinām · dāitîm · rathwîm · paẹma · ava-baraiti*[2].

'That governs the generation of all men (lit., purifies the seed of all men), that prepares the bodies of all women for delivery, that gives sufficient and well-timed milk to all women.'

To the fire and water *yazatas* may be added without hesitation VAYU or RĀMAN, and VĀTA, the *yazatas* of the air and the storm-wind.

Like all *yazatas* of nature, Vayu and Vāta are also thrown into the shade in the Avesta. The latter is designated 'the strong one,' and 'created by Mazda[3];' further than

---

[1] Yt. V, 89.   [2] Yt. V, 2.
[3] Vend. XIX, 13; Ys. XLII, 3.

this we learn nothing particular about him. Vayu occupies
a somewhat larger space, and is called the strong and the
swift one.   The influence of Vayu is tolerably extensive ;
however one can scarcely say whether it stands in closer
relation to his nature as the *yazata* ỏf the air or as that of
the wind.   Unmarried maidens pray to him for husbands
who may take care of them and beget offspring by them[1].
His name, however, is also invoked in the heat of battle
with hostile armies, when violent tyrants reign in the land,
when heretics attack the purity of religion, or when a person
is betrayed into the hands of his enemy[2].

On the whole, Vayu may be characterized as the strong,
robust, warlike helper in every danger.   With man and
horse he drives away anxious fear and suspense, he drives
away the demons[3], and hence it is said of him :—

> *Vayush · aurvô · uskāt · yāstô · derezrô · yaokhdhrô ·
> berezipādhô · perethu-varô . . . anākhrñidha-dôithra ·
> yatha · anyāoschit · khshathrāt · khshayamnão · hamô-
> khshathrô-khshayamnão*[4].

'Vayu is armed and warlike, powerful, martial, high-
footed, with a wide chest, and a tender glance, like
the others that rule over kingdoms as sovereigns.'

IV. STAR-YAZATAS.

Amongst the *star-yazatas,* the SUN (*Hvare*), the MOON
(*Mãoğha*), and the 'BEGINNINGLESS STARS' (*Anaghra
Raochão*), deserve to be first considered.   The rain-star
TISHTRYA is also worthy of mention, and in remote relation to them stand also the FRAVASHIS, the *manes* or
spirits of the defunct, so far at least as they were apparently considered to be stars.

I can and indeed must express myself only briefly upon
this subject, since I have had occasion to discuss it in my
'History of Civilization,' in the section upon '*The World.*'

---

[1] Yt. XV, 39.

[2] Yt. XV, 49–52.

[3] Yt. XV, 53.

[4] Yt. XV, 54.

The SUN, as the bearer of light, is the chief opponent of the demons. He is *the eye of heaven, the eye of Ahura Mazda*. The *Yazata of the Sun* is represented as driving in a bright shining chariot which is drawn by celestial horses.

The MOON is the lamp of the night. To her is ascribed a mysterious influence upon the growth of plants. Deserving of attention is her constant epithet *gaochithra*, 'containing the seed of cattle,' by which is perhaps indicated her influence upon the increase of herds.

By the name BEGINNINGLESS LIGHTS are probably meant the stars. Amongst them *Tishtrya* is the principal one. He is Sirius in the constellation of Canis Major. The veneration in which he is held is connected with the fact that he first rises in midsummer, and that the longer he remains in the heavens the sooner the heat will diminish and the autumnal rain appear instead of sultry weather and barrenness.

Thus Tishtrya becomes the dispenser of rain. It is he who opens the heavenly fountains, and thereby increases the waters in springs and rivulets, in rivers and in seas. His opponent is the demon of heat, APAUSHA, whom he conquers after a desperate combat. The helper of Tishtrya in the work of distributing the waters over the earth is the star SATAVAISA, which I believe to be Vega in the constellation of Lyra.

With the FRAVASHIS, the *manes*, we are again concerned more with the *cultus*. I have devoted a special chapter to the *cultus of the manes*. They are helpers in every necessity and danger. They protect habitations, supply them with water, and cause them to attain prosperity. They are helpers in war, and assist in the maintenance and preservation of the world's system and its laws. That they are regarded as stars is apparent from the description of them as wandering through the height of the firmament with a celestial escort.

V. ABSTRACT IDEAS AS NAMES OF SPIRITUAL BEINGS.

The Avesta religion differs essentially from the religion of kindred nations, more particularly in the fact that in it the sensible and the material appear to fall into the background when opposed to the purely spiritual, ethical, and ideal. The names of the six Amesha Spenta, the highest spiritual essences of the entire system, are indeed all abstract ideas, and are, moreover, still employed as such in the sacred writings.

Thus it cannot surprise us, if in addition a whole series of abstract ideas and ethical conceptions are formed into holy names, into more or less personal angels.

I shall not here discuss the fact that in the prayers and invocations of the Avesta are also named the *Daena*, the *Holy Doctrine*, *The Law*, or *Mâthra Spenta*, the *Holy Word*, or *Sauka* probably 'the Blessing.' They were exactly things which appeared in themselves worthy of veneration and at the same time desirable. If, therefore, any one in praying invokes them, or rather desires their coming, it is not thereby implied that they are real *yazatas*. Indeed it is difficult to draw the necessary distinction.

Such an abstract idea is ARSHTĀT or ARSHTI, who is invoked together with RASHNU[1]. Both these *yazatas*, as the etymological connection of their names of itself indicates, appear to be essentially cognate.

Rashnu, however, is undoubtedly the genius of justice. He is called *ashavan* 'the holy,' *razishta* 'the just,' *vaidhishta* 'the knowing,' *vichôistare* 'the discerning,' he who also perceives what is remote, *durae-darshtema* 'the far-seeing[2].' In short he is the *yazata* before whose penetrating eye nothing lies hidden. It may therefore be easily understood that he is a particular enemy of thieves, and above all

---

[1] Ys. I, 7 ; II, 7.

[2] Yt. XII, 7. *Vichôistare* from the root *vi* + *chit*; *parakavistema*.

of wicked men, whose deeds shun the light of day[1]. It is likewise clear why Rashnu appears amongst the Judges of the Dead. It is he who weighs the good and the bad deeds of each soul against each other, and who always passes sentence according to the result.

We will hardly err, therefore, in looking upon Arshtāt simply as 'Justice' personified.

The number of the abstract ideas in which, according to the doctrine of the Avesta, a certain sanctity is involved, and which therefore occur in invocations along with active and personal *yazatas*, is rather considerable. Many of them are not quite clear. Amongst the doubtful ideas I reckon UPARATĀT, perhaps 'Victory,' next DĀMOISH UPAMANA, about which I can say almost nothing for certain, then ĀFRITI 'Benediction' of pious men, possessing divine strength and efficacy, and lastly RASĀSTĀT, probably again something similar to Justice, and others.

VERTHRAGHNA, SRAUSHA and ASHI-VAČHVI are of a more definite character.

Verthraghna is without doubt 'Victory' or 'the *yazata* of victory.' This is quite evident from his being chiefly invoked in battle:

Kva · asti · verethraghnahę · Ahuradhātahę · nāma · azbāitish? kva · upastuitish? kva · nistuitish? Yat · spādha · haṇjasāoṇtę · rashtem · rasma · kataraschit · vishtāoğhδ · ahmya · nδit · vanyāoṇtę · jatāoğhδ · ahmya · nδit · janyāoṇtę . . . yatārδ · pourvδ · frāyazāitę · amδ · hutāshtδ · huraodhδ · verethraghnδ · Ahuradhātδ · atārδ · verethra · hachaitę[2].

'When occurs the invocation of the name of Verthraghna? When his praise? When his (conjuration) hearing? When armies dash against each other, drawn up in battle array, then to one of the two, not conquered, not smitten . . . who first invokes the well-created, well-formed Strength, Verthraghna, whom Ahura created: to his lot the victory falls.'

It is he, who 'commands amongst the lines of battle

---

[1] Yt. XII, 7, 8.   [2] Yt. XIV, 42, 43.

arrayed for the fight ¹.' It is he, who 'crushes the battalions, who separates and smites them, who shakes them violently².' He ties behind them the hands of the breakers of covenants, he blinds their power of vision, he deafens their ears, and unnerves their feet, so that they cannot offer any resistance ³.

It is remarkable that Verthraghna is also pictured ' in the form of a rich man who carries a sword with a golden hilt, a jewelled, an embellished and a richly ornamented one⁴.'

Finally, we must notice that he is identified with Vāta, the boisterous storm-*yazata*⁵. This carries us back to Indra, the *Vritrahan* of the Rig-veda, the god who fights in storm and thunder against the demons. Evidently Verthraghna may be traced to such a natural deity of the Indo-Irānian epoch, with this difference that that god was transformed after the Zoroastrian manner of thinking. His functions as a nature-god were lost sight of. Verthraghna is, according to the Mazdayasnân belief, no longer the fighter in the thunder-storm, but in general the genius of victory, and the pious are indebted to his help, if they overpower the unbelieving in battle.

A most characteristic figure in the Avesta religion is SRAUSHA. He too. exemplifies clearly. the ethico-philosophical spirit which predominates in the Zarathushtrian system. Srausha means 'obedience,' and especially obedience towards the Holy Word and its Commandments. Hence Srausha is the principal opponent of the demons, who endeavour to lead man to violate those commandments and to neglect his religious duties.

Ahura Mazda has created Srausha as the opponent of *Aishma*, the demon of 'violent wrath⁶.' Whoever follows

---

¹ [*Yô · vīrāzaiti · aṇtare · rāsh*la *· rasmana.*] Yt. XIV, 47.

² [*Yô · rasmanô · schiṇdayeiti · yô · rasmanô · kereṇtayeiti · yô · rasmanô · qaǧhayeiti · yô · rasmanô · yaozayeiti.*] Yt. XIV, 62.

³ Yt. XIV, 7–25.

⁴ [*Verethraghnô · vīrahe · kehrpa · raevaiô · baraṭ · kareṭem · zaranyô-saorem · frapikh*sh*lem · vīspo-paesaǧhem.*] Yt. XIV, 27

⁵ Yt. XIV, 1, 2.

⁶ Yt. XI, 15 (Comp. also Ys. LVII, 10), *aeshmahe · hamaestārem.*

d 2

the Zoroastrian Law must suppress the passion of anger. Srausha is, besides, the adversary of *Bushyāsta*, the evil spirit of 'indolence,' who, in the morning, entices man to give himself up to sleep[1]. 'Obedience' to the Law requires us to wake early and to set about our daily business; for even in the morning a series of ritual and religious duties await the Worshipper of Mazda. Similarly Srausha fights against the demons of 'drunkenness[2],' for the doctrine of Zarathushtra demands a frugal, prudent life.

If the name of Srausha means obedience to the Holy Law, it is very easy to explain why the introduction of certain ritual precepts is ascribed to him. It is he, who first of all recited the sacred hymns, who first tied together the *Baresma*, the consecrated sacrificial branches, in honour of Ahura Mazda, the Amesha Spenta, and Mithra; but he is also expressly styled the Teacher of the Law[3]. It is likewise intelligible why the holy prayers are the weapons with which he conquers the demons[4].

In other respects also the power of Srausha is naturally explained from that *single* point of view. Srausha pities the poor and the needy, since the Law commandeth charity towards the members of the same faith. He guards, like Mithra, the sanctity of covenants, as these are particularly sacred to the Zoroastrian. He takes part also in battles, for the Zoroastrian Law desires from its adherents an unswerving adhesion to its doctrine[5]. He is lastly called *tanu-māthra*[6], 'he whose body is the Holy Word,' because in him obedience towards the precepts of that Word and their fulfilment appear to be embodied.

Thus we have succeeded in deriving from one fundamental idea, which can be recognized in the very meaning

---

[1] Vend. XVIII, 16.

[2] Vend. XIX, 41 [*Sraoshŏ · ashyŏ · kundem · baŋgem · vibaŋgem · ava-janyāt*].

[3] Ys. LVII, 8, 2 and 24 [*Yŏ (sraoshŏ) daęnŏ-disŏ · daęnayāŏ. Yŏ · paoiryŏ · gāthāo · frasrāvayat · mat-āzaiṇtīsh · mat-paiti-frasāo*].

[4] Ys. LVII, 22.

[5] Ys. LVII, 10; Yt. XI, 14; Ys. LVII, 12.

[6] Vd. XVIII, 14.

of the name, all the powers of Srausha and all the notions which cluster round that *yazata* in the Avesta. Something similar is, perhaps, also possible with regard to the female *yazata* ASHI, or, more fully, ASHI-VAĠHVI. Ashi is 'Piety,' in the broad sense which the Mazda-yasnãn give to that idea—'the moral order.' Hence she is called, in an allegorical manner, the daughter of Ahura and of Spentā Ārmati, the Humble Devotion, and the sister of Srausha, Rashnu, Mithra, and of the Mazdayasnãn Religion[1]. She is most closely and intimately coupled with all the virtues which mark the Zoroastrian.

As the protectress of the moral order, Ashi bestows the human intellect, by which we must probably understand the faculty of distinguishing between good and evil[2]. She is, further, the defender of matrimony. She abhors courtesans and adulteresses, who violate this institute of the moral order. She hates those who keep a maiden by force from marriage, and thus withhold her from her destination[3]. In general she displays her activity chiefly in the house, probably because the entire moral order rests upon the narrow circle of the family. She is therefore invited into one's own house:

> *Ashi · srîra · dāmi-dāitę · mā · avi · asmanem · frashûsa · mā · avi · zām · niurvaęsę · itha · me · tûm · hãmcha-raḡuha · aṇtare · aredhem · nmānahę · srīrahę · khsha-thrô-keretahę*[4].

> 'Beautiful Ashi, created by the Creator, go not up into heaven, nor down to the earth; come thou to me into the interior of my house, of the fine, lordly one.'

The blessings which Ashi bestows are very multifarious.

---

[1] Yt. XVII, 16; XVII, 2 [(*dughdharem · Ahurahę · Mazdāo*). (16) *Pita · tę · yô · Ahuro · Mazdāo . . . māta · ārmaiti*sh · *spęṇta · brāta · te · yô · sraoshô · ashyô · rashnu*shcha · *mithrascha . . . qaḡha · daęna · māzdayasni*sh.]

[2] Yt. XVII, 2 [*Yā · (ashi) frasha · khrathwa · frāthanjayęiti · uta · āsnem-khratûm · ava-baraiti.*]

[3] Yt. XVII, 57–59.   [4] Yt. XVII, 60.

She confers power and riches, gold and silver, garments and shining rings, and to maidens she grants the beauty with which they please their husbands[1]. She was in close friendship with Zarathushtra as the founder of piety, but now too she presents herself to him who invokes her to unite herself with him[2].

By way of appendix we shall discuss in this section a genius that occupies a separate position and cannot be included in any of the groups treated of hitherto. It is GEUSH-URVAN, 'the Soul of the Bull,' also called DRU-VĀSPA.

We have under the name Geush-urvan undoubtedly an embodiment or concentration of the welfare and prosperity of herds. She is their representative, who has to defend their interests.

Just as in the oldest periods of Zoroastrian civilization the occupations of agriculture and cattle-breeding played a very important part, so is it easy to understand why Geush-urvan occurs already in the Gāthās. Here a song[3] is found, in which the 'Soul of the Bull' complains before the Deity of all the oppressions and dangers which are inflicted upon her by enemies, evidently the plundering nomads. Ahura predicts to her the future mission of Zarathushtra, who will indeed not merely be the founder of a new religion, but who will also confer upon men at the same time the blessings of civilization, imposing upon them as a duty a settled life, the cultivation of the field, and the careful rearing of cattle.

So also in the later Avesta, Druvāspa is the protectress of herds, though we do not learn any particulars regarding her. Her work is described in a general way at the beginning of the Yasht dedicated to her, where it is said :

Druvāspem · yasamaide · druvō-pasvām · druvō-stao-rām · druvō-urvathām · druvō-aperenāyukām · pouru-spakhshtīm · dūrāt-pathana · qāthravana · da-reghō-hakhedrayana · yukhta-aspām · vareth-rathām ·

---

[1] Yt. XVII, 6.   [2] Yt. XVII, 1, 21 ; Yt. XIII, 107.
[3] Ys. XXIX.

qanat-chakhrăm · fshaonīm · marezăm · amavaitīm · huraodhăm · qāsaokăm · baęshazyăm · druvô-stăitīm · druvô-varetăm · avaḡhę · narăm · ashaonăm [1].

'Druvâspa we praise, who keeps small cattle and large cattle, friends and children in vigour; who grants ample protection, appearing from afar, dispensing good-luck, long-continuing friendship; who yokes her steeds, makes her chariot roll, the wheels to rattle, granting nourishment, purifying, strong, well-shaped; who grants good profits; who renders powerful support; who possesses rich treasures for the assistance of the pious people.'

VI. MITHRA.

MITHRA is no doubt one of the most interesting genii of the Zoroastrian. In him are combined, as in no other figure of the Avesta religion, old and new, Arian and especially Irānian, symbolical parts of nature and ethical constituents. But Mithra is also at the same time a manifest instance of the manner in which, in the Avesta, the deities originating from a pre-Zoroastrian epoch are usually conceived and transformed according to the new spirit. Hence it would appear proper to devote a particular section to Mithra.

The great number of hymns which are united in the Mithra-Yasht, may of themselves prove the important place which the veneration of Mithra held in the nation. He was perhaps one of the most popular *yazatas*; and just for that reason, I believe, he had in the system itself to rank after the purely ethical genii and abstract ideas, as for example the Amesha Spenta.

Mithra has his physical and his moral sides. The latter is founded on the former, and proceeds from it. The two should be strictly distinguished.

Physically, Mithra is the *yazata* of the rising sun, or,

---

[1] Yt. IX, 1, 2.

more accurately, probably the *yazata* of the light radiating
from the sun.

> *Mithrem · yazamaidę . . . yô · paoiryô · mainyavô · yazatô ·
> tarô · harām · āsnaoiti · paurva-naęmāt · ameshahę ·
> hû · yat · aurvat-aspahę · yô · paoiryô · zaranyô-pīsô ·
> srīrāo · bareshnava · gerewnāiti · adhāt · vīspem ·
> ādidhāiti · airyô-shayanem · sevishtô*[1].

'We praise Mithra, who, as the first heavenly *yazata*,
rises above the Hara, before the immortal sun, the
swift-horse; who first, gold-modelled, surrounds the
beautiful mountain-summits and then looks over the
entire land of the Arians, the helpful.'

The description of sunrise, which forms the basis of these
lines, may be still clearly perceived. On the *Hara barzati*,
the mountain over which the sun rises, Ahura Mazda has
erected for Mithra a dwelling. Yonder there is neither
night nor darkness, neither cold nor heat, neither sickness
nor grief, and no fog ascends from the mountain[2].

As the *yazata* of sun and light, Mithra is called *vouru-
gaoyaoiti* 'the lord over wide fields[3].' He is also named
daḡhu-paiti 'the prince of the countries[4].' For the sun is
the king of the heavens, and he looks at the same time over
all the dominions of the earth.

The light is the symbol of truth. Hence the sun is called
the eye of Ahura, because with it he surveys the whole
world and perceives everything right and wrong. When once
such ideas exist, it cannot surprise us that also Mithra,
the *yazata* of the sun-light, should himself become a
guardian of truth and justice. If we look more closely
into the entire character of the Avesta religion, we shall
find it intelligible that this ethical part of the nature of
Mithra occupies a far wider space than his physical importance.

---

[1] Yt. X, 13; comp. also Yt. X, 95.
[2] Yt. X, 50.   [3] Yt. X, 1, 7, 10, 12, &c.
[4] Yt. X, 78 [*mithrô · raęvô · daḡhu-paitish*; Yt. X, 145, *mithrem ·
vīspanām · daqyunām · doḡhu-paitīm · yazamaidę*].

Mithra is the guardian of truth, the *yazata* of oaths and promises. As such Mithra is *adhaoyamna* 'the infallible,' and 'the undeceived one[1].' In an allegorical manner this is expressly indicated by the Avesta, when it says: 'he has a thousand ears (*hazagrô-gaoshem*[2]) and ten thousand eyes (*baēvare-chashmanem*)[3].' He neither rests nor sleeps, he hears and sees everything that happens[4]. His scouts are posted on high watch-towers and announce to him what passes on the earth[5].

As is usually the case with the deities of the sun in the Arian religions, so also in the Avesta is Mithra described as a warlike courageous youth who drives in a chariot through the spaces of the heavens:

Ahmya · vāshę · vazāontę · chathwārô · aurvantô · spaē-tita · hama-gaonāoǧhô · mainyush-qaretha · anaoshā-oǧhô[6].

'Four horses draw his chariot, white ones, of the same colour, which eat the heavenly food, (and are) immortal.'

In this chariot Mithra drives into the battle, in order to support his adherents and to annihilate the 'betrayers of Mithra' (*mithrô-druj*), by whom we must probably understand the enemies of the Zoroastrians in general:

Āat · yat · mithrô · fravazaiti · avi · haēnayāo · khravī-shyęitūsh · avi · hām-yanta · rasmaoyô · antare · daǧhu-pāperetānę · athra · narām · mithrô-drujām · apāsh · gavô · darezayęiti · pairi · daęma · vārayęiti · apa · gaosha · gaoshayęiti[7].

---

[1] Yt. X, 24 and often.

[2] Yt. X, 1, 7, 10, 12, &c. ; Ys. I, 3 ; II, 3.

[3] Yt. X, 1, 7, 10, 12, &c.; Ys. I, 3 ; II, 3.

[4] Yt. X, 102, 103 [*mithrem · aqafnem · jaghāurvāoǧhem . . . yô* (*mithrô*) *anavaǧhabdemnô · zaęnaǧha · nipāiti · Mazdāo · dāmān · yô · anavaǧhabdemnô · zaęnaǧha · nishhaurvaiti · Mazdāo · dāmān*].

[5] Yt. X, 45, 46. It should also be remarked that *Mithra* in the Yasna and the Vendidad simply means 'covenant, promise.'

[6] Yt. X, 125.

[7] Yt. X, 48.

'When Mithra thither drives against the terrible hostile armies, against those thus gathered together for fight, in the battle of the countries, then he binds the arms of the *betrayers of Mithra* to their backs, then he blinds their sight, and deafens their ears.'

This idea being amplified, Mithra becomes in general a *yazata* of war:

Vazrem · zastaya . drazhemnô · satafshtānem · satô-dārem · fravaęghem · vīrô-nyāonchem · zarôish · ayaǧ-hô · frahikhtem · amavatô · zaranyęhę · amavastemem · zaęnām · verethravastemem · zaęnām[1].

'He bears a club in his hand, with a hundred knobs, and a hundred edges, that sweeps downwards, crushing men, cast out of yellow brass, out of solid, gold-coloured (brass), which is the most powerful and most victorious of weapons.'

With his club he slays his opponents, the men and horses together[2]. He is, therefore, invoked by warriors both for strength for their teams and health for their bodies[3].

VII. DEMONOLOGY.

The question how evil, sin and guilt, grief and misfortune, come into this world has engaged Philosophy in all ages. For Zoroastrianism it was particularly important, since that system does not attribute to the divine beings any of the human passions and faults, but only recognizes in them pure, holy, absolutely good existences.

The Zoroastrian doctrine has accordingly solved that question by maintaining from the beginning a dualism of forces, one good and beneficent, and another evil and destructive.   The former is essentially represented by SPENTO MANYU; the latter by his opponent ANGRA MANYU.   As Ahura has a group of archangels and angels near Him, who support Him in His work, so is Angra Manyu surrounded by a body of evil spirits and demons.

On account of this opposition of good and evil, Zoroas-

---

[1] Yt. X, 96.   [2] Yt. X, 101.   [3] Yt. X, 94.

trianism has been often called a dualistic religion ; but the title cannot be considered correct [1]. It is true the evil power co-exists from the beginning with the good one, but as I have explained more distinctly in the chapter on the 'Eschatology' of the Avesta [2], it will be overthrown in the great decisive combat at the end of the world, and will be annihilated.

The highest amongst the evil spirits, the prince of the demons, is Angra Manyu 'the evil pernicious spirit.' That he existed along with Ahura Mazda (or Spento Manyu 'the blissful spirit') from the beginning, is expressed clearly enough in the Gāthās. The former rules over evil, and the evil-minded ones collect around him ; the latter is the Father and Creator of everything good. He is worshipped and followed by the pious and faithful.

[1] [Cf. Haug, *Essays*, p. 303 : ' The opinion, so generally entertained now, that Zarathushtra preached a Dualism, that is to say, the idea of two original independent spirits, one good and the other bad, utterly distinct from each other, and one counteracting the creation of the other, is owing to a confusion of his philosophy with his theology. Having arrived at the grand idea of the unity and indivisibility of the Supreme Being, he undertook to solve the great problem which has engaged the attention of so many wise men of antiquity, and even of modern times, viz. how are the imperfections discoverable in the world, the various kinds of evils, wickedness and baseness, compatible with the goodness, holiness, and justice of God? This great thinker of remote antiquity solved this difficult question *philosophically* by the supposition of two primeval causes, which, though different, were united, and produced the world of material things, as well as that of the spirit ; which doctrine may best be learned from Ys. XXX (*vide* pp. 149-151).'

Cf. also West, *Pahlavi Texts*, Part II, Introduction, p. xxiv : ' The reader will search in vain for any confirmation of the foreign notion that Mazda-worship is decidedly more dualistic than Christianity is usually shown to be by orthodox writers, or for any allusion to the descent of the good and evil spirits from a personification of boundless time, as asserted by strangers to the faith. No attempt is made to account for the origin of either spirit, but the temporary character of the power of the evil one, and of the punishment in hell, is distinctly asserted.' *Translator's note.*]

[2] *Vide* § 11. D. III.

At · tā · mainyû · paouruyę · yā · yēmā · qafnā · asra-
vātem ·
Manahichā · vachahichā · shkyaothanði · hî · vahyô ·
akemchā ·
Âoschā · hudāoḡhô · eresh · vīshyātā · nôit · duzhdāoḡhô ·
At · chā ·. hyat · tā · hēm · mainyû · jasaętem · paourvīm ·
dazdę ·
Gaęmchā · ajyāitūmchā · yathāchā · aḡhat · apemem ·
aḡhush ·
Achishtô · dregvatām · at · ashaonę · vahishtem · manô[1].

'The two spirits who first of all existed, the twins
proclaimed to me of themselves.

The good and the bad in thoughts, words, and works,

And of those two the intelligent selected the right
one, but fools did not so.

When the two spirits came first together, in order
to create

Life and death, and (to order) how the world should
be at the end,

Then the most evil one appeared on the side of the
impious, but the best spirit appeared on that of
the pious.'

It is likewise clear that the doctrine respecting the
powers co-existing from the beginning and standing diametrically opposed to one another, is expressed in the
following passage :

At · fravakhshyā · aḡhēush · mainyû · paouruyę ·
Yayāo · spanyāo · uitī · mravat · yēm · aḡrēm ·
Nôit · nā · manāo · nôit · sēṇḡhā · nôit · khratavô ·
Naędā · varanā · nôit · ukhdhā · naędā · shkyaothanā ·
Nôit · daęnā · noit · urvānô · hachainṭī[2].

'Announce will I the two spirits at the beginning of
the world :

Of them spake the blissful also unto the destructive:

---

[1] Ys. XXX, 3, 4.

[2] Ys. XLV, 2 ; here the evil spirit is designated by the word
aḡrēm.

"Neither our thoughts, nor our commands, nor our intelligence,
Nor our belief, nor our speeches, nor our deeds,
Nor our doctrines, nor our souls correspond."'

In all things Angra Manyu is the counterpart of Ahura Mazda (or Spento Manyu). The latter brings forth only what is good, the former only what is evil; the one creates life, the other death. Hence Angra Manyu is designated by the constant appellation *pouru-mahrka*[1], 'he who is entire death.'

Whoever causes goodness injures at the same time the evil spirit. No wonder then if Zarathushtra, who brought to men the true faith and the right piety, is regarded as the special opponent of Angra Manyu. With his birth the latter bursts out into the following cry of complaint and of rage:

*Zâtô · bę · yô · ashava · Zarathu*sh*trô · nmānahę · Pouru*shaspahę *· kava · hę · aoshô · viṇdāma · hāu · daęvanām · snathô · hāu · daęvanām · paityārô · hāu · drukh*sh-vīdrukh*sh . nyāonchô · daęvayāzô*[2].

'Born, alas! is the holy Zarathushtra in the house of Porushaspa. How can we contrive his destruction? He is a blow against the *Daivas*, he withstands the *Daivas*, he is an opponent of the *Drujas;* the worshippers of the demons shall fall down headlong!'

As Ahura Mazda is surrounded by the Amesha Spenta and Yazatas, the great majority of the beneficent spirits, so is Angra Manyu by the demons. The kingdom of the former is the light, the kingdom of the latter is the night and darkness.

The demons are designated by the names of DAIVA and DRUJ. The former are male, the latter are female devils. Of the great body of the evil spirits, some appear more conspicuous, others less. On the whole, it may perhaps be said that in the Avesta the kingdom of evil is not quite so exactly and fully described as that of the celestial spirits.

---

[1] Pahlavi, *pûr-marg.*   [2] Vd. XIX, 46.

It will therefore be necessary to say only a few words on this head. To the Amesha Spenta correspond a group of six demons, who in every respect, often even in very name, are opposed to the former, in the same way as their chief and prince himself is opposed to Ahura Mazda. They form the immediate associates, to some extent, the court of Angra Manyu. Against Vohu-manō there stands AKŌMANŌ, 'the evil mind;' against Asha-vahishta, ANDRA or INDRA, evidently an old nature-god, the Vedic Indra, who in the new religion was banished to the company of devils. The adversary of Khshathra-varya is SARU, perhaps 'the tyrant;' as an enemy of Spentā Ārmati, NĀOGHATYA is named, again a deity of nature of the pre-Zarathushtrian epoch. However, TAROMATI is also found, who is the type of 'arrogance.' To Harvatāt and Amertāt correspond TARU and ZARIJA, possibly 'hunger' and 'thirst[1].'

Among the rest of the Daivas, AISHMA, the demon of 'sudden anger,' should be particularly named. His destructive agency is indicated by the very epithet *khrvi-dru*[2], 'with a bloody weapon.' It is he who hurries men into rash and bloody deeds.

Along with him must be named ASTO-VIDHOTU, 'the crusher of the body.' He appears to be the demon who causes sudden and unforeseen death, availing himself for that purpose of the holy element of water and also of that of fire[3]. APAOSHA is the enemy of Tishtrya. He keeps back the rain and burns up, by the aridity and heat of summer, the vegetation of the earth. But he is defeated by Tishtrya after a hot combat, and now the refreshing and fertilizing rains pour down. Lastly, we may here notice BUSHYĀSTA, who seduces men in the morning to give themselves up to indolent sleep. His opponent is principally the vigorous Srausha and his faithful herald the domestic cock.

When we have briefly mentioned the PARIKAS and the

---

[1] Comp. Vd. X, 9.   [2] Yt. XIX, 95; Vd. X, 23.

[3] Vd. V, 8.

JAHIS, about whom I have had occasion to express myself frequently in my 'History of Civilization[1],' there remains only the terrible DRUJ NASUSH. She is the demon of decomposition. Immediately after death has taken place, she rushes in and takes possession of the body, which is thereby putrefied. Everything dead belongs to her and falls into her power, and whosoever therefore comes into contact with the dead has to submit to the ceremony of purification as prescribed by the Law.

It is hardly necessary for me to refer, in concluding this Introduction, to Spiegel's '*Eranische Alterthumskunde*,' in which the same subject has been treated. The section on the 'Religion of the Old Iranians' is a rich mine of information concerning that subject. That my exposition nevertheless essentially differs from that of Spiegel, is owing to the special object which I had in view. It has not been my main purpose to treat the matter exhaustively; my chief aim was rather to render the characteristic elements of the Avesta religion conspicuous. I wished to show how it occupies an independent and highly important position, through its entire tenor and through the process of intuition which manifests itself in it. I wished chiefly to prove how the purely ethical element preponderates, while everything besides, especially the activity of the world of divine beings in the phenomena of nature, falls into the background.

Finally, may I hope that I have succeeded in sketching a clear and correct picture of the faith which Zarathushtra created thousands of years ago, and which is still professed up to this day by the Parsees of India and Persia!

WM. GEIGER.

NEUSTADT, a. d. H.
April, 1883.

---

[1] *Vide* § 16.

CIVILIZATION

OF THE

EASTERN IRĀNIANS

IN

ANCIENT TIMES.

CHAPTER I.

ETHNOGRAPHY [1].

§ 1. *The Arians and their Extension.*

THE Avesta people, as we find them in the Sacred Texts, are pre-eminently a religious corporation. It is their attachment to the Mazdayasnian faith, or their hostile attitude towards it, which is the true criterion according to which all men are classified. To the priests, who composed these texts and whose ideas we may consider them to represent, the above was indeed the principal and cardinal question. He who did not accept the doctrine proclaimed by them, stood opposed to them as an enemy, as much perhaps as the members of foreign tribes with whom no relations were maintained. With the Irānians it was not the case, as it was with the Indians, that the whole nation adhered to *one* belief and *one* religion, prayed to the same deities, and offered sacrifice at the same altars. Nay more, the Irānian people were split up by the Zoroastrian Reform into two factions, which fought against each other with the greater enthusiasm, the closer had been the ties which had previously united them.

But whilst religion and religious unity appear in the fore-

---

[1] Geiger, *Osfīrānische Kultur*, bk. i, ch. 3, § 23.

ground, the element of nationality is by no means insignificant. The Irānians did not regard themselves merely as members of the Mazdayasnān Community, who revered their God-sent prophet in Zarathushtra, and their highest God and Master in Ahura Mazda; but they also felt that they belonged to *one* tribe and *one* nation, they recognized the ties of blood derived from their ancestors, their common descent, language and customs, and they called themselves accordingly by one common name, that of 'Arian.' This name probably indicates the nation as that composed of the Noble, the True, and the Pious, for they believed every virtue and every desirable and praiseworthy quality to be the peculiar heritage of their own tribe, whilst they undervalued the character of foreign peoples in the same proportion as they exalted their own[1]. If, in accordance with another view, 'Arian,' like the German '*deutsch*,' denoted simply 'the man of one's own tribe,' the meaning of the name would in that case be essentially weakened[2]. Hence I adhere to the first explanation, which seems to correspond thoroughly with the spirit of the age and the self-conscious and exclusive character of the Irānians as also of the Vedic Indians.

As the legendary hero *Jāmāspa* beholds the army of the enemy advancing to battle, he implores the *female-yazata* Anāhita to bestow victory upon him as upon *all the other Arians*[3]. A man of the name of Erkhsha 'the Bear' is called the best archer *among the Arians.*

'Thee Tishtrya we praise, the bright, radiant one, who goest as swiftly along the sea Voru-kasha as the arrow obeying the will of Heaven, which Erkhsha

---

[1] *Airya*=O.P. *airya* from root *ar*. The original signification is still often found in Skr. *arya*, 'true, devoted, and friendly to the gods' (Grassmann, *Wörterbuch*, s. v.), as well as in the counterpart to *airya*: N. P. *anēr*, 'prava indoles' (Vullers, *Lexicon*, s. v.). I must mention however that to the Av. *anairya* I give the meaning 'non-Arian' in all passages (also Vendidād I, 18).

[2] Roth, in the Petersburg *Sanskrit-Wörterbuch*, s. v. *arya*; Zimmer, *Altindisches Leben*, p. 100.

[3] Yasht V, 69: *Yatha · vispē · anyē · airē.*

has discharged, who shootest swift arrows, who shootest the swiftest arrows amongst the Arians[1].'

The territories inhabited by the tribes of the Avesta people are spoken of as 'the Arian Lands' or as the 'Homestead of the Arians[2].' The consciousness of unity of race and of equality of blood displays itself most clearly in the statement that from *Gaya-martan*, the first man according to Irānian belief (in the *Shāh-nāmeh* of Firdusi he is the first of the legendary kings under the name of Gayomard), Ahura Mazda created 'the race of all Arian regions, the seed of all Arian lands[3].' The Avesta itself, as we know, mentions *Aryana-vaija* (in which name that of the people is included) as the original seat and primitive home of the Irānians. With this name corresponds Strabo's 'Ariana,' which embraces the Eastern provinces, that is the primitive abode of the Irānian race, as well as the modern ' Irān,' which name is employed to the present day as the official designation of the whole kingdom of Persia. Herodotus also testifies to the antiquity of the name 'Arian.' He informs us that the Medes in earlier ages were universally named 'Arians[4],' a statement which may probably be taken in a somewhat wider sense than would appear from the author's own words to be intended; and the name may thus be applicable not merely to that single tribe, but generally to all the inhabitants of the Irānian highlands.

In the title 'Arian' is implied, according to our ideas, something distinguishing and honourable, a fact which explains its frequent occurrence in proper names. This might be adduced as a powerful argument in favour of the correctness of my own view; for if 'Arya' only meant 'fellow-countrymen,' it is difficult to believe that it would have been

---

[1] Yt. VIII, 6 and 37. I treat *Erkhsha* as a proper name=Ved. *ŗksha*, Rv. VIII, 68, 15. Cf. also Geldner and Noeldeke, *Zeitschrift der deutschen morgenländischen Gesellschaft*, vol. xxxv, p. 445.

[2] *Airyāo · daghāvō*, Yt. VIII, 9 and 56; X, 4, &c.; *airyō shayana*, Yt. X, 13.

[3] Yt. XIII, 87.   [4] Herodotus VII, 62.

found suitable for the formation of personal names. A whole series of such names as Ariobarzanes, Ariomardos, &c., is transmitted to us by Greek and Latin authors[1].

The Avesta nations are not actually styled 'Arians' in the oldest fragments of the Avesta, the Gāthās; but this absence may be explained from the character of the epoch of civilization represented by these hymns,—a period of the most embittered religious and economic struggles, in which the national element was entirely secondary. The reason cannot have been that the name was unknown; for it is primeval and older than the Irānian nation itself, which has received it from earlier ages. The Indians likewise speak of themselves in the songs of the Rig-veda as the 'Ârya[2],' and distinguish themselves as such from the dark-skinned aborigines of the land of the Indus and its five tributaries. During the contest with these—the enemy or *Dāsa*—the Arians, gradually advancing towards the East, occupy the plains of the Panjāb. It may be assumed, therefore, that even at the period when Indians and Irānians constituted a single undivided nation and when these two distinct tribes had not yet been formed, the name 'Arian' had been invented and was in use as a regular designation of the entire people. Furthermore, there are distinct traces extant which give it a still higher and more venerable antiquity. After the division of the Arian people had taken place, both the tribes, the Indian as well as the Irānian, retained their customary appellation and applied it in their usual manner.

It may not be without interest at this point to take a brief survey of the present distribution of the Arian race in the provinces of Central Asia, on the banks of the Oxus and the Jaxartes, as well as in Afghanistan. It is here

---

[1] Cf. Keiper, *Die Perser des Aeschylos*, p. 69.

[2] Ludwig, *Die Manthraliteratur und das alte Indien, als Einleitung zur Uebersetzung des Rig-veda* (Rv. vol. iii) 207; Zimmer, *AiL.* p. 100. In Indian the word *ārya* derived from the original form *arya* serves as a name of the people; however, cf. Böhtlingk and Roth, *Sanskritwörterbuch*, s. v. *arya*, as well as its compounds *aryajārā*, 'beloved of an Arian,' and *aryapatnī*, 'wife of an Arian.'

represented by that highly interesting class of people, the Tājiks, who have their abode in the midst of the Afghāns, Beluchees, and Uzbecks, as a tribe foreign to but tolerated by them and living in peaceful intercourse with them. They form the really settled part of the population, living by commerce, industry, and agriculture, and are therefore very often called *dihkāns* 'peasants' or *dihvars* 'villagers.' Similarly in the Uzbeckian principalities the name *Sart* denotes the settled portion of the people, the inhabitants of towns and villages, as opposed to the nomadic Kirghis ; while the Tājiks are understood to belong to the Arian race as opposed to the Turks or Tatars. Shaw on this point observes[1] : 'Among these various tribes there are two great cross divisions. The first is the division of Turk and Tājik, or of Tartar and of Arian blood. The other classification is that of nomads and settled people, Kirghiz and Sarts.' Hence it follows that by nature, and in all their habits of life, as well as in the development of the civilization of particular tribes, the Sarts are mostly composed of Tājiks, while the nomads are invariably Tatars. Thus it is explained why the Sart and the Tājik are very often regarded as identical. But this is quite incorrect ; 'for all the Khōkandis . . . agreed in affirming that Sart is merely a word used by the Kirghiz to denote all who do not lead a nomad existence like themselves, whether they be Tajiks or Uzbecks.' In a word, the name Sart has a purely historical import, while that of Tājik is rather ethnological.

---

[1] *Reise*, p. 21. Cf. Lerch (*Russische Revue*, vol. i, 1872, p. 30, seq.), who derives the name Sart from O. Ir. *khshathra* (by metathesis *khsharta* = N.P. *shahar*, 'city') and examines the history of the expression with his usual thoroughness. Its most ancient application is said to have been in the name of the Ἰα-ξάρται, whom Ptolemy mentions as living in the lowlands of the Sir (the Silis of the younger Pliny), where formerly more numerous towns, villages, and hamlets existed than at the present day. In Sogdiana the name Sart is obsolete, while it occurs again in Khiva. Sultān Baber denotes by it the populations of several towns and districts in Ferghānā.

Concerning the spread of the Tājiks in Afghānistan, I need not speak at length after what has been communicated to us regarding them by Elphinstone, and subsequently by Spiegel[1]. They are most numerous in the vicinity of the towns: they form the chief part of the population of Kābul, Kandahār, Herāt, and Balkh, while they are completely unknown amongst the inhabitants of the wilder portions of the land. In several districts, especially in Kohistān, that is to say, not far from the capital of Afghānistān, they have preserved their independence. Here indeed they do not exhibit any trace of the submissive and cringing disposition which they so readily assume in their intercourse with a ruling caste. They are on the contrary warlike and eager for the fray, and live in constant feuds amongst themselves. Another branch of the Tājiks inhabits the Lōgar valley, and a third, that of the Furmūlis, is in possession of Urghun, to which we look for the old *Urva* of the Avesta. In Seistān, where they are called *dihkāns*, they likewise form the more ancient portion of the inhabitants collectively, and are similarly spread over the whole of Baloochistān, distinguished by their fixed mode of life and by the fact that they speak the Persian language.

In the country of the Amu and the Sir the Tājiks are far more important. Ujfalvy, to whom we are indebted for detailed and authentic historical accounts of them, correctly points out that three classes must be distinguished : firstly, the native Irānians, who naturally claim our fullest consideration ; next, the Persian colonists ; and, lastly, the descendants of Persian slaves[2]. The indigenous Tājiks as a general rule have brown hair and beards, but there are also found individuals with fair or red hair. Khanikoff[3] describes them as tall people with black hair and beards. Their eyes are large and dark, the nose well formed, the

---

[1] Spiegel, *Eranische Alterthumskunde*, vol. i, p. 340 seq.

[2] Ujfalvy, *Expéd. scient.* vol. ii, pp. 33–34 ; Khanikoff, *Mémoire sur l'ethnographie de la Perse*, p. 92.

[3] *Mém. sur l'ethnogr.*, p. 103 ; comp. Spiegel, *E. A.* vol. i, pp. 339–340.

mouth rather large, the forehead broader, and the whole
structure of the body somewhat heavier than in the case of
the Western Persians. Shaw[1], to whom we are indebted
for most of our knowledge respecting the inhabitants of
the Pāmir, describes the Tājiks as follows :—

'The Tajiks are a very handsome race with high fore-
heads, full expressive eyes shaded by dark eyelashes,
thin delicately-formed noses, short upper lips, and rosy
complexions. Their beards are generally very large and
full, and often of a brown and even sometimes of a reddish
tinge. They differ from the high-caste men of Northern
India only, in being more stoutly and strongly built, and
in having fuller faces.

'Their kinsmen, the men of Badakhshan, bear even a
closer resemblance to the Northern Indians. . . . . The
Wākhanis partake of these characteristics, having also
some of them light hazel-coloured eyes, as have also the
Sirikulis whom I saw at Kâshghar. But the rough life
they lead in their highland valleys has given them a
certain harshness of feature as well as an asperity of
character, which contrasts with the good temper of their
neighbours, the Kirghiz.'

Ujfalvy further points out that 'the Tājiks of the mountains' are of a more independent and noble character than
the inhabitants of the plains. This, as well as their exterior
and the primitive customs which are preserved amongst
them, permits us to recognize in them the genuine descendants of the old Mazdayasnān. As everywhere else,
so also in Central Asia, the secluded and inaccessible
character of the high mountainous districts helped to preserve and perpetuate the peculiar characteristics of their
inhabitants.

The Tājiks of the mountains are collectively called by
the name of Galcha[2]. I do not think we can with justice

---

[1] *Reise*, pp. 22–23.

[2] The name probably means 'mountaineer,' if the derivation of
Tomaschek (*Pamirdialekte*) from Pers. *ghar*, O. Ir. *gairi*, is correct.
Ujfalvy : 'le Galca qu'on a appelé jusqu'à présent aussi Tadjik des

accept any fundamental distinction between the Galchas and the Tājiks of the plains[1]. All the differences that exist between them, whether extrinsic or intrinsic, may be explained by the fact that the former, being isolated in their mountains and high valleys, preserve the type of the Arian race in a purer and less impaired state, while the latter, through their intermixture with Tatarian elements, have lost much of the purity of their blood.

The Galchas are described as individually handsome, with brown, and occasionally red or even light flaxen hair; while the *brachycephalous* skull-formation and considerable skull-capacity form a striking peculiarity, which but seldom appears prominently in the pure Tājiks[2]. Galchas are found in the valleys of the mountains surrounding Ferghāna; they dwell in the country round the sources of the Zerafshān, particularly in the valley of Yaghnōb and along the Oxus as far up as its sources in the Pāmir; and even in the eastern parts of the plateau of Pāmir itself, that is to say, beyond the Neza-tash ridge, we meet with them in the district of Siri-kul. Not less interesting are the natives of the southern declivity of the Hindūkush, in Chitrāl and Kafiristān, but they appear to belong mostly to the Indian race.

The language of the Galchas, which has been of late the object of careful investigation[3], is divided into several dialects, which have a particularly close connection with

montagnes' ('the Galca who was called also up to now the Tajik of the mountains').

[1] Cf. Van den Gheyn in the *Bulletin de l'Athéné Oriental*, 1881, pp. 221-223.

[2] Tomaschek, *Pamirdialekte*, p. 5 seq.

[3] Tomaschek, in his *Zentralasiatische Studien*, vol. ii, has worked up the materials collected by Shaw ('On the Ghaltcha Languages,' 'Journal of the Asiatic Society of Bengal,' vol. xlv, 1876, pp. 139-278; xlvi, 1877, pp. 97-126). He holds the inhabitants of the Pāmir to be the descendants of the Saks, and 'such a linguistic research is to serve above all as a valid support to the following historical proof that these Saks were a purely Irānian tribe, which had preserved the old Irānian mode of life and the genuine Irānian type in greater

the old Eastern Irānian, and thus with the language of the Avesta. If it shows an admixture of Indian words, the reason for this probably lies only in their primitive condition, in consequence of which they still suggest to us more of an original affinity with the Indian than with Modern Persian.

Of the Pāmir dialects the Mungī or Mindshāni is the most important. It is spoken in Mungān, the neighbourhood of Karān, Paryān, Shangān, and in the still unknown valleys on the frontiers of Kāfiristān, and is distinguished by a peculiar resemblance to the Avesta language. In the valley of the Panja, according to the different districts, the Wākhi, the Ishkāshamī, and Shigni are spoken. Besides this, the Sanglichī, the dialect of Sanglich (between Mungān and Ishkāshim), is worthy of mention, as well as the Yaghnōbī, the language of the Galchas in the mountains near the upper Zerafshān. I must not pass over the report of Mushketoff[1] upon the Galchas dwelling in the vicinity of the glaciers of Zerafshān. He regards them as the direct descendants of the ancient Persians. Their civilization is a highly primitive one. They do not occupy themselves with agriculture; their houses and chattels are made of stone, the former without lime or cement. Their sole domestic animal is the *Ishak*, a kind of wild ass, which they use for carrying burdens.

We have just spoken of members of the Irānian stock, who have remained in a very low stage of civilization. Of the other Galchas this cannot be asserted in the same degree. I incline to believe that we may recognize in them the descendants of the Zoroastrians. The Avesta expressly described the primitive home of the Irānian people, the most holy *Aryana-vaija*, as being situated in the mountainous countries drained by the Sir, the Zerafshān, and the Amu. Into these almost inaccessible valleys the faithful adherents

purity than the Medo-Persians, who were strongly influenced in every way by the Semites.'

[1] 'Proceedings of the Royal Geographical Society,' vol. ii, 1880, pp. 765–766.

of the Mazda religion may have retired further and further before the attacks of the Tatars and the Arabs. There they still cherished for a long time the ancient and venerable *cultus* which they had inherited from their ancestors. Many antiquated customs, preserved to the present day, point to this conclusion. For instance, Wood[1] relates that he observed among the inhabitants of Badakhshān and Wakhān a peculiar disinclination to blow out a light. This is in conformity with the ideas and usages of the Zoroastrians, and, more important still, of the Zoroastrians alone. Fire was notoriously regarded by them as the most sacred element, which must be preserved as much as possible from any kind of profanation. Even the breath of man or his spittle is sufficient to desecrate it. Therefore even the priest before the fire-altar must perform his ceremonies and recite his prayers with his mouth covered. I can allude but briefly to the peculiar customs of the Kāfirs : their practice of exposing the dead, and also their peculiar treatment of women after delivery and during their courses, which correspond so closely to the similar precepts of the Avesta that we can scarcely admit the possibility of a merely accidental resemblance[2].

Finally, our theory is corroborated by native legends. In Shignān a tradition[3] exists that the inhabitants of that land were, so late as from 500 to 700 years ago, *Zardushti*, adherents of the Mazda religion, and that only then were they converted to Islām by Mahomedan emissaries from the neighbouring western provinces. Certain buildings in the valley of the Oxus are dedicated to the *Ātashparastagān*, or 'fire-worshippers[4].' Even if this statement be not altogether accurate, it still proves that people have preserved in the Galcha provinces down to the present day the remem-

---

[1] 'Journey,' pp. 177, 218 ; comp. therewith Spiegel, *E. A.* vol. i, p. 339.

[2] Masson, 'Narrative of Various Journeys in Baloochistān, Afghānistān, and the Panjāb,' vol. i, p. 224 seq. ; Spiegel, *E. A.* vol. i. p. 397.

[3] Gordon, 'Pāmir,' p. 141.   [4] Wood, 'Journey,' p. 218.

brance of their former connection with the old national religion.

If at a future time the veil which still hangs over the territories of the Oxus, viz. Shignān, Roshān, and Darwaz, should be lifted by a courageous traveller and inquirer, we may expect to receive new and abundant information concerning the highly important questions of Central Asiatic Ethnography and Irānian Antiquity.

§ 2.   *The Adversaries of the Avesta People.*

THE life of the Avesta people was by no means one of peacefulness and tranquillity.   The Gāthās themselves present a picture of continual combats and feuds, and show us how the existence of the newly-founded community of the Mazdayasnān remained for a long time most precarious and uncertain.   By degrees, however, all opposition seems to have broken down, the Mazda religion throve and increased, the number of its adherents grew larger from year to year, and in the more recent part of the Avesta they appear no longer as a maligned and persecuted people, but as victors and rulers.

This brings us to a cardinal question in the history of the civilization of the Avesta people, a question which we may briefly state as follows.   Are we to concede that the Irānians, at the time of their immigration into the settlements described in the Avesta, did not there meet with an aboriginal people not akin to them?   Do we learn from the Avesta itself anything of conflict with tribes of non-Arian race?   Or do all the descriptions of hostile surprises and warlike undertakings, which occur in the Avesta, refer solely to the feuds carried on amongst the Irānians themselves; and are consequently the names of nations (to be hereafter enumerated) handed down to us in the Avesta to be all explained as designations of particular tribes (and their subdivisions) of the Irānian people?

As regards the first part of this question, it is evident that in the Avesta a very marked social and religious opposition is exhibited from the beginning, a contrast between the settled population and the nomads, between the adherents of the Zoroastrian doctrine and their enemies. And from that time forward it is unquestionable that this opposition is of paramount importance, and is most strongly emphasized by the authors of the Avesta. However, I believe that all the circumstances bearing on this point have not yet been explained. As the inhabitants of Turkistān are divided according to descent into Turks and Tājiks, into members of the Arian and Tatarian races, and according to occupation into Sarts and Kirghiz; so, side by side with the economic separation of the population into wandering herdsmen and agricultural settlers, there exists also a national schism which affords us proof of the existence of a non-Arian element in old Irān. It is true, the national opposition, so far as it seems to be indicated in the Avesta, does not belong to the present, but rather to the past—at least more frequent mention is made of the battles fought with the race foreign and hostile to the Arians in the legendary stories than in the form of genuine historical narrative. However, all this none the less tends to prove the existence of a non-Arian aboriginal people.

The religious and economical schisms more or less coincide, as we shall see presently. The Zoroastrian doctrine thrives among the settled population, who first accept it, while the nomadic tribes mostly decline to submit to its binding and restraining laws. The Avesta on this account invariably extols the settled life of the peasant and the careful tending of cattle, and recognizes a religious merit in the cultivation of the soil and in the reclaiming of land still lying waste, as also in the gradual promotion of civilization.

But the social contrast can be as little mistaken for the national one in old Irān, as it can in the present age in the principalities near the Sir and the Amu. It is probable, from internal evidence, that the non-Arians were mostly nomads; but there is no doubt that a considerable part of the old Irānian nation also followed the same roving manner of life.   They had as yet by no means universally taken to agriculture and permanent settlements.

I begin with the Gāthās, the only part of the Avesta the contents of which are exclusively devoted to contemporary events and the description of existing circumstances. Here the contrast is manifestly the economic and religious one. I shall refer to this more in detail, when, in the economic portion of my work, I have to speak of the mutual relations of agriculture and cattle-breeding, as well as of the contrast between the nomadic and the settled populations.

On the one side stand the husbandmen, the pious, the faithful, truly devoted to Ahura Mazda and the Good Doctrine, who distinguish themselves particularly by the care which they bestow upon the sacred cow.   On the other side we behold the impious, who do not plough the field, and who cause injury and harm to the cow: these are the nomads, who have no knowledge of the systematic rearing of cattle, the unbelievers who do not accept Zarathushtra's doctrine.   That these too were Irānians is proved by the mere fact that the prophet argues with them, propounds his doctrine to them, and calls upon them to decide in its favour.   This at least presupposes a community of language and a certain measure of relationship which we could not admit as existing between Arians and non-Arians.   We have only to remember the sublime passage in which Zarathushtra, or one of his first adherents and followers, preaches the new faith (evidently in the midst of a large gathering of peasants), beginning with the words—

'I will announce it: Now hear and understand,
Ye who have come from near and from far[1]!'

Between the believers and the unbelievers, the husbandmen and the nomads, bloody conflicts ensued:

'He shall not disturb our prayers,
Who said how one beholds in the worst manner (*or profanely*)

---

[1] Yasna XLV, 1.

The cow and the sun with one's eyes;
Who bestows gifts upon the wicked,
But causes the pasture-grounds to lie waste,
And hurls his weapons against the pious [1]!'

The prophet even summons his adherents openly to the fight:

'None of you shall listen to the words
And precepts of the wicked;
For into his house and into his village,
Into his estate and his country
Will he bring grief and death.
Therefore slay them with weapons [2]!'

The separation of the people into believers and unbelievers begins in the Gāthās, and continues throughout the whole of the Avesta. It is highly characteristic of the tone of the Avesta, and the language possesses a complete series of expressions whereby the adherents of the Zoroastrian religion and their opponents are designated [3]. From the wicked, who are ignominiously compared even with noxious and loathsome animals [4], originated every kind of evil, viz. hatred, enmity, and discord [5]; the faithful, on the contrary, distinguish themselves by their pious and holy spirit and their humble devotion towards Ahura Mazda [6].

---

[1] Ys. XXXII, 10.   [2] Ys. XXXI, 18.

[3] The most important amongst them are: *Asha* or *ashavan* (Skr. *r̥tāvan*), 'pious, righteous;' *anashavan, drvat* (in the Gāthā-dialect *dregvat*, where *g* strengthens *v*, as in *hvōgva*, identical with *hvōva* of the common dialect), 'impious, unrighteous;' *hudaçna*, 'adhering to the good doctrine;' *duzhdaçna*; *Mazdayasna* 'Mazda-worshipper;' *daçvayasna*, 'demon-worshipper;' *dahma*, 'pious;' *adahma*. Fellow-believers are called *hāmō-daçna* or *hva-daçna*, the believers in other faiths *anyō-varena* or *anyō-tkaçsha*.

[4] Hence *khrafstra-mashya*, 'men like *khrafstras.*'

[5] *Açnaǧh*, 'hatred,' proceeds from the wicked (Ys. XXXII, 6–8); the wicked are designated as *tbishvañtō*, 'malignant, hostile' (Ys. XXVIII, 7); their resistance is called *paiti-rema*, *açshma* (Ys. XLIV, 20; XLVIII, 7; XLIX, 4, &c.)

[6] Hence the abstract terms *asha, vohu-manō*, as well as *ārmaiti*

The constantly recurring prayers of the Avesta, therefore, are especially those which call down blessings and happiness upon the faithful, and misery and misfortune upon the wicked.

> 'According to desire, power over all good that originates from piety is given to the pious; but no power is given to the wicked! Master of his wishes be the pious, impotent in his wishes be the wicked! Joy and prosperity do I wish for the world of the pious, but distress and adversity do I wish for the entire world of the wicked[1].'

The religious and the economic schism in the population of old Irān is thus beyond question illustrated clearly enough. It is undoubtedly far more difficult to prove the existence of a race-opposition between the Arians and the non-Arians.

The plains near the Caspian and Aral Seas, as also those along the northern shores of the Black Sea, were, even in the most ancient days, inhabited by a large number of wandering tribes, which are usually classed under the general appellation of 'Scythians' by the Greeks. They may be considered as consisting chiefly of the aboriginal population of Irān. If they were of Tatarian descent, like the present inhabitants of the steppes—and certain analogies in their mode of life and customs with those of the present Turkomans and Kirghiz cannot but be recognized—the diversity of race would be thereby established. However, it is almost agreed that the Scythians were of Arian descent, as appears particularly from the proper names transmitted to us through the medium of Greek writers. The southern tribes appear to have belonged to the Irānian, the northern perhaps to the Sclavonic branch of the Indo-Germanic family[2]. Concerning

---

(in the Gāthās=āramaiti), are frequently used as concrete for 'the pious, righteous;' Ys. XXXIII, 3; XXXIV, 2 and 3; XLVI, 16, &c.   [1] Ys. VIII, 5, 6, 8.

[2] Duncker, *Geschichte des Alterthums*, vol. ii, p. 430 seq.; Spiegel, *E. A.* vol. ii, p. 333 seq.

the Scythian nation of the Saks, which dwelt in the mountainous countries near the upper banks of the Amu-daryā, Tomaschek[1] specially undertakes to adduce proofs that it was a genuine Irānian tribe, and that it has preserved the characteristics of the Irānian nation in a purer and more genuine form than perhaps the Persians or the Medes. Here again then we have no national contrast, but merely another instance of that economical separation of the Irānian people into nomads and settled colonists, which is indicated by the most ancient fragments of the Avesta. The Scythians represented only those tribes which still wandered over the steppes as migratory herdsmen; whilst the Sogdians, Persians, Medes, Bactrians, Arians were those who had taken to the cultivation of the soil and to permanent dwellings. But if the Scythians of ancient times exhibit many striking points of resemblance in customs and ways of life to the modern Tatarian inhabitants of the steppes; if they, like the latter, distinguished themselves as bold riders, delighted in continual battles and feuds, drank mares' milk as their favourite beverage, and lived in the most astonishing and repulsive uncleanliness,— all this must have been on account of the identity of external circumstances in the nature of the soil and climate, whereby both have been influenced, and the same results were brought about at different times and among different nations.

I do not wish to deny the Irānian, or at all events Arian, nationality of a large portion of the Scythian tribes, least of all that of the Saks[2], but I would remark that the name 'Scythian' is used rather vaguely by Greek writers. It strikes me that the name had more of an economic import, and comprehended all the nomadic nations of the Eastern

---

[1] *Pamirdialekte*, p. 4.

[2] According to Grigorjeff ('On the Scythian Tribe of the Saks'), as well as according to Cuno ('Inquiries in the Region of Ancient Ethnography, part i, 'The Scyths'), the Saks are a Sclavonic people; while in other quarters this view is disputed (cf. *Russische Revue*, vol. i, pp. 103–105).

European and the Central Asiatic lowlands, without taking
into consideration whether any differences of blood and
language existed.   In short, the notion contained in the
name ' Scythians' is co-extensive with the vague and general expression 'Tūrānians,' much in favour with modern
writers, or perhaps with the term 'Kirghiz' in the case of
modern Turkistān.   If, therefore, it can be proved with
certainty of a part of the Scythians, that they belonged to
the Arian race and spoke an Arian language, it does not
follow that there were not also tribes of a foreign race,
perhaps Tatars, amongst the Scythians and reckoned as
belonging to them[1].

This is merely by the way.   As we are here dealing
only with a possibility, I shall omit further mention of
the Scythians, and shall attempt to discover whether
no other traces of a non-Arian aboriginal population may
be discovered.   And such traces are undoubtedly to be
found.   The best Assyriologists are agreed that the Semites,
on their immigration into the plains of the Euphrates
and the Tigris, found a people foreign to them, with a
culture, language, and writing of their own.   From the
blending of the two tribes, the Sumir and the Akkad, the
aborigines and immigrating Kushites or Semites, arose the
Chaldæan people.   This gradual intermingling may have
taken place only after fierce struggles and contests, but no
tradition reaches back to those warlike ages of the past.
Even in the oldest monuments we find Sumir and Akkad
already forming one nation.   The language of the Sumir
became gradually extinct, and only survived as a sacred
dialect still preserved in temples and schools.   But the
writing invented by the aborigines, viz. the cuneiform
character, was now accepted as the predominant and only

---

[1] To my delight I here find myself in accord with Maspero, who
asserts positively ('History of the Oriental Peoples in Antiquity,'
p. 129): 'The Scyths, the oldest among mankind, belong at
least partly to those tribes of the Tūrānian race, which even at
the present day inhabit the north of Europe and Asia from the
marshes of Finland to the banks of the Amur.'

current language of the Semites; it was adapted to the wants of the Kushite dialect, and served thenceforth for their writing, as it had done before for that of the Sumerian dialect. Every symbol now corresponded to a new sound, without however losing its old signification. The symbol which, in the Sumerian language, meant the sun and the day, still retained its Sumerian phonetic value in *ut, ud, par* and *para;* it may however be also read *shamash* or *yum*, which are the Semitic words for 'sun' and 'day.' Thus the writing of the Chaldæan cuneiform characters of itself reveals to us the striking intermixture of two dissimilar elements, pervading in a similar way the entire civilized life of the tribes of the Mesopotamian lowland[1].

It is therefore clear that we must assume the existence of an aboriginal population of foreign race before the appearance in the East of the Semites, and even before that of the Arians. That it did not confine itself to the districts round the Euphrates and the Tigris, but that it spread likewise over the entire plateau of Irān, is to be accepted as pretty certain. Whether that original population was a Tatarian one, cannot indeed be proved absolutely, but it is not improbable, if we consider the character of the Sumerian language. If, relying upon Chinese sources, we allow that the present Khānātes, Khiva, Bokhārā, and Khōkand, as well as Eastern Turkistān were inhabited in the most ancient times by an Arian population, and that the Mongol-Tatar race first occupied those districts in a comparatively recent period[2], I must declare myself altogether incompetent to decide this question. However, this does not seem to me to touch the root of the matter. If we speak of an aboriginal population of Western Asia, we are dealing with an epoch of time for which direct historical testimony cannot be demanded, and which indeed stands at the very dawn of history. If, then, the Tataric-Mongolian nations which

---

[1] Cf. Maspero, 'History,' pp. 135 seq., 152; Duncker, *Geschichte des Alterthums*, vol. i, p. 247 seq.; Spiegel, *E. A.* vol. i, p. 381 seq.
[2] Cf. *Russische Revue*, vol. ix, p. 328.

now possess Central Asia found Arian tribes there before
them, very likely the Arians in their turn met in their
first immigration with a primitive population of Tatars,
which naturally, at the time when the new Mongolian
invasion began, had been absorbed long ago by the
ruling classes.

I would moreover suggest that no more weight be attached
to these details than I myself allow them. For in order
to attain to a really definite judgment on this difficult
and complicated question, one must have made the most
extensive studies regarding very different countries. Only
the *possibility* that, side by side with the Arian population
of old Irān, an older non-Arian one existed, may be considered as assured. This brings me to the principal point
of my argument : How does the Avesta bear upon this
question ?

I shall later on adduce some indirect proofs, which
seem to establish the existence of a primitive non-Arian
race. That slavery existed in old Irān follows, as well as
from other causes, from the fact that industry, in spite of
the absence of a peculiar class of manufactures, had reached
a degree of development by no means insignificant. The
slaves may have been either captives taken in war from
among the hostile Arian tribes, or, what is more probable,
descendants of the conquered aborigines who had been deprived of their lands, but were allowed to follow trades which
to the conquerors appeared less honourable than agriculture.
We shall find further on that, in the houses of the Mazdayasnān, daughters of unbelieving tribes lived as maid-servants
and concubines, a practice denounced in the Avesta with
such abhorrence, that we may conclude therefrom that, like
the *dāsa-women* of the Rigveda, these must have been
women belonging to the non-Arian tribes, against whom
the priests of Mazda preached with such holy indignation.

But in the Avesta we have also proofs of the most direct
kind. *Non-Arians* are often expressly named, and, twist
and turn them as we will, these facts cannot be ignored, and
we are thus actually compelled to assume the existence of
non-Arian tribes in old Irān. The non-Arian countries

are attacked by the Arians, they are destroyed through the
glory of Zarathushtra[1]. This is a clear allusion to the war
of races which the Irānians, especially the pre-Zoroastrian
Irānians, waged with their enemies, and in which they
proved victorious. Of the province of *Varna* it is expressly
said that it contained non-Arian inhabitants[2]. Varna was,
in my opinion, situated in the north-western parts of the
country possessed by the Irānians, perhaps in the present
district of Tāberistān. And it may be hence conjectured
that the non-Arian tribes gradually withdrew before the
victorious Arians into the almost inaccessible mountains of
the Alburz, in order to maintain there, for at least some
time longer, their ancient independence.

This non-Arian tribe in Varna I hold to be identical with
the 'wicked people of Varna,' frequently mentioned elsewhere in the Avesta, who stand in close relation to the
'demons of Māzenderān[3].' As Māzenderān is not very
distant from Tāberistān, there is good reason for believing

---

[1] Yt. XVIII, 2 (*anairyāo · danhāvō*); Yt. XIX, 68.

[2] Vd. I, 18; *anairyācha · danhēu*sh · *aiwishitāra*. I read *aiwishitāra* instead of *aiwishtāra* according to the Vendidād-sāde and the
Pahlavi translation. The latter has *anārich malāān madam mānash-
nīh*. The word thus comes from the root *shi* = *khshi*, and we need
only be surprised that the root-vowel is not increased before the
suffix *tar*.

[3] *Varenya · drvañlō* and *māzainya · daçva*. It has probably a
similar sense, when it is said of *Urva* in the south-eastern boun-
daries of the territories of the Avesta people, that 'evil inhabitants'
dwelt there (*agha · aiwishitāra*) Vd. I, 11; for its reading *vide* the
preceding note; (Pehl. *sharītar avarmānashnih*). Here we must
probably think not of non-Arian but of Indian tribes. Very interesting also is the expression 'malignant or hostile tribes' (*danhēu*sh ·
rākhshāilhyāo and *rākhshyēilī*sh *danhāvō*. Yt. X, 27 and 78, as
anairyāo · danhāvō). The epithet is derived from the rt. *rakhsh* = Skr.
raksh, and is thus akin to Skr. *rakshas*, which also serves in the Rig-
veda as a designation for hostile tribes. The meaning 'demon'
which is usually found in dictionaries is certainly only the secondary
one, as in the case of Dāsa and Dasyu. *Vide* Zimmer, *Altindisches
Leben*, p. 109 seq.; Ludwig, *Einleitung zur Uebersetzung des Rig-
veda*, p. 211.

in the connection, and we are also entitled to recognize in the demons mentioned above only foreign aborigines, the remnants of whom maintained themselves longest in the swampy forests on the narrow coast-district between the Caspian Sea and Alburz.

The war of races is moreover assigned by the Avesta to a very ancient period. The tradition respecting that period of bloody warfare is attached to the half-mythical figure of *Haushyangha* — Hōsheng in Firdūsī — one of the oldest princes of the line of the heroic kings of the Avesta and of the Shāh-nāme :

> 'To the Ardvi-sura Anāhita did Haushyangha, the Paradhāta, sacrifice on the foot of the Hara, and he prayed to her : "Grant me this gift, O Ardvi-sura Anāhita, that I may become the supreme ruler over all demons and men, . . . and that I may slay two-thirds of the demons of Māzenderān and of the wicked people of Varna[1]." '

As we know, Strabo also makes mention of a tribe of the Anariaks, who according to him were settled on the coast of the Caspian Sea. Here we have the corrupt form of that name *Anarya* by which the Irānians of the Avesta could scarcely have meant merely an individual tribe dwelling near the Caspian Sea, but rather all the tribes that belonged to a race foreign to their own[2].

If my view is correct, the aborigines of the land are frequently designated as *daiva*, demons. They were to the orthodox Irānians only the earthly image of the superhuman, wicked powers. In an analogous manner the two ideas which indicate demons and foes belonging to foreign tribes are continually intermingled in the Rig-veda, and we cannot always easily distinguish, in the different passages, which of the two designations is the correct one. If in the

---

[1] Yt. V, 22.

[2] Strabo, pp. 507, 508 (here a city Anariaka is also mentioned), 514 near the Marders, the Hyrcanians, the Cadusians and similar tribes. The ʾΑναριάκαι of Strabo would correspond closely enough to an Old Irānian *Anairyaka*, a derivative from *anairya*.

Avesta a distinction is made between daiva and men[1], we must naturally understand the former to mean superhuman monsters. It may be shown, however, that in the Rig-veda, too, the primitive population of the Panjāb, the people of the *Dāsa*, are frequently placed in direct opposition to the tribe of Manu, to the human race[2]. That the daivas of the Avesta may likewise be beings of flesh and blood we might be inclined to infer from the fact that even Maz-dayasnān, when they grossly violate the commandments of Zarathushtra, degenerate into demons, and become like the rudest, most abject, and most profligate of men[3]. However, I may here assume a similar use to that of the German word *Teufel* (devil).

The struggle of the Arians with the daivas, the subjection of the primitive inhabitants of the Irānian highlands, naturally accompanied the first immigration of the Arian tribes in the earliest epoch of their history. Accordingly, the native legend assigns those events to the reign of King Yima, by whom also, as we shall see further on, the systematic breeding of cattle is said to have been introduced. His person at all events represents a very early and primitive stage of the civilization of the Irānian people. The Avesta makes him pray to Anāhita :

> 'Grant me that I may snatch away from the demons both wealth and plenty, both fields and herds, both nourishment and splendour[4].'

For the arable lands and pasture-grounds the course of the struggle is as follows. Yima tries to take by force from the daivas the districts suitable for thriving settlements in order to make them over to his own people. This was undoubtedly

---

[1] Ys. XXIX, 4 ; cf. also supra, Yt. V, 22, next the formations *daçva, mashya, yātu, pairika, kavi, karapan*, near them we also find sātar 'the destroyer, the enemy,' Ys. IX, 18 ; Yt. I, 10; V, 13 &c.

[2] Rv. II, 20, 7 ; V, 31, 7 ; VI, 21, 11, &c.

[3] Vd. VII, 56, ' . . . he is a *daiva*, a worshipper of the *daivas*, one who holds intercourse with the *daivas*, one who adheres to the *daivas*.' Cf. Vd. VIII, 31.

[4] Yt. V, 26.

the beginning and the earliest phase of the war of races. The legend then goes on to ascribe to Zarathushtra the complete destruction of the daivas. Formerly they roved in human form about the earth, but after the advent of the prophet they disappeared and could only exercise their destructive influence as disembodied beings[1]. Where the Irānian people thus gradually emerge from the dawn of legend into the brighter light of an historical age, the daivas and the battles with them are removed to a supernatural and superhuman region, and lapse into all-deforming myth. At the period of the foundation and of the flourishing estate of the Mazda-religion the dominion and independence of the non-Arian tribes are already broken down; they have either disappeared from the soil and been destroyed by the Irānians, or they still subsist merely as the last survivors who have adapted themselves gradually to the laws and ideas of the victors, and who pursue a peaceful trade amidst the ruling classes of the Arians, without being any longer savagely persecuted by them but yet without enjoying equal rights.

We have already spoken of the *Māzanian daivas*. Whether their name bears any relation to that of the present province of Māzenderān cannot be proved with certainty; however, it is not impossible. Māzenderān, on account of its extremely unwholesome climate and its marshy soil, which was certainly covered in olden times with impenetrable forests, may have remained free from the settlements of the Arians, and have served as a place of refuge to the conquered aborigines. In the legend of Firdūsī, also, Māzenderān is regarded as the dwelling-place of demons, as prominently appears from the narrative of the march of Kaikāus to that country[2].

It is with the *Māzanian daivas* that Haushyangha

---

[1] Ys. IX, 15, 'Thou, O Zarathushtra, didst make * all demons, * who before roamed about the world in human forms *, conceal themselves in the earth.'

[2] *Firdūsī, Shāh-nāme*, ed. by Vullers, vol. i, p. 315 seq.; Spiegel, *E. A.* vol. i, p. 585 seq.

principally fights—the very hero of the Irānian legend who subdued the wicked people of Varna. He thus invokes the genius Druvāspa:

> 'Grant me, that I may overpower all *Māzanian daivas*, that, terrified, I may not give way through fear before the demons. Before us may all *daivas* in alarm give way against their will, terrified may they fly unto darkness[1].'

Together with the *daivas* are to be named the *drujas*, monsters which are also, as I believe, to be understood in very many cases as human beings, and indeed as race-enemies of the Arians. We read frequently in the Gāthās:

> 'For that reason do I ask Thee; give me a correct reply, O Ahura:
> How can I deliver the monsters into the power of the pious
> In order to slay them according to the commandments of Thy Doctrine,
> In order to cause a mighty overthrow among the wicked?
> I will deliver them up, O Mazda, to Danger and Misery[2]!'

So also in the later Avesta, when the bullock, carried off by the nomads of the steppes, complains to Mithra that he has been led away into the abode of monsters[3]; or, when the 'monsters of Varna,' who may probably, however, be identical with the evil people of Varna, are expressly distinguished from the 'invisible monsters,' the wicked spirits[4].

Two results may be deduced from the above facts. The Avesta in no way contravenes the belief in a primitive race in Irān foreign to the Arians, but lends it a noteworthy confirmation. 'Non-Arian' tribes are expressly mentioned in the Zoroastrian documents. We furthermore

---

[1] Yt. IX, 4; XVII, 25; cf. Vd. XVII, 9.
[2] Ys. XLIV, 14.   [3] Ys. X, 86.
[4] *Varenya · dravaiñti · druj, mainyava · druj*, Yt. I, 19.

arrive, through the Avesta, at the result to which modern interpretation of the Rig-veda has brought us. In many passages where mention is made apparently of monsters or demons, we have to deal, not with superhuman incidents, but with absolutely real and to a certain extent historical events. The same expression which designates the dark powers of Hell, the demoniacal enemies of the bright, beneficent deities of light, denotes also the enemies of mankind, and, indeed, especially those enemies with whom the Arians were united by none of the ties of blood, custom, religion, or language, and who might therefore, with some show of reason, be regarded by them as the embodiment of the power hostile to God—the non-Arian tribes whom they subdued in the earliest period of their immigration in the fierce war of races.

§ 3. Character of the Adversaries of the Avesta People.

IN particular cases it is naturally no easy matter to distinguish between those enemies of the Avesta people who, living as nomads, differed from them only in their economic status, and those who belonged to a foreign tribe. The following may be considered as a criterion at least occasionally applicable. As the war with the primitive race is as a rule laid in the legendary period, that is, in a past time remote from that of the Avesta, we are probably right in holding, where the Avesta speaks of existing circumstances, that the conflict is generally one between husbandmen and nomads. But where the events of an earlier epoch are described, there remains the possibility of allusion being made to a difference of race. At all events it is beyond question that in the Avesta national conflicts, as opposed to social ones, are only of secondary importance.

In this Section, therefore, I shall only mention in general those enemies who threatened the peace and security of the Avesta people, without considering whether they belonged to the Arian race or not.

These enemies were bodies of horsemen, who had their real abode and place of refuge in the desert. Mounted on swift horses, they broke suddenly into the settled and well-cultivated districts of the Zoroastrians, and surprised their villages and hamlets. Whoever offered resistance was slain, the remainder, as well as the women and children, were carried off into captivity. The main object of these inroads, however, was simply to make booty of the herds of cattle, which were driven off by the robbers into the oases of the steppes, where all pursuit was vain[1].

Such conditions of life vividly recall to mind those which existed down to very recent times on the north-eastern frontiers of Persia, and which have only very lately been gradually brought to an end through the extension of Russian dominion in Central Asia. As in ancient times the settled dwellings of the Avesta people were invaded by the no-madic tribes of the North, so in Khorāsān up to our own times the villages and estates of the Persians were liable to the inroads of the Turcomans. The object of the plun-dering excursions of the Turcomans is likewise to rob their more wealthy neighbours, and to carry off cattle and slaves. They owe their success more to their sudden and unex-pected attacks, which cause the greatest panic and con-fusion among the Persians and cripple their power for resistance, than to their personal courage and resolution. The effects of such attacks are horrible, and travellers like Ferrier, Vámbéry, M'Gregor and others are able to describe dreadful scenes, which they have either heard of or witnessed with their own eyes[2]. The insecurity of life and property has here reached such a height, that the most flourishing and most fertile districts of Irān have become gradually

---

[1] The dwellers near the banks of the Rangha, the Jaxartes, pro-bably nomadic tribes of herdsmen, are expressly designated (Vd. I, 20) as *taozhya* (= N.P. *tōz*) 'robber-like, rapacious;' *taozhyācha · daghēu*sh · *aiwishitāra*.

[2] Comp. the collections by Marvin, 'Merv,' p. 177 seq.; on the system of attack and the mode of fighting of the Turcomans see particularly Ferrier, *Voyages*, vol. i, p. 162 seq.

depopulated, and remain wholly uncultivated and useless. In many districts ruined villages are met with in close succession. The remains of waterworks and canals show that industry is declining. In some parts hardly a single family is to be found which has not had to lament the loss of one or more of its members, who have either perished during a raid or are pining in slavery among the Turcomans.

If however the Persians at the present day are everywhere at a disadvantage on the frontiers of Khorāsān, and do not even show themselves capable of making corresponding reprisals, the case must have been different in more ancient times. According to the Avesta, the princes of the Arian districts assembled and opened a regular campaign against their enemies, in order to exact a bloody vengeance for all their encroachments[1]. If we were to press this passage, we might even infer from it that the enemies referred to must have belonged to a non-Arian tribe.

An allusion to the marauding and plundering expeditions of the northern barbarians is contained in the following passage : —

> 'What is, fifthly, most unpleasant to this earth ?—When pious men, O Spitama Zarathushtra, and women and children are driven into captivity along the sandy, waterless way, and, complaining, raise their voice[2].'

Here is evidently represented such a band of robbers on their way back to their sandy steppes from a successful raid. The captives are dragged away in fetters, and with tears and wailings they follow their cruel victors to a hard, life-long bondage. We can scarcely believe that two or three thousand years have intervened between the time when these descriptions were written and quite recent days, when the missionary Wolff, in his well-known ' Travels,'

---

[1] Yt. X, 8.

[2] Vd. III, 11. Observe the expression *varaithīm · pañtām · pāsnvāoğhem · hikvāoğhem,* 'the dry and dusty way leading to captivity,' i. e. into the desert !

depicted scenes in every way similar, experienced and witnessed by himself in the same land[1].

As a designation of the nomads of the deserts who set out for plunder, the word *haēna*, 'army' or 'hostile army,' is pretty often used in the Avesta. In this context the word corresponds perhaps to the modern *Al-amān*, the expression for the plundering expeditions of the Turcomans. It may be conceived that nothing was so much feared, nothing so much an emblem of horror and terror, as a surprise by the *haēna*: —

> 'Whoever should give a wicked, impious enemy of the pious, the pressed juice *Hauma*, or of the consecrated food for the sacrificial festival meal, does no better work than if he led the *haēna*, consisting of a thousand horse, against the villages of the Mazdayasnān, slew the men, and dragged away the herds of cattle into captivity[2].'

The nature of the *haēna* is clearly characterized in this passage, more especially by the descriptive epithet 'consisting of a thousand horse.' Elsewhere it is styled 'with broad lines of battle, malicious, surprising[3].' The enemy

---

[1] Wolff, in Marvin, 'Merv,' p. 238. I cannot forbear quoting the description which the passage before us so strikingly recalls: 'Wolff was accompanied by Bokhara merchants, who had bought at Sarakhs two Persian boys as slaves, whom they were going to bring to Bokhara to sell. The one was seven years of age, and the other nine. The Turcomans universally call the Persians Guzlbaash, i.e. "Red-head." Wandering through the desert the two poor Guzl-baash slaves were singing in the morning, and during the day, and in the evening, in plaintive strains, the following words:

> "The Al-amaan has taken us,
>   Poor, poor Guzl-baash!
> And carry us, and carry us
> In iron and chains, in iron and chains
>   To Oorgantsh and Bokhārā."

Thus they proceeded through the desert, continually hearing that plaintive strain.'

[2] Vd. XVIII, 12; *hazaḡrō-aspǎm · haēnǎm.*

[3] *Haēnayāoscha · perethu-ainikayāo · davāithyāo · paṭāithyāo.* Ys. IV, 18.

is thus a force of cavalry, scouring the country in detached bands, not fighting man to man, but conquering through cunning surprises and sudden attacks, not by heroic valour. The *haęna* also bears banners and standards[1]; and I may here remind the reader that the Turcomans also, I believe, carry field-ensigns, although their employment generally presupposes a certain amount of tactical knowledge and an organized mode of fighting.

On the other hand, it appears somewhat incongruous to find the *haęna* mentioned as using war-chariots[2]. The nomads of the steppes certainly fought in that age, as they now do, on horseback only ; the use of war-chariots points to more civilized nations. The writer therefore is either speaking of hostile armies in general, and not especially of the hordes of the deserts, or else he arbitrarily transfers the conditions and methods of his own people to other tribes.

The appearance of the enemy, as it was mostly a sudden surprise, naturally inspired terror and consternation[3]. Only through divine assistance was it possible to master the dreaded and hated foe :

'When Mithra drives against the terrible, hostile armies, against those so assembled for fighting in the battle of the country : Then does he fasten behind their backs the arms of those who have broken their engagements ; then does he veil their sight and deafen their ears[4].'

---

[1] 'Before the wicked armies of the enemy, they bear the bloody banners (*khrūrem · drafshem*),' Yt. X, 93; Ys. LVII, 25. Cf. *perethu-drafsha, uzgereplō-drafsha, khrūrem · drafshem · barat.* Yt. XIII, 136.

[2] *Ratha · haęnya.* Yt. VIII, 56 ; XIV, 48.

[3] *Vōighna* ; comp. Skr. *vij*, part. *vigna*, 'perplexed, confounded.' Ys. LXVIII, 13, *pairi · haęnayāoscha · vōighnābyō*, 'before the terror which 'the *haęna* calls forth.' In Ys. LVII, 14 *vōighna* is akin to *aghāo · ilhyęjāo*, 'evil, corruption ;' in Ys. VIII, 56 ; XIV, 48 near *haęna, pāman, kapasti, haęnya ratha, uzgerepta · drafsha.*

[4] Yt. X, 48, *avi · haęnayāo · khravīshyęifīsh* · (similarly Yt. XV, 49; XIX, 54).

Naturally, it was the herds of the settlers that the nomads more especially hankered after. The main object of all the plundering incursions and surprises of the nomadic hordes was to gain booty, as was generally the case in all the wars of those remote ages. They found it more convenient to seize from their settled neighbours what they required, than to occupy themselves with the troublesome work of rearing cattle in a regular and systematic manner. If we consider what value the Avesta people attached to their herds, we can conceive why the loss of those dearest of possessions is lamented in the following strain :

> 'On that blood-stained path into captivity wanders the cow, that goes upon hoofs, when she falls into the power of the breakers of covenants [1].'

> 'The cow that is driven away as booty, implores him (Mithra) for help, longing to return to her stalls: "When will the valiant one, driving us from behind, bring us back into our stall, O Mithra, the master of wide fields? When will he lead us to the paths that belong to the pious, us who are dragged away into the abode of the demons [2]?"'

§ 4. *Names of Nations in the Avesta.*

WE have an interesting passage in the *Farvardin Yasht* which enumerates the most important nations in Irān. It runs as follows, omitting superfluous repetitions :

> 'We praise the *manes* of the pious men and of the pious women of the Arian countries, of the Tūrānian countries, of those of the Sarima, of those of the Sāni, and of those of the Dāhas [3].'

---

[1] Yt. X, 38. The 'breakers of covenants' *mithra-drujō* (as elsewhere occasionally *anashavan, drvat,* &c.) stand evidently for *haçna* here, as in the passage (Yt. X, 48) translated above.

[2] Yt. X, 86, *vide* Geldner, *Metrik,* § 104.

[3] Yt. XIII, 143–144.

If we take this passage quite literally, we must at any rate assume that the Arians are here contrasted with the Tūrānians, the Sarima, the Sāni, and the Dāhas, and that the latter, therefore, do not belong to the Arian race. Here, however, I must first of all observe that so far as I am aware no further proof can be adduced from the Avesta for the non-Arian descent of the nations above-named.

I begin with the Tūrānians. At present we use this name ethnographically for the Tatarian nomadic tribes of Central Asia. But this application is arbitrary, and is in nowise confirmed by hints gathered from the Avesta. Nor is the practice justified by Firdūsī. Indeed, the name *Tūra* appears to have always been regarded by the Irānians, from the Avesta to the Book of Kings, as a collective idea which did not indicate any ethnographical division, but comprised the peoples of the steppes from the Caspian Sea to the Sir and beyond it. The remains of an aboriginal population of Tatars may thus indeed have formed part of them, just as may have been the case also with the Scyths of the Greek authors, but they must in all likelihood have been chiefly Arians.

The Tūra are mentioned in the Gāthās ; but, owing to the recognized difficulty of those texts, we must not attach too much importance to such an isolated passage. I believe it to mean that a family from that tribe, namely that of the *Fryāna*—the name is altogether Irānian—became converted to the Zoroastrian faith and adopted a settled life :

'When pious people in the family and amongst the kinsmen
Of the praiseworthy Tūrānian *Fryāna* arose,
Who increased zealously the settlements of the good :
Then settled with them together with the Spirit of the Good Mind
Ahura Mazda, and ruled over them, to their joy[1].'

---

[1] Ys. XLVI, 12.

Elsewhere also the Avesta speaks of pious men amongst the Tūrānians as well as amongst the Dāhas[1], and if this does not prove the non-Arian descent of those tribes to be an impossibility, it at least renders such a belief essentially more difficult.

As horsemen the Tūra are characterized by the epithet 'with swift horses,' but the passage in which it occurs is not perfectly clear[2]. Against the 'Tūrānian countries' Tūsa, the Tūs of Firdūsī[3], takes the field. But all the oppressions and injuries which the settlements of the Avesta people had to endure from their turbulent neighbours of the Caspian deserts are personified in the Tūrānian prince *Frangrasyan*, the Afrāsiāb of the Shāh-nāme, who, after protracted and desperate struggles, was finally overpowered by *Kavi Husrava*, Kai Khosrav, the king of the Irānians. Firdūsī naturally pictures these events in his accustomed manner as great wars in which innumerable heroes appeared on both sides in order to mutually test their strength and valour—thus altogether in the tone and style of a chivalrous epoch. The substance of these ancient legends he transforms with artistic hand according to the taste and conceptions of his own age[4]. In the Avesta the case is otherwise. It describes the battles with Frangrasyan and the Tūrānians more mythically, a proof that they had taken place in a

---

[1] Yt. XIII, 113, 123, 143. The names *Arejağhat* and *Frārāzi*, which occur here, have a thoroughly Irānian sound.

[2] *Āsū-aspa*, Yt. XVII, 54.

[3] *Tūiryāo dahhāvō.* Yt. V, 54; comp. Spiegel, *E. A.* vol. i, pp. 576, 620 seq.

[4] When Firdūsī describes the state of civilization among the Tūrānians in entirely the same terms as that of the Irānians; when he makes them dwell in towns and castles with magnificent buildings, walls and towers; when he represents the king as standing at the head of his people surrounded by his retainers—all this is manifestly a simple modernism, an anachronism frequent in the ˙Shāh-nāme. According to Firdūsī, Irānians and Tūrānians are moreover cognate. They derive their descent from Frēdūn, whose three sons—Selm, Tur and Eraj—were the ancestors of the Western people, the Tūrānians and Irānians. *Vide* Spiegel, *E. A.* vol. i, p. 546 seq.

period even then remote, and were at least almost at an end when the Avesta was composed. Thus it is the *yazata* Hauma himself, who delivers his enemy into the power of Husrava :

> 'To her, to the Druvāspa, did Hauma sacrifice . . . and beg of her this boon! "Grant me . . ., that I may fetter the destructive Tūrānian Frangrasyan, and that I may bring him bound and in chains before the Kavi Husrava, so that Kavi Husrava may kill him behind the sea Chaichasta, the deep, wide-flowing[1]."'

Further on, the battle with Frangrasyan is pictured in a mythico-symbolical way and is described as a struggle for the ' majesty ' or the ' heavenly splendour '—the *hvareno*. This is evidently the symbol and token of supreme power. When Frangrasyan fruitlessly endeavours to seize the *hvareno*, we are probably to understand merely the tribes of the deserts that vainly strive with and endeavour to subdue the settled population.

That *Tūra*, however, has a tolerably general and comprehensive signification[2] we gather from the simple fact that the name is interchangeable with similar collective appellations, or may appear in the place of names of individual tribes. Thus it is used as quite synonymous with *Dānu*, which evidently designates only the enemies of the Avesta people, be they Arians or non-Arians, in one word the ' barbarians : '

> 'We adore the good, sublime, blissful Fravashis, the *manes*, who form many armies, carry hundreds of weapons, who bear banners — the radiant ones, who in mighty battles come rushing down, who, armed and steadfast, fight battles *against the Dānu*. Ye have overpowered the resistance of the *Tūrānian Dānu;* ye have subdued the enmity of the Tūrānian Dānu[3]!'

---

[1] Yt. IX, 17–18.

[2] Justi (*Handbuch der Zendsprache*, s. v.) derives *tūra* from *taurv*, *tarv* = Skr. *turv*, *tūrvati*.

[3] Yt. XIII, 37–38.   According to Yt. V, 73–74 (*yat · bavāma ·*

In the course of this description the Dānu are styled
'having ten thousand (i. e. *innumerable*) princes.' This
name shows that they were divided into a multitude
of small sections and bands, each of which was ranged
under one single chief unrestrained in his absolute power
by any higher authority. This is a common feature of
nomadic life, while settled tribes aspire to a concentration
of authority by which the heads of the several individual
sections of the people are in turn subject to one prince or
king who stands above them ; it is also particularly
characteristic at the present day of the populations
inhabiting the steppes of Turkistān.

From a historical point of view the word *Dānu* is of
special interest, for this name is also found in the Rig-veda,
as well as Dānava, another form of it. According to the
dictionaries, it is a designation of the demons, foes of
the gods, who are opposed by Indra. But I believe that here,
as with the name Dāsa—of which we shall speak further
on—we must accept as the original meaning 'opponent,
enemy[1].' The united Indo-Irānians seem to have designated as *Dānu* the tribes not akin to themselves with whom
they came in contact during their march from North to
South. After the separation, the Irānians retained the
name as a comprehensive appellation for all Tūrānians, that
is, nomadic tribes on their northern frontiers ; the Indians
applied it chiefly to the non-Arian aborigines of the valley
of the Indus and of the Panjāb, and extended it also to the
enemies of the gods after the usual manner of ascribing
earthly conditions to the supernatural world[2].

---

aiwi-vanyāo · *dānavō* · *tūra* · *vyākhna* ·) the Dānu are vanquished
by *Ashavazda* and *Thrita*. Here are also mentioned, as it
seems, the names of Dānu-heroes—*Kara Asabana, Vara Asabana,*
and *Duraȩkaȩta*—of which the last at all events has a true Irānian
sound.

[1] *Dānu* is to be derived, just as *dāsa*, from rt. *dā*, 'to cut, to cut
into pieces, to annihilate' (cf. Grassmann, *Wörterbuch*, s. v.).

[2] *Dānu* designates a demon, e. g. Rv. V, 32. 1, 4, 7, where it is
used together with *Çushna* (*vide* Ludwig, *Einl.* 337), further I, 32, 9,
and perhaps X, 120, 6.

For us the former, or historical meaning, so to speak, of
Dānu, is more important than the mythological one. It is
found in a song abounding in references to actual events :
    'Wast thou not also, *Vritra-killer*,
    O sublime one, quite filled with wrath,
    When thou didst slay the *Dānu* (the enemies)[1]?'
In another hymn, moreover, the subduing of the Dānu
is placed on the same level with the overpowering of the
Dasyu. That by the latter name the non-Arians of the
Panjāb are meant probably no scholar will deny. I do
not therefore see any reason why we should not recognize
historical events in the entire strophe, instead of assuming
a strange amalgamation of things human and superhuman.
    'Take, O strong one, the strength with which the enemies
    Thou didst slay, the spider-brood of the Dānu ;
    With which thou didst reveal the light to the Arian
        tribe ;
    On the left sank the Dasyu tribe, O Indra[2]!'
That *Tūra* must be understood as a collective name, we
see further from the fact that the tribe of the *Hunu* is also
spoken of as a Tūrānian one :
    'To Ardvi-sūra Anāhita did the armed Tūsa, the
    warrior, sacrifice, sitting on the back of his horse,
    imploring strength for his teams, and health for him-
    self, protection against his enemy, the defeat of his
    adversaries, the entire subjection of his opponents,
    the wicked, hostile ones. And he prayed to her for
    this boon : " Grant me, O good, beneficent Ardvi-sūra
    Anāhita, that I may vanquish the armed *Hunu* in
    Vaiska near the defile Khshathrō-sauka, that lies
    high up in Kangha, the sublime holy one ; that I
    may kill them in the Tūrānian countries in hundreds
    and in thousands, in myriads and in innumerable
    multitudes[3]."'

---

[1] Rv. IV, 30, 7.
[2] Rv. II, 11, 18, *dānum - aurṇavābham*. With the last word comp.
Grassmann, *Wörterbuch*.
[3] Yt. V, 53–54, 57–58 ; according to the obscure and difficult

The above translation of the passage, according to which *Hunu* would be the name of a tribe, is at all events a simple and approximate one. But it is often disputed, as *hunu* is considered to be the Irānian equivalent for the Indian word *sūnu*, and is translated by 'son.' I must admit that in the present case that sense does not quite satisfy me. Whose sons are thus vaguely referred to? There is a genitive wanting, which is absolutely necessary to complete the sentence. If, on the contrary, my own view is correct, the passage contains a most remarkable hint well deserving of attention. It mentions a tribe of horsemen[1], who are grouped with the Tūrānians, the tribes of the Northern steppes, and mentions as their dwelling-place the territories lying half-way up the Sir-daryā, where the existence of a Tatar tribe may be most easily and safely accounted for. Under such conditions one feels inclined to compare the Hunus of the Avesta with the later Hunns. In that case there would probably be no older testimony than the religious documents of the Zoroastrians to prove the existence of that energetic tribe, which later on exercised such a mighty influence on the history of mankind. But it is very dangerous to argue similarity of name, and it cannot be denied that weighty historical reasons are opposed to this hypothesis. The Hunns belong, in fact, to a much later epoch than the period of the composition of the Avesta, which moreover places the battles with the Hunns in the heroic age of the Avesta people. Even the white Hunns, who are mentioned by Haug, first appear in the last few centuries before the Christian era, when they drove the inhabitants of the Northern steppes towards the South[2]. We need only assume that the Hunns, as a nomadic tribe, roved all about the steppes

passage Yt. XIII, 100 ; *Kavi Vishtāspa* also was engaged in war with the Hunus (Yt. XIX, 86).

[1] Hence *aurva · Hunavō.* Of interest is also Yt. XIX, 41, *Hunavō · yat · pathanya* (Skr. *patheshthā,* 'being on the road, waylayers') 'the predatory Hunus.' The context of the passage is indeed very difficult and obscure.

[2] Comp. particularly Justi, *Handbuch,* s. v. *hunu.*

of Central Asia even in the remotest antiquity, and that they made themselves dreaded by isolated incursions long before they became notorious by their inroads on a large scale and by immigrating in large numbers amongst the tribes of Western Asia and of Europe. But under all circumstances I strongly maintain my view that the word *hunu* is the name of a tribe, whether or not that name be identical with that of the later Hunns. The interpretation of the text itself is not at all affected thereby.

As regards the *Sarima* and *Sāni* little can be positively asserted, since they are never named in the Avesta except in the passage cited above[1]. We must thus confine ourselves to conjectures, based upon the greater or less similarity to the sound of the name. By the *Sarima* tradition apparently denotes the peoples of the West. At least Firdūsī makes Selm, whose name may be identical with Sarima, a sovereign of the Western countries. According to the Book of Kings, the kingdom of Frēdūn was divided among his three sons, Selm, Tūr, and Eraj; the first received the West, Tūr the North, and the last Irān Proper[2]. As there is evidently a play upon the name here, we should do well not to overrate the historical value of this statement. The Sarima have been compared with the Sarmatians or with the Solymi[3]. As the former, according to the statements of Ptolemy and Strabo, must have dwelt on the plains near the lower course of the Don and the Volga[4], we should have at least to assume that they had wandered in course of time from East to West. For if they had already dwelt, in the period represented by the Avesta, where the Western writers look for them, the Avesta people would scarcely have been able to come in contact with them. In

---

[1] *Sairima* indeed occurs in the *Vishtāsp-Yasht* (Yt. XXIV, 52), which is admitted to be thoroughly corrupt.

[2] Spiegel, *E. A.* vol. i, p. 546.

[3] Justi, *Hdb.* s. v.; Spiegel, *Avesta übersetzt*, vol. iii, p. 139, n. 1 and 2; Windischmann, *Zoroastrische Studien*, pp. 229–230: cf. also de Harlez, *Av. tr.*, iii, 41, n. 2.

[4] Kiepert, *Alte Geographie*, § 306; Forbiger, *Handbuch der alten Geographie*, vol. ii, p. 452 seq.

the same way I believe that the Solymi who had settled in Lycia[1] were too remote. Personally I am inclined to consider the name Sarima to be a similar collective expression, like Tūra, for the different nomadic tribes of the North, and to give it as general a meaning as possible. I should translate it by 'archers[2],' which meaning appears to be applicable from the fact that nomadic tribes are generally distinguished for their use of the bow, a peculiarity which is specially recorded of the Scyths.

As regards the *Sāni*, they have been identified with the Soanes on the south of the Caucasus. Justi reminds us of the city of Sān, which, according to Persian lexicographers, is supposed to be situated in Kābulistān or in Balkh. But no cogent proof can be brought forward in support of either view[3].

We now come to the *Dāha*. It is probable that the Avesta denotes by this name the Daai of the Greek historians and geographers. They are reckoned amongst the Scythian tribes that dwelt in Northern Hyrcania, east of the Caspian Sea. They extended as far as the Oxus and the Jaxartes, and Herodotus even speaks of the Daai as inhabiting the province of Persis. Consequently, they were widely spread and considerable in number, and, moreover, at the same time a 'warlike people, who served Darius Codomanus as cavalry, and Alexander and Antiochus as mounted archers[4].'

In the Rig-veda the name of Dāha is found under the equivalent Indian form Dāsa, and here we meet with linguistic coincidences similar to those we have already become acquainted with in the case of the Dānu.

---

[1] Forbiger, *H. a. G.* vol. II, p. 248.

[2] From Skr. *çarya* or *çaryā*, 'arrow.'

[3] I derive *Sāni* from the rt. *sā*, which is also the origin of the word *sālar*, 'the enemy.' Thus the name generally bore the same meaning as Tūra.

[4] Kiepert, *a. G.* § 61; Forbiger, *H. a. G.* ii, p. 570, note 13; Strabo, pp. 304, 511, 515; Herodotus, I. 125; Arrian III. 11, 28 ('the Daai living on the other side of the river Tanais—this river is mistaken for the Jaxartes,—the Daai on the banks of the Tanais,' cf. III. 30); V. 12; Curtius, viii. 3.

Scholars were formerly inclined to hold the fundamental meaning of Dāsa to be 'monster, demon hostile towards the gods,' and that meaning was adopted in the majority of passages. The aboriginal inhabitants of the Panjāb are said to be only secondarily designated *Dāsa*, because they opposed the immigrating Arians in a hostile manner. This view interpreters have more and more tended to abandon[1]. The correct process is quite the reverse. The natural course to follow is not that which leads from heaven or the ethereal regions down to the earth, or from the realm of the supernatural to that of the sensual, but the opposite one. Men took the circumstances of their own immediate surroundings, what they daily saw and experienced, for their starting-point, and transferred human conditions, representations, and ideas to spiritual and heavenly objects. By Dāsa in the Rig-veda is meant first of all an enemy, especially an enemy of the Arians, an enemy of foreign race, and this is certainly the sense in the great majority of passages. It is only in a secondary sense that it is used as a designation for the enemies of the benevolent gods—the demons, whose destructive influence the fancy of mankind recognizes in scorching heat and drought, in the raging storm-wind, in the burning and destructive lightning-flash, in the dark night of the thunder-clouds. As regards the use of the word *Dāsa* in the Indo-Irānian period the same remarks are applicable as those above which concern the name *Dānu*. After the separation of the two Arian tribes the name appears to have been used so far differently by the Irānians, that it was evidently restricted to a special tribe, and no longer used as a designation for all the enemies of the Irānian people.

---

[1] Ludwig, *Einl.* p. 207 seq.; Zimmer, *AiL.* p. 100 seq. The former has described the state of affairs quite clearly in the words: 'Wherever Dāsa and Ārya stand opposed to each other, we may invariably consider the former to belong to the aboriginal inhabitants; where, on the contrary, demons alone should be understood, cannot in that case be easily settled. Only so much appears to us certain, that the latter are to be understood much more rarely than is done in the present system of interpretation.'

Names of tribes may be further contained in *Adhyu* and *Dadhika*. The latter have been excellently compared by Spiegel with the Dadikai of Herodotus[1]. As they are constantly named together with those mentioned above[2], we may well regard the Adhyu as a tribe likewise, provided the comparison be correct. The Avesta does not furnish us with any more precise explanation; at most we may regard it as probable that they belonged to the Irānian nation, and that the Zoroastrian doctrine had found entrance among them. According to Herodotus, the tribe of the Dadikai seems to have taken part in the great campaign of Xerxes against the Greeks. It was closely united with that of the Gandars who were settled among the present Suleiman mountains, and formed one assessment district with them[3]. Their place of abode is thus probably to be looked for in the neighbourhood, perhaps in the dominion of Ghazna, though in other cases also tribes living at a distance from each other belonged to the same district.

The *Vardhaka* and the *Hyauna* were enemies of the Avesta people, and were conquered by Kavi Vishtāspa. However, it is not easy to interpret the passage in which this fact is strikingly suggested[4]. Under the name of Hyauna are reckoned *Arjat-aspa*, as well as *Tānthravat*, ‘the dark one,’ and *Peshana*, ‘the fighter.’ These names are purely Irānian, and if their bearers neither assumed the titles themselves nor received them from the Avesta people, the Arian nationality of the Hyauna can no longer be doubted.

‘The armed Kavi Vishtāspa subdued the *Tānthravat*, the adherent of the false doctrine, and the *Peshana*,

---

[1] *E. A.* vol. ii, pp. 380–381, note.

[2] *Aidhyu, Daidhika*, Ys. XXXIX, 2; Yt. XIII, 154; but in Yt. XIII, 74 *daidhika* is represented in a somewhat striking connection.

[3] Herodotus, VII. 66; III. 91.

[4] *Varedhaka, Hyaona*, Yt. IX, 30–31; XVII, 50–51 (here also *hyaunimām · dahyunām*, ‘of the Hyaunian districts’). Spiegel (*E.A.* vol. iii, p. 283 note) compares with the Hyauna the Chionites who lived on the western side of the Caspian Sea.

the demon-worshipper, and the *Arjat-aspa* and all the other wicked *Hyauna* bent upon harm[1].'

I am conscious that I am putting forward a mere hypothesis; but it seems to me deserving of examination. In the list of countries of the Vendidād (often mentioned) the counter-creations of the Evil Spirit are named, as we know, together with each district: in *Aryana-vaija*, extreme cold; in India, excessive heat; in *Haitumat*, the 'sins of *yātu*.' But at the same time it is also said with regard to several provinces, that in them unbelieving and hostile tribes were the scourge of the land ; *Urva* has evil people, the country near the *Rangha* predatory inhabitants, and *Varna* in the Alburz mountains a non-Arian population. This leads me to consider whether the names of tribes might not be directly conjectured from other expressions which are found in that connection, and which frequently offer a formidable *crux interpretum.*

In the case of *Moru* (Merv) *maredha* is denoted as the calamity created by Angra Manyu[2]. Herein I recognize the name of the tribe of the Mardoi. These must have lived within the limits of Moru and must have harassed that district by pillaging expeditions. Their character is sufficiently indicated by their name ; for *maredha* signifies 'murderer[3].'

The Mardoi or Amardoi—for even Strabo expressly declares that the two names are identical[4]—had, like the Daai, spread very widely and were found, according to Greek authorities, in the most diverse countries of Western Asia. We meet with Mardoi in Hyrcania, where

---

[1] Yt. XIX, 87 ; comp. Yt. V, 109.

[2] It is said in Vd. I, 6 ; *āat · ahē · paityārem · frākereñtat · Agrō-mainyush · pouru-mahrkō* : *vīthushāmcha · maredhāmcha.* To my mind a correction into *maredhācha* or *maredhācha* is absolutely necessary; *ām* actually served only as a sign of the nasalized *ā* in the accusative plural. One is tempted also to hold *vīthushāmcha* to be the name (perhaps mutilated) of a nation.

[3] From root *mared*; comp. also Haug, in Bunsen, *Aegyptens Stellung in der Weltgeschichte*, v, p. 129.

[4] Strabo, p. 523.

they dwelt in the inaccessible mountain-passes of the Alburz, perhaps in the vicinity of Demāvend; and also in the mountains of Persis. Against both those tribes Alexander the Great fought; against the former he took the field from Zadrakarta the capital of Hyrcania, against the latter from Persepolis. There were Amardoi in Bactria and Scythia; they may also have dwelt in Margiana; Mardyeni are mentioned as living in Sogdiana[1]. They were probably the mere remnants of a distinct tribe which formerly roved about the border of the habitable districts of Eastern Irān towards the deserts.

More interesting still is the name of the Derbikes, which I find again in the Old Irānian *Driwika*. The Driwika are regarded as a counter-creation in *Haraiva*[2], which seems to be in complete harmony with the statements of Western writers, according to whom the Derbikes dwelt in the north of Margiana[3]. They may perhaps have occupied the territory between Merv and Sarakhsh. They are described as a nomadic people in so low a stage of civilization and with such coarse and strange manners and customs that they can hardly be considered Arians. 'They worship the Earth as their deity, sacrifice and use as food no female beasts, slaughter and eat (!) old men of over seventy years of age[4]; whilst they hang old women and then bury them.' This sounds too cannibalistic not to rouse a suspicion that it is incredible. Still the narrative cannot be wholly without foundation, and if true only in part, it is still sufficient to set in a clear light the barbarous condition of the Derbikes.

There is a very striking correspondence between the

---

[1] Forbiger, *H. a. G.* vol. ii, p. 595, note 20; Spiegel, *E. A.* vol. ii, p. 538 note.

[2] Vd. I, 9, *āat · ahễ : paiṭyārem · frākereñlat. Ağrō-mainyu*sh · *pouru-mahrkō : saraskemcha Driwikācha* ('hail-storms and the people of the Driwika').

[3] For particulars, see Forbiger, *H. a. G.* vol. ii, p. 566.

[4] The same is recounted of the Massagetae (*H. a. G.* vol. ii, p. 467, note 16) and of certain Indian tribes (p. 494).

name Derbikes and the proper name *Dṛbhika* in the Rig-veda to which Ludwig refers[1]. This occurs only in a single passage and there indeed in a somewhat mythical sense, which however is also sometimes the case with Dāsa and Dānu :

> 'Their priest, to him who slew the Dṛbhika,
> Liberated the cows, opened the prison ;
> To Indra, who resembles the storm in the atmospheric space,
> Covered with Soma, as the horse with trappings[2]!

Through the discovery of the same name, as that of a tribe, in the Avesta, the history of the word is completed, and is found to be identical with that of Dāsa or Dānu. Originally, in the Arian period, the word may have had a pretty general meaning. I would translate it by 'beggar folk, poor rabble[3].' The Arians, who were proud of their well-cultivated fields and their rich stock of cattle, seem then to have contemptuously designated by this expression the homeless nomadic people without possessions, whom they met on their marches. Among the Indians the meaning of the name was evidently forgotten during their migration into the Panjāb; and this fact would explain how it came to be used by them in a semi-mythical sense. It was merely a relic of antiquity. It still retained indeed the idea of the frightful and the terrible, but its proper application, its original significance, was no longer known. Among the Irānians on the contrary Driwika served, as we have already seen to have happened in the case of Dāha, no longer as a general designation of all nomadic tribes, but as the special name of a single race[4].

---

[1] *Einleitung*, p. 207.

[2] Rig-veda II, 14, 3, Roth's translation (*B. R.* sub voce *jū*); quite differently Ludwig, Rv. II, 57.

[3] Cf. Avesta *driwi*, 'trash or trifle,' *drighu*, 'poor,' Skr. root *darbh*.

[4] By the way, I am here giving only a conjecture regarding the obscure word *bravara* or *barvara* in Vd. I, 7, which is called *paiyāra* in Bākhdhi. I have long held it to be a name of a tribe;

The tribes which have so far been mentioned, dwelt either in Irān itself or in the countries on its northern border, which are generally comprised under the name Tūrān. Here, where desert and fertile land are in such close contiguity, the rivalry between the settled population and the nomads, and, at least partly, that between Arians and non-Arians must naturally have been keenest. Here from the earliest times occasion was given for continual quarrels, and here broke out in remote antiquity that desperate conflict, which, as the war between Irān and Tūrān, engrosses a great part of the legendary history of Persia, and which, though in an altered form, continued down to modern times.

The question now arises whether the Irānians were not also engaged in contest with hostile tribes in the East and West. In the region of the Suleiman mountains their territories apparently bordered on those of the kindred tribes of the Indians; and in the South-West, though indeed at a considerable distance, the Semites had established in the low country round the Euphrates and the Tigris a mighty kingdom whose military power was frequently felt by the inhabitants of the Irānian highland.

The Avesta seems to furnish hints of at least passing conflicts with Indian and Semitic nations; these, however, are in any case very doubtful and shrouded in myths and legends of many kinds. The Indian tribes are, I believe, comprehended in the *Gandarwa*, whose name can scarcely be separated from that of the mythical being Gandharva of the Rig-veda. The home of the Gandarwa is placed in the extreme East; he was re-

---

perhaps it may be the Irānian equivalent for the Greek Βάρβαροι (?) Now to my surprise I find the following notice in Grodekoff ('Ride,' p. 79): 'The road was intersected by the River Balkh, locally known as the Bandi-Barbari. Bandi means "beyond the pond" (?) —the dam is constructed at the town of Balkh itself—and the term Barbari is applied to the wild people living among the northern spurs of the Paropamisus and the Hindukush' (? comp. also Mod. Pers. *barbar*, for which the meaning 'fight' is given by the lexicographers : Vullers, *Lex. sub voce*).

garded as a terrible monster[1], bent upon killing the faithful, who was vanquished and slain in the valley of *Pishin* by the hero *Kersāspa*[2]. We may perhaps place Pishin in the province of Urva, belonging to the list of countries where 'wicked inhabitants' are expressly spoken of. We know also that the scene of other adventures and exploits of Kersāspa is laid in the South-Eastern territories of the Avesta people[3].

It is, further, generally assumed that the sufferings and miseries which came upon the Irānians from the Mesopotamian countries, particularly from Babylon, were embodied in the figure of *Aži Dahāka*[4]. How much of a mythical element is contained in the legend of Dahāka may be clearly seen from the following passage describing the combat between Dahāka and his opponent *Thraitāna*:

> 'This blessing fell to the lot of Āthwya, this boon was given him that a son was born to him: *Thraitāna*, from his mighty race, who slew the dragon *Dahāka* with the three jaws and the three heads, with the six eyes and the thousand limbs, the all-powerful, devilish monster; whom Angra Manyu created on the living world as the strongest monster to annihilate the people of the pious[5].'

Many a passage may however be cited in confirmation of the historical basis of the myth of Dahāka. If the usual interpretation be correct, Babel, which is called *Bawri* in the Avesta, should be regarded as the dwelling-place of

---

[1] Comp. the Κένταυροι.

[2] *Yō · ajana*t · *Gaṅdarewem* * *yō · apala*t · *vizafānō* * *merekhshānō · ashahē · gaēthāo* · 'who slew Gandarwa, who rushed downward with open jaws to annihilate the people of the pious,' Yt. XIX, 41. *Gandarewa* may be perhaps regarded as the name of a tribe (Yt. XIII, 123), just as *Tūra* which immediately precedes it.

[3] See pp. 81 and 113 of *Ostīrānische Kultur*.

[4] Justi, *Geschichte des alten Persiens*, p. 31; Spiegel, *E.A.* vol. i, p. 543 seq.

[5] Ys. IX, 7–8. The description of Dahāka as *daēva* and *druj* is interesting: compare what is said above in pp. 20–21.

Dahāka[1]. Another locality with which he stands in closer
connection would be *Kvirinta*, which has been ingeniously
identified by Justi[2] with the *Karina* of Isidor of Charax,
the present Kerend at the top of the pass of Zagros. In
perfect accord with this is the epithet 'difficult to approach,'
indicating the strength and strategical value of the place,
which was indeed of importance, since the Assyrian princes
must have led their armies through it, when they took the
field against the inhabitants of the Irānian highland.

The name of Bawri as well as that of Kvirinta may have
been known to the Avesta nation only from hearsay, for no
passage in our texts justifies the supposition that they had
then advanced so far to the South-West.

The historical evidences of a real, though only transient
supremacy of the Assyrian princes over Eastern Irān are,
it must be confessed, very deficient. The Medo-Persian
epic can indeed boast of mighty expeditions which Ninos
and Semiramis undertook against the kingdom of Bactria,
and tell of the fierce battles which preceded its subju-
gation. But these accounts can scarcely be regarded as
genuinely historical, though they may have some foundation in fact. The Assyrian cuneiform writings only tell us
of Tiglāth-Pilesar, who lived in the eighth century, that in
one of his expeditions he advanced a considerable distance
towards the East. In them also appear some highly interesting names : Arakuttu, evidently Arachotos-Harahvati,
Nisaa-Nisaya and Zikruti, the Sagartians, in the list of
conquered territories and nations ; but these disappear
again in the inscription containing the account of a later
campaign and its result, a proof that the Assyrian dominion
in Eastern Irān was not at all events of long duration[3].

---

[1] *Bawrōi*sh · *paiti* · *daḣḣaoȳ̆* (?) 'in the country of Bawri,' Yt. V, 29.
Therewith agree Hamza and the author of Mujmil, Spiegel, *E. A.*
vol. i, p. 532.

[2] *Hdb.* sub voce. *Tem · yazata · Ashi*sh · *thrijafāo. Dahākō · upa .
Kviriñtem · duzhitem,* 'unto him did the three-headed dragon
Dahāka offer up a sacrifice on the scarce accessible Kvirinta.
Yt. XV, 19.

[3] Duncker, *GdA.* vol. ii, p. 261; Maspero, 'History,' pp. 366—368.

Nevertheless, it is by no means incredible that the more powerful among the rulers of Babylon and Assyria endeavoured at least to bring under their sway the Eastern districts of Irān, and that they reached so far in their more distant expeditions. Furthermore, it is not impossible that such attempts gave occasion for the rise of the myth of Dahāka or in some way caused its transformation. The later legend also represents Zohāk as coming from Arabia[1]. That there was no permanent supremacy is proved by the Avesta itself. Dahāka is only for a limited period master over the Irānian nation; foreign rule soon gave way again to the national dominion originally founded by the hero *Thraitāna* or Frēdūn. Thraitāna had concealed himself among the heights of the Alburz, that is to say in the lofty mountains to the Eastward, which were at all times the place of refuge of the Irānians during hostile invasions. From hence, followed by the valiant body of his faithful adherents, he took the field against the usurper, defeated and killed him, and thus brought the foreign domination to an end.

If this view of the saga of Dahāka be correct, we have in it a peculiar commingling of legendary and purely mythological elements. If, on the one hand, it contains an historical nucleus, on the other it is certain that ‘the dragon’ signifies by natural symbolism the serpent of the clouds, and is identical with the *Ahi* of the Rig-veda, the demon of tempest, against whom the beneficent genii fight in storm and bad weather, in lightning and in thunder. Everywhere, in the Avesta as well as in the Rig-veda, the combats on the earth and in the air are confounded together. The Avesta also represents Dahāka in the figure of a serpent, while the later rationalistic legend describes him as a man with serpents' heads growing on his shoulders; it makes him three-headed with three jaws and six eyes, while he is also represented in the Yashts[2] as sitting upon a golden throne like an earthly potentate and king.

---

[1] Spiegel, *E. A.* vol. i, p. 531.
[2] Yt. XV, 19.

The relations, then, between the various populations of Turkistān and of Eastern Irān present a somewhat motley picture even in the earliest period. By far the larger portion of the land was inhabited by tribes of Arian race. These, however, did not form a concentrated and united whole, but were divided into hostile parties through differing habits of life and forms of religion.

The upholders of civilization were those Irānian tribes which professed the Mazdian faith. They mostly dwelt in fixed settlements, cultivated the fields, and practised the regular breeding of cattle. By way of exception, the Zoroastrian doctrine seems likewise to have made its way among semi-nomads.

In sharp contrast to the Avesta people stand the bulk of the nomadic tribes of Arian blood. They are mostly comprised under race-names such as Tūra or Dānu, perhaps also Sarima or Sāni. Certain individual tribes are to be understood by the names Driwika, Hyauna, Mardha, Dāha, etc.

At the same time we must admit the possibility that many of these tribes, e. g. the Hunu, belonged to a foreign, possibly the Tatarian, race. That close to the Irānians an aboriginal population not akin to them existed, is beyond a doubt. In the beginning this may have been powerful and numerous. But it gradually became reduced in numbers and withdrew before the victorious Arians into the more inaccessible mountains. The conquered portions became merged in the mass of the victors.

Finally, in the South-East as in the South-West, the Irānians came into contact with foreign nations : in the former with the Indians, in the latter with the Semites. Between them and the Indians of the border provinces continual but unimportant feuds and petty forms of warfare evidently prevailed ; but the Semites made themselves hated and feared only by brief occasional campaigns.

CHAPTER II[1].

PRIVATE LIFE.

§ 5. *Physical Characteristics of Men and Women.*

. . . . . WE have examined the nation itself as a whole
with its division into the believing and the unbelieving, into
husbandmen and nomads ; we have discussed the opposition
in which in Irān the Arians, who had immigrated, stood to
an aboriginal population of foreign race. We now return to
the narrowest circle and consider the old Irānian as a single
individual, the general circumstances of his life, and his
position in the house and in the family.

What he was in outward appearance, we cannot easily
state. The Avesta offers scarcely anything tangible, as it
only touches occasionally upon this question. A comparison with the present descendants of the Avesta people
is more profitable.

I will endeavour to delineate the ideal type which seems
to have held the mind of the old Irānian. Naturally the
reality cannot have invariably corresponded with the type.

In man the principal stress is laid upon bodily strength
and health. Zarathushtra therefore prays for these to Verthraghna, the genius of victorious battle, whom fancy
naturally endowed with extraordinary strength. They
are the gifts for which one also implores Hauma, the
yazata, who keeps away sickness and death[2].

Wide chest, broad hips, high feet, and above all a clear
sharp eye, are the glory of man. These are the attributes
which distinguish the king who is to surpass his people

---

[1] Ch. iv, § 27, *Ostīrānische Kultur.*

[2] Yt. XIV, 29 : *bāzvāo · aojō, tanvō · vīspayāo · dravatātem, tanvō ·
vīspayāo · vazdvare.*—Ys. IX, 19.

not only by higher intelligence but also in bodily vigour and beauty[1].

The descriptions of the divine beings may also be made use of, as they are certainly [*metaphorically*] spoken of as men perfectly well-formed. The Amesha Spenta, the highest spirits next to Ahura Mazda, are represented as ' endowed with sharp eyes.' The *manes*, the Fravashis, are called ' clear-sighted,' and the star Tishtrya-Sirius ' sharp-eyed [2].' These epithets sufficiently prove the importance which the Irānian attached to the shining brightness of the eye.

Tall in stature, slender in form, strong, able, clear-eyed, having small heels, long arms and handsome calves; all these are in the Avesta honourable epithets for *yazatas* and men [3].

In woman, beauty and elegance of figure are most conspicuous. Symmetry of shape, a slender waist and large full eyes, which are still admired at the present day in Irānian women, are esteemed as the principal of maidenly beauties. Other feminine graces are light complexion, especially about the arms, small slender fingers and a well-formed bosom [4].

It is remarkable that the fifteenth year of a man's life is esteemed as his ideal age, which is regarded as the period during which he who is still in the freshness of youth approaches the work and miseries of life, not with a weak body but in full vigour, the time when the youth comes to

---

[1] *Perethu-vara, perethu-sraoni, berezi-pādha, anakhrüidha-döithra,* Yt. XV, 54.

[2] *Verezi-döithra,* Ys. XXVI, 3 ; *verezi-chashman,* Yt. XIII, 29 ; *drvō-chashman,* Yt. VIII, 12.

[3] *Berezat, huraodha, amavat, hunairyach, spiti-döithra, kasupāshna. dareghō-bāzu, hvaschva,* Yt. VIII, 14 ; XIV, 17 ; XVII, 22, &c.

[4] Comp. the epithets *huraodha, urvaęsō-maidhya, vouru-döithra ;* Vsp. II, 7 : *gh.nāo · hubaghāo, hufedhrīsh, huraodhāoğhō,* ' the lovely women of good family (elsewhere *āzāta*), the well-grown up.' *Vide* Yt. V, 127, *yathacha · hukerepta · fshtāna · ağhen · yath-acha · ağhen , navāzāna* (= N.P. *nuvāzān,* ' the lovely, charming, alluring ').

the age of puberty[1]. As youths of fifteen, men wandered on earth in the golden age during the reign of Yima, the father like the son. In like youthfulness also appears Verthraghna, the genius of victory[2].

Bodily development ought to be very rapid when such an early age is esteemed the most beautiful one, and this fact stands in the closest connection with climatic circumstances. What we know of the Persians of the present day accords with the above statement. Youths as a rule attain to puberty in their fourteenth year, and are in the habit of marrying shortly after. In old Irān these circumstances must have been quite the same, and the youth was already in full manhood at an age in which, in colder latitudes, he has scarcely passed the age of boyhood.

The statements of the Avesta respecting the exterior in the old Irānian, are, as we see, of a very general kind, and as deficient as insignificant. On just the most important and most decisive points, such as the colour of the hair, the structure of the skull, and the size of the men's beards, we know nothing. It is therefore necessary to supplement the incomplete description of the Avesta by a study of the present descendants of the old Irānian nation. Important to us is the description of the Eastern Irānians, which I have already given above. By means of the same we may perhaps more or less correctly describe the external appearance of the old Irānians in the following manner[3]:

The men were of middle, often of high stature, and were strong-built, with broad and well-developed chests. With the girls and women the general tendency was towards a slender and supple formation of body, the colour of their skin was brighter and more delicate, particularly on those parts of the body which were protected from the influence of the sun. Large shining eyes distinguished both men

---

[1] 'At the age (ayu) in which man first grows up to manhood, first comes to strength, first attains to puberty.' Yt. VIII, 14.

[2] Ys. IX, 5; Yt. XIV, 17; comp. also Yt. XXII, 9.

[3] Comp. Ch. I, § 1, pp. 6–7.

and women. The beards of the men were of luxuriant growth. The majority of the people had probably dark-brown hair; but light brown and red hair were not uncommon. Both types, the dark and the light, are generally to be distinguished among the Arians. The brachycephalous structure of the skull was general, the form of the face was oval; nose, mouth, and forehead, and even the extremities, hands and feet, were well-shaped.

---

§ 6. *Dwelling, Clothing, and Food.*

THE general circumstances of life in which the old Irānian people lived were throughout plain and simple, so far as we can learn from the Avesta. Here we observe nothing of that luxury which prevailed later on in the courts of great Persian kings and in the palaces of Persian nobles. The Avesta people consisted of herdsmen and peasants, and the richest amongst them were distinguished from the humbler and less important class only by their larger estates and herds. Money, the first requisite of commerce, even of the rudest kind, was unknown; cattle formed the means of barter and payment. No mention is made of the importation of foreign goods. The natural products which the Avesta mentions are without exception indigenous.

The soil of Irān itself was poor, yielding only scanty crops, a fact which rendered sloth impossible and enforced diligence, perseverance, and thrift. The chief sources of luxury, fruitfulness of soil, and extensive mercantile intercourse, were consequently denied to the Avesta people, and the conditions of a simple, frugal and unostentatious life were alone known to them.

Hence we can say that the wants of the Avesta people, in reference to dwelling, dress, and food, hardly went beyond the necessaries of life. Compared with the things which were necessary and useful for human life, everything

that tended to its embellishment and refinement was of
subordinate importance.

*   *   *   *   *   *

§ 7. *Birth, Education, and Admission into the Community.*

WE now trace the career of the old Irānian during the
years of his youth, from his birth to the solemn act by
which he was admitted, as a duly recognized member, into
the Zoroastrian community.

'The desire for progeny' (*puthrō-īshtī*) is the motive for
marriage-conclusion[1]. If a marriage proves childless, the
real object has been frustrated. It was regarded as evidently a divine visitation. Childlessness is a curse, which
the yazatas inflict upon those who sin against them:

> 'Hauma accurses him who shall drink it: "Childless
> shalt thou become and infected with ill-repute, thou
> who withholdest my juice like a profligate thief[2]."'

Posterity is a gracious favour bestowed by Heaven as a
reward for virtuous behaviour and piety. 'The blissful holy
Fravashis, the *manes*, grant bodily offspring to those who
do not violate agreements.'[3] It is particularly Mithra who
blesses with children. Hence he is called *puthrō-dāo*, 'the
bestower of sons.'[4] He allows the progeny of his adorers

---

[1] Vd. III, 33.   [2] Ys. XI, 3; Geldner, *Metrik*, § 116.
[3] Yt. X, 3. [Rather those who do not violate the sacred bonds
of marriage. It is indeed a fact worthy of notice in the sacred
lore of the Avesta nation that even the Fravashis, of the departed
adherents of the religion of Zarathushtra, bear ancestral love and
good-will towards their survivors on earth after their exit from this
world. *Tr.*]
[4] Yt. X, 65. [Mithra, the *yazata* presiding over love and friendship or love itself, blesses faithful wives and husbands with offspring,
i. e. those who duly observe the holy ties of wedlock. The violation of such ties, it is said metaphorically, brings misery and
misfortune upon the family. *Tr.*]

to increase and prosper; while he annihilates the offspring of those who transgress his commands and excite his displeasure:—

' Blood-stained are the settlements, the abodes deprived of their offspring, in which promise-breakers dwell.'
' Who will revere me, who will deceive me, who will hold me worthy of veneration with good or evil sacrifices? On whom shall I bestow wealth and fortune, to whom shall I give health of body, I who am able to do so? To whom shall I grant blissful plenty, I who am able to do so? To whom shall I grant the happiness of bodily offspring? To whom shall I send sickness and death, to whom want and misery, I who am able to do so? Whose bodily offspring shall I destroy at one stroke?'[1]

Naturally it is for sons especially that the yazatas are invoked. Daughters are certainly less desirable. Moreover sons are also the proper defenders of the house. They must guard it from enemies and adversaries, they must stand round their father when he goes into battle, they must propagate his race and improve and increase his estates. The greater the number of sons the better secured was the stability of the house and of the family. ' Which is, secondly, the place where the earth is most delightful? Where a pious man builds a house in which there are fire, cattle, women, *sons*, and menials. Henceforth also shall there be in that house abundance of cattle, bread and fodder, dogs, women and children, and every enjoyment of life[2].'

When the Irānian prays for wealth in men (*vīryăm-ishtīm*) and numbers of men[3] (*vīryăm-văthwăm*), he

---

[1] Yt. X, 38, 108, 110. Comp. Geldner, *Metrik*, § 127.

[2] Vd. III, 2, 3; comp. *ZddmG*. vol. xxxiv, p. 416. Here ' *asha* ' cannot possibly mean ' piety.' From the context and from a comparison of Vd. V, 52 where ' *yaomcha · ashem* ' occurs, I infer the meaning to be ' bread ' or ' food.' The Greek word ἄρτος need hardly be referred to. Comp. also Hübschmann, *ZddmG*. 1884. p. 428.

[3] Yt. VIII, 15; comp. also Vd. XVIII, 27 : ' Thee shall follow herds of cattle and a multitude of heroes.'

certainly and particularly means brave sons who offer him the best guarantee for the perpetuation and prosperity of his family. Therein concentrating all his wishes, he addresses himself to the genius of fire[1], that forms the centre of all family life, with the words: 'Give me bodily offspring who may found habitations, who may gather around me, who may grow up strong to be a protection in danger, consisting of heroes, who will promote the welfare of my house!'[2]

Hence it is an occasion of joy in the house of the Mazdayasna, when the wife has conceived[3], and a child is hoped for. At this time the woman requires more than ever heavenly protection, that her offspring may be unharmed, and herself propitiously delivered. For this reason she appeals by means of her prayers to Hauma, and still more to the special tutelary *yazata* of the female sex, Ardvi-sūra Anāhita. The former protects women at the time of delivery, and bestows on them brave sons and pious children[4]. Of Anāhita it is said in the hymns addressed to her, that she aids the generation of men and prepares all women for childbirth, that she helps all women towards a happy delivery and bestows on them sufficient and well-timed milk[5].

During pregnancy, and even for some time after delivery, women should hold aloof from conjugal intercourse[6]. The tenth month was the normal time for confinement.

The first ceremony performed on a new-born child,

---

[1] [As it is a religious custom amongst the Zarathushtrians to invoke the blessing and help of the Deity and other spiritual genii, with their faces turned towards the sacred fire (be it the hearth-fire or that of the sacred altar), so also here the adorer, asking for heroic sons of the above description, prays to Ahuramazda indirectly through the hearth-fire which he regards as the emblem of God. *Tr.*]

[2] Ys. LXII, 5; comp. Yt. XIII, 134; XIX, 75.

[3] *Aputhra*=*ā+puthra*; Geldner, *Kuhns Zeitschrift*, XXV, p. 193, note 3.

[4] Ys. IX, 22: *Haomô · āzizanāitibïsh* * *dadhāiti · khshaçtô-puthrîm* * *uta · ashava-frazaiñîîm.*

[5] Yt. V, 2.

[6] Vd. XV, 8.

appears to have been the washing of its hands[1]. The fundamental idea involved in this symbolical treatment is that the impurity which is contracted by conception, and which communicates itself also to the child, must be washed off with the purifying element of water. This clearly explains why a woman after confinement is for some time looked upon as unclean.

The antiquity of this custom is proved by quite similar ceremonies among the Indians, who were accustomed to wash a child on the eighth day after its birth; nay more, it is even proved by those practised among the old Germans[2].

The birth of a son was celebrated as a festival in the family of a Mazdayasna. Such old customs are retained in our own time among the Mahomedan Tājiks, in Kohistān, in whom we can safely recognize the remnants of the old Arian population[3]. Among them the parents prepare a feast when a child comes into this world. The mother keeps her bed for five or six days, and a week after the child receives its name in the presence of the Mullān.

With respect to the giving of names amongst the Avesta nation and the ceremonies usually connected therewith, we

---

[1] Vd. XVI, 7 : Yezi · aperenāyūkō · frāshnavāt · zasta · hē · paoirīm · frasnādhayen · aetahē · yat · aperenāyūkahē, 'when the child comes into appearance (is born), they shall wash first the hands of it, viz., the child.' [Here we differ from the author's meaning and would render the passage thus : 'If a child should touch her, they should first of all wash both the hands of it, (that is) of the child.' Here the context plainly shows that we have to do not only with a woman who has just been delivered but one who is in her courses, and consequently the question does not refer only to a child just born but to any child that is supposed to have become unclean by coming in contact with its mother. The precept of the Vendidād, therefore, refers to the first washing of the hands of any child that has touched a menstruating woman. Tr.]

[2] Zimmer, AiL. 320–321 ; Weinhold, Altnordisches Leben, p. 262.

[3] Ujfalvy, Expéd. scient. i, p. 15. Upon the birthday festival among the Western Irānians, vide Duncker, GdA. iv, pp. 164–165; Spiegel, E. A. vol. iii, p. 706.

know nothing at present. Among the modern Parsees it certainly takes place under solemn formalities[1].

The mother suckled her child at her own breast; the father's duty was chiefly to preserve it from every danger. Both the parents together sought by offerings and prayers to the divine beings to induce them to take the child under their special protection, and to allow it to grow and thrive in strength and happiness[2].

As to the child's education, their first aim was to make of him an able and useful member of their community, and to implant in him those virtues for which the old Irānian people were principally remarkable, and which the Avesta sums up in the words: 'piety in thought, word and action.'

It is pretty clear that the special training of boys for future callings went hand in hand with their religious education, and that it was chiefly regulated according to the profession of the father. The warrior would have his son instructed in the handling of weapons, and the use of the bow, the lance and the sword. The peasant took his children out with him to the field and showed them how to manage the plough, to scatter seed, or gather in corn. Lastly, the priest initiated his sons in the understanding of the Holy Scriptures and their commandments, and fostered in them the consciousness of the sanctity and dignity of their peculiar position.

As even now the *vis inertiae* is a great factor in the choice of a profession, how much more powerful must it have been before the existence of that universal intercourse which destroys all class-distinctions.

---

[1] Dossabhoy Framjee, 'The Parsees,' pp. 64–65; Spiegel, *E. A.* vol. iii, p. 700. [No formalities to my knowledge are generally observed by us at the present day. By the by, it may be said that the initiation into the historical knowledge of our ancestors has led to one social reform, viz., that the mother is not so much inclined to name her child after the manner of Hindoos, as to call it by one of the glorious names of her heroic ancestors. Now-a-days, I believe there are more *Rustams, Jehangirs,* and *Shirins* than there were thirty years back. *Tr.*]

[2] This is evident from the idea contained in Vd. III, 31, upon which compare my remarks in *ZddmG.* vol. xxxiv, p. 423.

It was evidently also no uncommon practice to commit children to the care of a priest for training and instruction in the same manner as the Indian Brahmins were wont to do. This practice must certainly have prevailed most among those who were destined for ecclesiastical functions, and the most essential subject of instruction was of course the interpretation of the Holy Text, the right performance of ceremonies, and the ritual of sacrifice. The relation between these teachers and their pupils is not often mentioned in the Avesta, yet we see that it was one of love and friendship[1].

Youths or maidens were solemnly admitted into the Zoroastrian community by investing them with the sacred string[2]. . . . The girdle is the symbol of the spiritual tie which binds together the whole Zoroastrian community. Men as well as women were wont to wear it continually. . . . The modern Parsees call it *kosti*. The *kosti* is a woollen string consisting of seventy-two threads, the manufacture of which is accompanied by certain ceremonies. The season of investiture is now earlier than it used to be in ancient times[3]. In other respects the ideas of the present Parsees with reference to the object and importance of the *kosti* correspond, so far as we know, with those of the Avesta.

From the religious point of view, investiture with the sacred girdle may be compared with confirmation in the Christian Churches, and, from the legal point of view, with a declaration of majority, i.e. with the coming of age. Whoever wore the *kosti* belonged to the adult members of the community and was entitled to all its privileges. He was then relieved from parental discipline, and naturally took upon himself, with his personal independence, also the entire moral and civil responsibility of all his actions, which the parents had hitherto borne wholly or in part.

---

[1] Yt. X, 116. The pupil is called *hāvishta* or *aēthrya*, the teacher *aēthrapaiti*.

[2] *Aiwyāoğhana*, 'girdle.'

[3] Dossabhoy Framjee, 'The Parsees,' p. 67 ; Spiegel, *E. A.* vol. iii, pp. 700–701.

The religious importance of this act is evidently far
more interesting to the composers of the Parsee Scriptures than its civil aspect. Nevertheless we assume that
the youth was admitted by this act, not only into the
religious community of the Zoroastrians, but also at
the same time into the army and to new family ties,
and was regarded as capable of bearing arms and quali-
fied to vote. Henceforth he was entitled to bear arms and
to take a part in the meetings and councils of the village
community, he could acquire landed property and manage
his own domestic concerns; in short, he became a perfect
citizen of the state.

Of the ceremonies accompanying the investiture with the
kosti nothing is mentioned in the Avesta; however, we
know that this custom is very ancient, in no way invented
or first introduced by the Avesta people, but only developed
and modified to suit their particular ideas.

Amongst the Indians the so-called '*conveyance*'[1] corresponds with it. By this the sons of the three higher
castes were entrusted to the care of a Brahmin teacher
when they had attained a certain age. Like the Irānian
youths they were invested with a sacred string, and the
ceremony took place under solemn consecrations and
prayers. Here also this act originally marked the admission of boys and youths to the right of contracting
family ties. In the Brahmanical period, however, the holy
thread became the distinguishing badge of the *dvija*, 'the
twice-born,' and the investiture itself was regarded as the
sacred new-birth which distinguished the three higher
castes from the Sudras, and was considered as the badge
of their higher enlightenment.

---

[1] *Upanayana* (*B. R.* s. v.); Manu, II, 36; *vide* Deslongchamps,
Loi de Manu traduite, 33, note 1; Spiegel, *E. A.* vol. iii, p. 136.

§ 8. *Love and Marriage.*

THE fifteenth year of age was the normal time of marriage for girls[1].

As the raising of children was considered a duty and their acquisition a blessing, it was naturally wrong and monstrous if a woman did not fulfil her vocation[2]. Besides, it was deemed a grievous sin forcibly to hinder a maiden from contracting marriage :—

> ' For her third complaint mourns the good *Ashi*, the sublime : " That is the worst deed which hostile men commit, when they keep a maiden from marriage and immure her as an unmarried one[3]." '

Hence, no doubt, it was considered a matter of course, as it is still in Persia[4], that a girl should be married on reaching the years of puberty. A young woman who lost her bloom and grew old unmarried, was merely a useless burden in the house of her parents. It even seems that she was frequently subject to taunts and mortification, at all events to general disrespect.

For this reason the thoughts and aspirations of the young daughter of a Mazdayasna were directed towards obtaining a lord and husband, who would take her to his own house ; and this most heart-felt of all wishes is expressed with simple candour.

---

[1] Vd. XIV, 15.

[2] The tract *Shāyast-la-Shāyast* says : ' The rule is this, that a man, when he does not wed a wife, does not become worthy of death ; but when a woman does not wed a husband it amounts to a sin worthy of death ; because for a woman there is no offspring except by intercourse with men, and no lineage proceeds from her ; but for a man without a wife, when he shall recite the Avesta as it is mentioned in the Vendidād, there may be a lineage which proceeds onwards to the future existence.' West, 'Pahlavi Texts,' part I, pp. 322–323 ; comp. Vd. XVIII, 51.

[3] Yt. XVII, 59.

[4] Polak, *Persien*, vol. i, p. 205.

Loud and silent prayers arise to the *yazatas*, especially to Ardvi-sūra, of whom it is said : ' Thee, maidens, when they are fit for marriage, implore for strong men and valiant husbands [1].' But the *yazata* of wind, Vayu, who otherwise usually has nothing to do with such matters, is also invoked :

' Grant us this grace, that we may obtain a husband, a youthful one, one of surpassing beauty, who may procure us sustenance as long as we have to live with each other, and who will beget us offspring ;— [a wise, learned, ready-tongued husband [2]].'

In extreme cases Hauma also is a helper in need, and ' grants to the maidens, who have long remained unmarried, an able, wise husband, who quickly courts them [3].'

The *courting*, or, as it is strictly translated, the *solicitation* [4] for the hand of a maiden, was made to those persons under whose care she stood, that is, above all, to the parents or their representatives. Sometimes, however, women appear to have been independent, and to have been thus able to dispose of themselves as they chose [5].

Whether the motive for marriage was at times real love, or merely the natural impulse and wish for a home, we can hardly ascertain. However, it would be better not to judge merely from modern ideas and views of so old a period and of the peculiar sphere of the East. If the marriage of a grown-up daughter with an orthodox husband may be reckoned as a merit to the Mazdayasna, if it may even

---

[1] Yt. V, 87. For a surely very doubtful attempt at interpreting this extremely difficult passage *vide Handbuch*, p. 132.

[2] Yt. XV, 40. This passage is evidently corrupt. The correction *yavānem · sraçshto-kehrpem* for *yavāna · sraçshta* (var. ō) *kehrpa* can scarcely be avoided. Similarly I read *huberefīm* instead of *huberetām*.

[3] Ys. IX, 23. Unmarried women are called *aghru*, which has naturally nothing to do with rt. *garew*, as I have wrongly taken it in my *Hdb. Glossar*. s. v.

[4] *Jadh* in *moshu-jaidhyamna*.

[5] So at least according to Vd. XV, 9, if here *stātō-ratu* and *astātō-ratu* may be translated by ' standing under the care of any one ' and ' not standing under the care of any one.'

be prescribed to him as a penance for certain transgres-
sions[1], such marriage assumes indeed the character of a
purely business-like transaction, in which the sentiments
and feelings of the persons most interested are generally
not taken into account.

Contrasted with the foregoing, a stanza in the *Gâthâs*, if
rightly interpreted, appears to contain a higher and purer
idea of marriage, and to regard it as an intimate union
founded on love and piety. On the occasion of the cele-
bration of a marriage, the priestly Singer addresses, as I
would believe, the young people, with these words:

*Sâqênî · vazyamnâbyô · kainibyô · mraomî ·
Khshmaibyâchâ · vaedemnô · menchâ · î · mâzdazdûm ·
Vaédôdûm · Daênâbi*sh· *abyaschâ · ahûm · yê · vaghču*sh·
*managhô ·
Ashâ · vê · anyô · ainîm · vîvaghatû · tat · zî · hôi ·
hushênem · aghat.*

'Admonishing words I say unto the maidens, who will
    enter into marriage,
And to you (the youth) I, who know it; take them to
    heart;
Learn to know, through Religion and of these (the
    parents?), the life of a good mind;
In piety you shall both seek to win the love of each
    other, only thus will it lead you to joy!'[2]

The courtship was followed by the *betrothal*, through
which the girl was entrusted to the man[3]. Between the
betrothal and the nuptials some further time elapsed.
Among the Gebers in Kirmân, a girl is betrothed at the

---

[1] Vd. XIV, 15.

[2] Ys. LIII, 5. In stanza 2, of Gâthâ, 64, Bartholomä reads
vaedemanô instead of the certainly much better verified *vademanô*.
If we accept the last reading, this stanza would be appropriate
in the mouth of the bridegroom. Touching this I refer also to the
Pahlavî translation which must have likewise read *vaedemanô*, for it
renders the word by *âkâsîh.* I identify *vîvaghatû* with Skr. *vivâs.*

[3] Thus *paradhâta* and *aparadhâta* (Vd. XV, 9), 'betrothed' and
'unbetrothed,' come from rt. *dâ* with *para.* Also in Skr. *parâ-dâ,* 'to
give up, to surrender,' is mentioned.

age of nine, and married at thîrteen. With the Parsees of India the betrothal takes place still earlier. The marriage ceremony consists in joining the hands of a young man and woman, while prayers and holy formulas are recited[1]. Through the touching of their hands the union is made a legal compact.

Of a similar kind were most likely the holy rites which were observed at the *conclusion of a marriage* (*nāirithwana*)[2]. Therewith, the bride, magnificently adorned[3], was conveyed, under various solemn customs and observances, from the house of her parents to that of her husband, which was to become henceforth her new home. Hence the Irānian speaks of a 'taking home' of the wife[4], just as the Greek does of the ἄγεσθαι γυναῖκα and the Roman of a *ducere puellam in matrimonium*[5].

It is characteristic, as bearing upon the legal and moral position of the wife in the old Irānian house, that she bears from the marriage-day the title of *nmānō-pathni*, 'the mistress of the house,' just as the husband is called *nmānō-paiti*, 'the master of the house[6].' The wife ranks thus more as the equal of the husband than his dependent. She is not his slave but his companion, entitled to all his privileges, sharing with him the direction and management of the household.

Whilst the man has chiefly to procure through the labour of his hands the necessary means of maintenance for his

---

[1] Dossabhoy Framjee, 'The Parsees,' p. 76 ; Spiegel. *Av. üb.* vol. ii, p. xxviii. seq. ; *E. A.* vol. iii, p. 677.

[2] Vd. XIV, 15.

[3] Comp. p. 226 of *Osîrānische Kultur.*

[4] *Vadh,* 'to lead.' This verb itself has disappeared from old Indian, and it is only preserved in its derivative *vadhū,* which has no connection with *vah.* Besides in the Avesta *vaz* is also used to denote 'to marry, to take home (a bride).'

[5] Respecting the marriage customs prevailing amongst the Indians I refer to Zimmer, *AiL.* pp. 312–313 ; Lefmann, *Geschichte des alten Indiens,* p. 99 seq.

[6] Actually corresponding to the Rv. *gṛhapati* and *gṛhapatnī.* In Vd. XII, 7 *nmānō-paiti* and *nmānō-pathni* are as 'husband' and 'wife.'

family, and therefore moves more out of doors, the wife's sphere of action is indoors. As the cultivation of the field, the chase, and war are incumbent upon him, so does she tend the domestic herd, devoting herself to the care and primary training of her children, and to the preparation of food, and the making of needful clothing and other articles of home manufacture.

We shall therefore not err in conceding to woman in ancient Irān nearly the same social position as that occupied by the wife among the Vedic Indians, the Germans, or the Greeks of the age of Homer. Among all these peoples we meet with the same social relations. It is true the man represents the highest power in his small house-state, and the wife too must be willing and obedient to him like his children and domestics, but she is in no way degraded to the rank of a maid-servant or slave, as was the case in Eastern countries even at a very early period[1].

In the Avesta both sexes appear constantly as possessing equal rights; there is no difference as to their respective importance. Pious men and women are frequently named together. As in this world, so also in the next, they live together, enjoying in common the pleasures of Paradise[2]. Wives are an honour to the house[3]; and the good spirits,

---

[1] I give here as an appendix the names of relations occurring in the Avesta: *pitare*=Skr. *pitṛ* 'father,' *mātare*=Skr. *mātṛ* 'mother'; *puthra*=Skr. *putra* 'son,' *dughdhare*=Skr. *duhitṛ* 'daughter'; *nyāka*=N.P. *niyā* (not corresponding to the Indian) 'grandfather,' *nyākē* 'grandmother'; *napāt*=Skr. *napāt* 'grandson,' *napti* 'granddaughter'; *brātuirya*=Skr. *bhrātṛvya*, masc. 'uncle,' fem. 'aunt'; *tūirya* 'nephew, niece.' Hence further on we avail ourselves of a circumscription, viz., *tūirya puthra* and *tūirya dughdhare*, *tūirya puthra puthra* and *tūirya dughdhare dughdhare* relations in the fourth and fifth generation. Comp. Vd. XII. Comp. further *hvasura* 'father-in-law'=Skr. *çvaçura*, and *zāmātar* 'son-in-law'=Skr. *jāmātṛ*; *brātare* 'brother'=Skr. *bhrātṛ*, and *hvaṅhar* 'sister' =Skr. *svasṛ*.

[2] Vd. IX, 42; Ys. XXVI, 8; XXXIX, 2; Yt. XI. 4, &c.

[3] Vd. III, 3.

particularly Ahura Mazda, are represented as being in the company of female yazatas [1].

As in the Vedic antiquity, so also amongst the Avesta people, women took part even in the holy ceremonies and solemn offerings. The ladies of the house who cherish good thoughts, utter good words, and perform good actions, who are obedient and subject to their lords, are invited in the Vispered at the offering ceremony equally with pious and orthodox men [2]. Further on it is said that both wife and husband naturally pray together, with uplifted hands, to Mithra for his protection and support [3]. The following remarkable saying of the Rig-veda is also in accordance with Irānian custom : 'Already from olden time the wife has attended the common sacrificial offerings and festive gatherings, she, the fosterer of the holy law [4].'

The first and strictest demand which the bridegroom made of the bride was, that her name and reputation should be pure and unspotted [5], and her virginity before marriage unstained [6]. This demand is enforced with unrelenting severity among the Persians of the present day, though their morality is rather lax. The simple accusation of the husband is sufficient to divorce a young wife and to expose her to misery and shame [7]. This peculiar destiny

---

[1] Ys. XXXVIII, 1.

[2] Vsp. III, 3; *yavānem · humanaǧhem · huvachaǧhem · hushkyaothnem · hudaęnem · āslāya* . . . *nmānahę · nmānō-pathnīm · āslāya, nāirikāmcha · āslāya · frāyō-humatām · frāyō-hūkhtām · frāyō-huvarsh*tām · *hushhām-sāstām · ratu-khshathrām.*

[3] Yt. X, 84. Very obscure and doubtful. The word translated by me by ' both wife and husband ' is *pithę.* Cf. Spiegel, *Commentar,* vol. ii, pp. 566–567; C. de Harlez, *Av. tr.* vol. ii, p. 236.

[4] Rv. X, 86, 10; Zimmer, *AiL.* pp. 316–317.

[5] *Nāmēnī* (Vd. XIV, 15) is certainly correctly translated by de Harlez by ' elle doit être de bonne réputation ' (she has to be of good reputation).

[6] Vd. XIV, 15, *anupaęta* and *askeñda,* the former from root *i* with *upa* (also Skr. *upa-i* means *coire cum femina*), the latter is supposed to be connected according to Geldner (*K.Z.* vol. xxv, p. 211, note 1) with Skr. *skanda,* ' profusio seminis.'

[7] Polak, *Persien,* vol. i, p. 213.

of women, which naturally paves the way for the most shameful abuses, has at least this one advantage that offences against morality are very rare amongst unmarried girls in Persia.

Marriage between blood-relations was forbidden among the old Indians. They exhibit even a religious dread of consanguinity in marriage. As to the Rig-veda, this idea is clearly demonstrated by a remarkable song already often quoted, which contains a dialogue between Yama and his sister Yamī[1]. Here the latter tries to decoy her brother into love, but she is rejected by him with an express appeal to the gods who had forbidden such sin.

How entirely different is the case in the Avesta! Here the marriage of relations is not only unforbidden but even recommended, and described as a meritorious and pious action. It is esteemed as an institution that has proceeded from Mazda and Zarathushtra, and is thus sanctioned as a very ancient custom and a divine ordinance [2].

---

[1] Rv. X, 10; Zimmer, *AiL.* p. 323.

[2] The technical expression is *hvaētvadatha*; comp. particularly Ys. XII, 9; Vsp. III, 3. [We understand the passage (Ys. XII, 9) quite differently. Here *hvaētvadathām* is to be taken as a noun used adjectively and qualifying *Daēnām*. *Āstuyē · Daēnām · Māzdayasnīm · fraspāyō-khedhrām · nidhā-snaithishem · hvaētvadathām · ashaonīm ·* 'I extol the Mazda-worshipping Religion (i. e. the Religion that commands its followers to adore the Wisdom of the Creator), that is far from all doubt, that levels all arguments (disputes), the sacred one which is itself a tie that unites (the spiritual man with God).' Here *hvaētvadathām*, we believe, does not properly refer to marriage among mankind, as Dr. Spiegel and others have endeavoured to interpret it, but it rather signifies that the Religion revealed to Zarathushtra by Ahura Mazda is the only medium on earth, the sincere belief in which infallibly conduces so to exalt the human mind as to bring it to a clear conception of the Deity. Whatever might be the view of the later Pahlavi writers with regard to the word *khvetudas*, we have no single instance in the Avesta which can suggest the idea that amongst the Avesta nation there ever was a marriage contracted between brother and sister. See the question fully examined by Dr. West, 'Pahlavi Texts,' part ii, Appendix.—*Tr.*]

Later writers also of the traditional Parsee literature frequently expatiate upon kindred-marriages. The *Bahman Yasht* plainly puts the following words into the mouth of Ahura Mazda : 'The most perfectly righteous of the righteous is he who remains in the good religion of the Mazdayasnân, and continues the religious practice of kindred-marriage in his family ;' and, according to the *Shâyast-la-shâyast*, such a marriage is in itself capable of expiating mortal or heinous sins, and serves as an efficient and powerful weapon against the evil spirit Ahriman[1].

It is frequently observed that the Avesta people set a high value on the preservation of the purity of their blood, and stood in great fear of its intermixture with foreign elements. This principle was followed to the utmost extreme in the introduction of marriage among relations . . . .

Among modern Persians kindred-marriage is not rare. It is here evidently a remnant of antiquity which has been preserved to the present day, with the tenacity peculiar to such family institutions, in spite of the entirely altered circumstances under which they now live. Besides, this custom, as we learn from well-informed judges, is by no means attended with results disastrous to the children[2].

In conclusion, I come to the question whether monogamy or polygamy existed amongst the Avesta people.

I premise that the bare principle only is here to be treated of, and not its practical application. Persons in poor and embarrassed circumstances, who were not in a position to support several wives and a larger number of children, were perforce obliged to be content with *one* wife. We must absolutely set aside the question concerning concubines or persons who lived in a state of concubinage. Polygamy properly so called is only spoken of where several women occupy towards one man the same lawful

---

[1] *Bahman Yasht*, chap. ii, p. 61 ; *Sh.-lâ-sh.* VIII, 18 ; XVIII, 3. *Vide* West, 'Pahlavi Texts,' part i, pp. 213, 307, 387.
[2] Polak, *Persien*, vol. i, pp. 200–201.

rank, and where the children of all of them are considered to have been begotten in lawful wedlock.

Unfortunately in the Avesta there is a lack of positive testimony as much concerning the one (monogamy) as concerning the other (polygamy), and we must therefore content ourselves with merely indirect proofs and conclusions drawn from analogy.

Sons and wives are esteemed as an ornament to a house, and the *yazatas* bestow them upon the pious in abundance. This might be construed as an indication that polygamy was customary and a great number of women a mark of opulence and divine blessing [1] . . . .

However, it would be better not to lay too much stress upon such isolated passages of almost universal import, nor to draw from them any far-fetched conclusions.

The Parsees of India live, as we know, in monogamy. But that is in no way an original custom. A short time ago bigamy was in general use [2]. So too we learn of the Tājiks living in the mountains of Zerafshān that with them polygamy is indeed not the rule but is by no means forbidden [3].

The modern Persians and their marriage customs may therefore be used for comparison only with great reserve, since they naturally come under the influence of Islāmism. But amongst the old Persians polygamy was commonly practised . . . .

I shall go even further. Among the old Indians, also, it

---

[1] [The passage wherein the Avesta esteems ' sons and wives as an ornament to a family,' does not imply the wives of a single man but all the married women living in the same house. Just as is the case now in Parsee families, so also in the age of the Avesta may we conceive a Zoroastrian family as having married daughters, daughters-in-law, and even granddaughters-in-law with the *mater-familias* at their head, all forming a group of more than a dozen women. Even when the Zoroastrian prays for sons, he does not generally pray for sons only but for sons and wives, i. e. sons who should be sufficiently well settled in life to afford to marry as well as to maintain households of their own. *Tr.*]

[2] Dossabhoy Framjee, ' The Parsees,' p. 88 seq.

[3] Ujfalvy, *Expéd. scient.* i, p. 16.

is supposed on the authority of some passages of the Rig-veda, and indeed evidently with full justice, that at least men of rank frequently enjoyed a plurality of wives[1]. There is likewise no doubt that in ancient Germany, particularly in the case of princes and grandees, polygamy was an old and primitive custom which was only in course of time replaced by monogamy[2].

We have here numerous analogies and grounds of probability which appear to speak in favour of the antiquity and priority of the custom of polygamy. In support of any contradictory opinion I have nothing to bring forward.

Under such circumstances I consider it almost certain that plurality of wives was not prohibited to the Avèsta nation. Probably every one was free to do as he liked. Whoever was able to maintain more wives and a larger household, could marry several ; whoever could not afford it, contented himself with only *one*. The precepts of their religion left this question wholly untouched, because there was no question at all of that custom being allowable or not allowable, or of its being right or wrong, but simply an accidental or personal ability or inability. In this way the silence of the Avesta is most simply explained. Had the Avesta prescribed monogamy, thus being in conflict with the custom which we know to have prevailed elsewhere in the country of Irān, there would have been certainly no lack of passages which opposed and attacked polygamy, and which represented the new institute of monogamy as sacred and divinely established.

Finally, I must further add that polygamy is not at all against the natural order, and as regards its practice in the Orient it is even explained and justified by the nature of the climate. It is even doubly intelligible in a nation that lays so great a value upon a numerous posterity as is known to have been done by the Avesta people.

---

[1] Zimmer, *AiL.* p. 324 ; Lefmann, *Geschichte des alten Indiens*, p. 98 ; Kägi, *Der Rig-veda*, XV.

[2] Weinhold, *Altnordisches Leben*, p. 248 seq.

§ 9. *Prayers and Household Customs.*

THE scantiness of our references unfortunately does not allow us to describe, on the basis of the Avesta-text, the daily life of the Zoroastrian, the arrangement of his household, his professional and religious duties and occupations, and the change from labour to relaxation.

We can here only discuss the most important customs and ceremonies which are prescribed to the Mazdayasnân, men as well as women, as a regular exercise, or to meet certain occasions of daily life.

The whole life of the faithful man was, according to the view of the Avesta, a conflict with the powers of darkness, with Angra Mainyu and his demons. He was threatened on all sides with their persecution. He had to remain ever on his guard lest he should have to yield to the evil power through some transgression. He was however enjoined to extend and strengthen the kingdom of light and to impair and diminish that of darkness, through his active interference in the great struggle between the heavenly and the infernal spirits.

Thus he had to be vigilant, alert, and active. Sloth and laziness induced to vice. Even sleep itself was really a mere concession to the demons[1], and therefore one had to endeavour to limit its power over him as much as possible. As soon as, at early morning, with the break of day, the good spirits had overpowered the demons of night and had begun to exercise their power anew, the pious had also to rise and to go to their daily work. In this they were chiefly assisted by Chanticleer, whose call scared away slumber. It is to this circumstance, I believe, that the domestic cock owes the great attention which is paid to it among the Zoroastrians. I shall dwell upon this more fully in my description of the domestic animals.

In the war against vice the divine beings bring succour to men in various ways. This succour they grant as a

---

[1] Comp. however Vsp. VII, 3.

mighty weapon through which man can avert and annihilate the destructive influence of the demons[1]. Such is the Holy Word which Mazda has revealed to Zarathushtra; such are the prayers which he has taught him.

The conception of the nature of prayer seems to us rather an extrinsic one. It is not [always] the internal elevation of man towards God, nor the degree of devotion and fervency, which makes it efficacious. To the words themselves belongs mysterious, one might almost say magical, power; the mere recitation of them, if correct and faultless, brings that power into action.

These prayers are not to be recited merely on particular occasions; they do not secure help and deliverance in times of imminent danger and difficulty alone. As the demoniacal powers are constantly lurking in ambush to do injury unto men, it is commanded to say prayers, even as a sort of preservative, regularly at fixed hours of the day, and in all constantly-recurring occupations and actions.

For the modern Parsees the precise forms of prayer are strictly laid down; a brief survey of them will be sufficient[2].

On rising, washing, and dressing, especially on tying the sacred string, a series of prayers are to be repeated. Next follows the special morning-prayer. Before and after each meal, likewise, prayers are said; and in the evening, before the Parsee goes to sleep, he has, further, to reflect upon and examine what he has done in the course of the day, and then only, after reciting certain prayers, he retires to rest.

---

[1] Thus it is said of Zarathushtra that he by means of the prayer *Yathā-ahū - vairyō* frightened away the demons who, having plotted his ruin, had surrounded him (Vd. XIX, 2). Zarathushtra exultingly says further on: '(I will conquer) by means of the (sacred) mortar, and the cup and the *hauma*, and by the prayer (*vacha*) taught to me by Mazda. My weapon is the *Vahishtem-prayer*; with this I will conquer and frighten away the demons. This weapon is an excellent one, O thou profligate Angra Manyu!' Vd. XIX, 9.

[2] Spiegel, *Av. üb.* vol. ii, p. l. seq.

To the prayers, which form part of the order of the day, are further added a number of others which must be said on certain occurrences, viz. after sneezing, after connubial intercourse, after satisfying natural purposes, after pollutions during sleep, after the cutting of nails and hair, as well as after the lighting of candles.

Several of these cases are anticipated in the Avesta[1], and if others are not mentioned, it may be owing perhaps to the incompleteness of the text. Besides these, prayers are naturally also prescribed for the different ceremonies of purification. They should be repeated, according to circumstances, twice, thrice, four times, or even oftener, and must alternate with the recitation of strophes or sayings from the Gāthās[2]. For deceased relations also, and all relatives, near and distant, it is a solemn obligation to say prayers and to recite the sacred hymns[3].

There are, on the whole, four prayers which can be adapted to the most diverse occasions. Three of these are composed in the antique dialect of the Gāthās, the fourth, the prayer *Yẹ̄ghẹ̄-hātãm*, shows the same language as the later Avesta. The prayer *Airyema ishyō* is of subordinate importance, whilst the efficacy of the two others is commended in the Avesta in inspired words. Unfortunately the text is extremely difficult and obscure, so that none of the attempts hitherto made to interpret it can be considered as perfectly satisfactory[4].

The prayer *Ashem vōhū* is translated by Haug in the following manner:—

'Righteousness is the best good;
A blessing it is; a blessing be to him
Who is righteous towards *Asha-vahishta*.'

---

[1] Vd. XVIII, 43 and 49; XVII; *vide* Duncker, *GdA*. iv, pp. 158–159.

[2] Vd. VIII, 19; XI and XII; XIX, 22.

[3] Vd. XII.

[4] Spiegel, *Comm.* vol. ii, p. 466 seq.; Haug and West, 'Essays on the Parsis,' p. 141, note 2. The text is found in Bartholomä, *Gāthās*, pp. 65–66. Comp. now also Roth, *ZddmG*. XXXVIII, p. 437.

Its meaning is praised in the Hādokht-Nusk[1]. All that is good and excellent is comprised in it, and all other prayers are, so to say, included in it. But foremost amongst all the forms of prayer is the *Ahuna-varya*, or, as it is called by the Parsees, the *Honover*:

'Just as a heavenly lord is to be chosen,
So is an earthly master for the sake of righteousness,
As a giver of good thoughts, and of the actions of life towards Mazda.
The dominion belongs to the lord whom he has appointed as a protector for the poor.'

Regarding this prayer it is said that Ahura Mazda first uttered it, and that it existed before the heavens, before the water, before the earth, before the animals, the plants, and mankind[2]. One should recite it without any omission, and not intermix it with anything foreign, if it is meant to have its full effect. Whoever recites it in the manner prescribed, his soul crosses over the bridge which separates this world from the next, and reaches the highest paradise, the most brilliant stars.

The *Honover* is the best prayer that ever has been and ever will be spoken. As long as the earth exists it must be recited, and it will protect from death him who says it and who remembers it.

Lastly, it is expressly declared in another passage that this prayer, which had the Highest God for its author, was also recited by the prophet Zarathushtra:

'Renowned in the country of Aryana Vaija hast thou first, O Zarathushtra, said four times the *Ahuna-varya*, dividing it into verses[3].'

---

[1] In Westergaard, Yt. XXI, note; Haug and West, 'Essays,' p. 218 seq.

[2] Ys. XIX; Haug and West, 'Essays,' p. 185 seq.

[3] Ys. IX, 14; cf. Haug and West, 'Essays,' p. 179. In my *Handbuch* I have wrongly interpreted the epithet *viberethwat*; it is certainly derived from root *bar* = Skr. *bhar bhṛṇāti*, N.P. *burīdan*. Comp. also Geldner, *Metrik*, p. 127: 'four times with the transposition of parts.'

Besides prayers, sacrifices and offerings may also be noticed here. But as these were only of a private nature, offered only in the rarest cases, and conducted mostly by priests, they will be discussed hereafter.

On the other hand, I must here mention the tending of the hearth-fire, as this was undoubtedly the daily and constant duty of every master of a house, and consequently belonged to household customs in the proper sense of the word.

With the employment of fire begins the civilization of mankind, and this beneficent element, the use of which, like speech and reason, distinguishes men from beasts, enjoys on that account divine veneration everywhere on our globe. To the Avesta people, however, it is something more than the mere foundation of civilized life. With them it is at the same time the holiest and the purest element, the reflection of their Highest Deity, Ahura Mazda. It is moreover the symbol of moral purity, and a strong weapon of defence against the demons. During night and darkness, when the wicked demons are at their work, fire produces light and brightness, and frightens away these hellish spirits.

Fire is directly called *Ahurahę Mazdāo puthra*[1], 'the son of Ahura Mazda'; he is His earthly image, of the same nature and essence with Himself. He is a genius who, after the creation was completed, first spontaneously descended upon the earth in order to protect the creatures devoted to Mazda against the powers of evil[2]. This is proved by the fact that Asha-vahishta, the genius of 'the best piety,' is at the same time the genius of fire. Hence also the hearth-fire, as the centre of the house, is the symbol of a fixed settlement; and the latter, on the other hand, is the characteristic or token that distinguishes the righteous and faithful from the impious.

The worship of the hearth-fire amongst the Indo-Germans deserves a succinct description. Amongst the

---

[1] Spiegel, *E. A.* vol. ii, p. 41 seq.
[2] *Vide* Spiegel, *Traditionelle Literatur der Parsen*, p. 332.

Irānians it is called *nmānō-paiti*, 'the master of the house,' amongst the Indians, *grhapati*, which means the same thing. With the Greeks and Romans also it is the centre of their family-life. Round the ἑστία, the consecrated hearth, assemble the family on the Apaturian and Amphidromian festivals. The *pater-familias* or the *mater-familias* looks after the cult. All libations that are offered begin with the *Hestia*.

Near the hearth of a Roman house stand the images of the Lares and Penates. The marriage-ceremony is performed near it, as was customary among the old Indians. The young couple are received at the entrance into the new house with the fire of its altar. Near the hearth is placed the nuptial couch.

Similarly, in the house of the old German an ever-burning fire blazed on the hearth, as an emblem of the everlasting duration of his family and his race. Round about this fire stood the images of the household gods carved in wood. It was the centre of the family worship. A remnant of this old custom survives still in the sports of children.

The mighty Fire which is useful to the pious in a multitude of ways, but which annihilates the vicious in the form of deadly flashes of lightning, is commended in the Gāthās :

'After Thy Fire, O Ahura, the powerful, do we yearn in a pious manner,
After the swift, mighty, that rejoices the creation, and lends manifold assistance,
But which, O Mazda, works the destruction of the enemy through the bolts of his hands[1].'

From the smoke and the flame of Fire it was believed that the Will of the Deity could be recognized. His crackling flame was the means whereby He spoke to men. In doubtful cases especially the oracular decision of Fire appears to have been often invoked[2].

The hearth-fire, however, must also be preserved and

---

[1] Xs. XXXIV, 4.
[2] Ys. XXXI, 3 and 19. Cf. further *infra*.

tended by men. According to a certainly very ancient idea, it must at no time, not even in the night, be extinguished. It must continually blaze and shine as a never-resting champion against demons. When the bright flame becomes extinct, the good spirits, who protect the house from the terrors and dangers of darkness, disappear from it.

The fuel must be dried before it is used[1], in order not to contain any moisture which would cause the two elements, water and fire, to clash. Moreover, the proper kind of wood must be selected, some fragrant species, such as *Hadhānai-pata*, being most desirable. The bark was probably stripped of the wood before burning[2].

The wood must be carried with clean-washed hands, and this is a duty which is to be fulfilled at the beginning, middle, and end of the night, but particularly at early morning when people rise from their beds with the first crowing of the cock. Otherwise *Āzi*, the demon of want and lust, would cause damage to the fire and it might die out from lack of fuel.

Furthermore, Fire actually shows his gratitude to him who bestows due care upon him. As to the master of the house, he blesses him above all things in his domestic life, allows a goodly number of able sons to grow up, and all that belongs to him to improve in power and importance.

‘ May herds of cattle follow thee and men in numbers!
　　May a powerful mind and an active soul follow thee!
　　Mayest thou pass thy life with a merry heart all the
　　days that thou livest!’
‘ This is the benediction of Fire unto him who brings
　　him fuel, dry, picked out at daylight, rightly prepared
　　with the intent of the holy commandment[3].’

---

[1] Comp. the whole section Vd. XVIII, 18 seq.

[2] Ys. LXII, 10; Vd. VIII, 2; Vd. XVIII, 27 (the stripping of the bark is perhaps meant by *yaozhdāta*). We may compare the statement of Strabo (p. 732), that the Persians offered sacrifice to the fire by laying one over the other pieces of wood without rind. Windischmann, *Zoroastrische Studien*, p. 295. The fuel is called *aẹsma*.

[3] Vd. XVIII, 27; cf. also Ys. LXII, 10.

The numerous commandments of purification, which are given by the Avesta for almost all imaginable occurrences, have a direct and important bearing upon the daily life of the Zoroastrian. They are multiplied to such an extent, that the excess of formalities and ceremonies must necessarily choke the deeper sense which underlies them.

The Indians, also, look upon a variety of objects as impure, and believe that their impurity may be transferred by contact to men, who have then to remove it by means of prayers, ablutions, and other similar remedies. But this idea is among the Irānians of the Avesta carried to its furthest extreme, and has consequently, as affecting ordinary life, a still greater importance and meaning. The notions of the Brāhmanical Indians and the Eastern Irānians, moreover, exhibit in this respect a striking resemblance even as to details, and, indeed, in such a manner that we have a right to regard them as very ancient, and to trace them at least to certain common fundamental aspects, which have been transmitted to us from Arian antiquity.

In the Avesta, *dead bodies* are pre-eminently considered as impure. However, the logic of this view is very sensible and excellent. Impure are only the corpses of originally good and pure beings, and they are so, indeed, on the ground that the party of light has sustained a loss on account of their death. If, on the contrary, a vicious person dies, it must be regarded as a gain ; his dead body cannot therefore exercise any corrupting influence[1].

Thus it is principally the dead bodies of pious human beings and those of particularly holy animals, such as the dog, from which contamination issues. Immediately after

---

[1] Thus it is said in Vd. V, 36 : '*Living* a destructive, evil person, as for example an *ashemaugha*, directly or indirectly causes pollution to the creatures of the blissful spirit, O son of Spitama, Zarathushtra ; *living* he smites the water, extinguishes the fire, and carries away the cattle ; *living* he inflicts upon the pious man such a wound as robs him of his life or disfigures his body . . . *but not* [*so when*] *dead.*'

death has taken place, the demon of putrefaction[1] prevails and enters the corpse in the shape of a fly, and therewith the dead body has fallen into the grasp of the evil powers and pollutes whatever comes in contact with it.

The different degrees of pollution are laid down most minutely[2]. The principal distinction is that made between immediate contamination, when one comes into direct contact with the impure object itself, and the indirect pollution which spreads of itself from a defiled person or thing[3].

Not only men, but beasts also, may be polluted; and even utensils, particularly those which are used in religious ceremonies, clothes, etc.

Water is impure when a dead body has been rotting in it, or when it has been poured upon a carcass; the roads upon which corpses are conveyed also become impure, and so do houses in which anybody has died; in fact, any piece of land upon which a dead body has lain.

Above all, the holiest element, fire, was naturally most exposed to defilement, and it had to be therefore preserved with great care, so that it might not come into contact with anything impure. It is always water or fire which must be taken to a safe place when a death or similar occurrence of polluting influence takes place[4].

Even by its employment in daily life, more particularly by its application to industrial purposes, fire became unhallowed, according to the notions of the Avesta. Hence it had to be purified from time to time, and to be brought back to the 'lawful place,' the holy fire-altar of the community, and by fetching thence a fresh brand wherewith to revive the fire of the home-hearth[5].

---

[1] *Druj-nasush.*

[2] Comp. Spiegel, *E.A.* vol. iii, p. 693 seq.; *vide* Vd. V, 27 seq. and the remarks in my *Hdb.* pp. 85–86. Duncker, *GdA.* IV, pp. 161–162.

[3] *Hãm-raęthwa* and *paiti-raęthwa.*

[4] Comp. Vd. VIII, 73 seq., upon the treatment of the fire with which a corpse was burnt; Vd. V, 39 seq.; XVI, 1 seq.

[5] Vd. VIII, 82 seq.

Here also we come across the traces of a very ancient fire-cult. Analogies of the most striking kind to this custom of the Avesta people are to be found among the Greeks and Germans.

In Lemnos, the most holy centre of the worship of Hephæstus, it was a custom annually to extinguish for several days all the fires in the whole island. A sacred ship then brought from the altar at Delos a fire-brand with which fresh hearth-fires were kindled throughout the island amid the loud rejoicings of the people.

In Germany also, there existed until modern times in several districts (as in the country of Marburg and in Lower Saxony) the custom, manifestly descended from the heathens, of extinguishing now and then all the hearth-fires. By rubbing a piece of wood on a wheel, that is, in the old solemn manner, fresh fire was then kindled, from which everybody ignited his own piece of wood and carried it home[1].

The common fundamental idea of this custom amongst the Irānians, Greeks, and Germans, is that the fire in daily use, communicated from one log to another, must have lost in purity through the service of men in course of time, and had therefore to be restored and renewed by fresh fire, the pure, celestial, and still unpolluted element.

The pollution of men, clothes, implements and such like, had to be removed by washing with water and cow's urine. The latter is regarded also by the Indian as miraculously efficacious, and is frequently prescribed in the code of Manu as a means of purification[2].

Besides such ablutions, rubbing with earth and fumigation are employed. The latter remedy is used, besides the recitation of sacred *māthras* (sayings), for the purification of dwellings[3] . . . . . .

---

[1] With this comp. A. Kuhn, *Die Herabkunft des Feuers.*

[2] Manu, V, 59 seq.; for particulars *vide* Duncker, *GdA.* IV, p. 128 seq.

[3] Vd. VIII, 2; XII; IX, 32 and XIX, 24 (with this comp. my *Hdb.* p. 107).

The fire had to be conveyed outside the house polluted by the death of an inmate, and it could only be brought back after the lapse of a month during summer, or of nine days during winter[1].

Defiled land had to lie fallow, defiled water had to be baled out and thrown away. Roads, after a dog had been led over them, had to be reconsecrated by the priest reciting certain prescribed prayers[2].

The purification of vessels was to be repeated the oftener the more valueless the material was of which they were made. Vessels of lead and wood, when even once polluted, remained impure for ever[3].

Nor do only dead bodies cause pollution. According to the view of the Avesta, women after childbirth are likewise unclean. Among the modern Persians the period of forty days is fixed for a woman lying-in, and during that time she must remain apart from her husband. Analogous to this are also the precepts current among the Parsees of Bombay. The woman is brought to the ground-floor of the house before her delivery. After the child is born, she remains in the same place for forty days. It is only after the lapse of this term, and after performing ablutions with cow's urine and water, that she can again associate with other members of her family, and devote herself to her husband[4].

The Mosaic law determines a period of thirty-three days after the birth of a boy, and of sixty-six days after that of a girl, during which time the woman who has been confined is regarded as unclean, and remains within doors[5] . . . .

During their menses also women are impure, and to a certain extent in the power of evil. They are unclean, and impart pollution to objects and persons surrounding them. Consequently they are lodged during that time in a special

---

[1] Vd. V, 39 seq.

[2] Vd. VI, 1 seq.; VI, 33 seq.; VIII, 14 seq.

[3] Vd. VII, 73 seq.

[4] Polak, *Persien*, i, p. 220; Dossabhoy Framjee, 'The Parsees,' p. 63.

[5] *Leviticus*, XII, 4 seq.

place, where they remain perfectly secluded from all that could be exposed to defilement.

Their place shall be covered up with dry dust, and be cleared of all plants and weeds: it shall be situated higher than the surface of the rest of the house, so that the eye of the woman may not fall on the hearth-fire and defile it. Fifteen steps distant must that place be from the sacred elements, water and fire, as well as from the sacred chattels used in offerings; and only as far as three steps distant can pious men approach it.

Even now in [a few] Parsee houses such a resting-place is found for unclean women, which is called *Deshtānistān*. It is an apartment void of every comfort, and from which one can neither perceive the sun, nor the moon, nor the stars, neither fire nor water, nor sacred vessels, much less any men[1].

Three days were regarded as the normal period of menstruation, and the ninth day was its utmost limit. If it continued still longer, it was the work of the demons, an appearance of sickness. Under ordinary circumstances the isolation of the woman continued for four days, and only after fitting ablutions could she return amongst other people[2].

In modern Persia it is enjoined that women should refrain in such cases seven or eight days long from bathing and from holding any intercourse with their husbands. The Mosaic law prescribes a separation of seven days, during which time women are unclean and are forbidden to men[3].

Of course the Avesta likewise forbids men conjugal intercourse with their wives during their courses; the infringement of this prohibition seems to have been at first

---

[1] West, 'Pahlavi Texts,' part i, p. 277, note 4. Very detailed statements regarding the treatment of menstruating women are contained in the Tract *Shāyast-lā-Shāyast*, chap. 3.

[2] The statement essentially rests on the beginning of Vd. XVI, where the management of a *nāirika · chithravaiti, dakhshtavaiti, vohunavaiti* is discussed . . .

[3] Polak, *Persien*, i, p. 203; *Lev.* XV, 19.

considered even as an inexpiable sin. Later on a milder view was taken of it, for another penalty, though indeed a very high one, was set upon it. If the guilty one avoided the punishment, he was regarded as one damned, and was abandoned to the infernal powers[1].

A similar rule of conduct as that for menstruating women is also prescribed by the Avesta for such as have miscarried. These must also be lodged in a separate place, furnished with an enclosure, and thirty steps distant from fire, water and sacred utensils; the ground being as dry as possible, and cleared of plants. People must again remain three steps distant from it. During confinement they receive as food first only milk, then fruits, and later on, after the lapse of three days, meat, bread, and *madhu*, but no water[2].

The ceremonies through which impurities were removed were of very different descriptions. Sometimes they consisted in the washing of the head, sometimes in that of the hands and arms, sometimes in that of the entire body[3]. Particular importance was attached to the cleaning of the nine doors or openings of the human body, viz. of the eyes, ears, and nostrils, of the mouth, &c., because through them, so to say, the interior of the human being is connected with the exterior world[4].

In the higher and more unusual cases of pollution the Zoroastrian could not even undertake to perform the ceremony himself, but had to call in a priest. Particular efficacy was held to belong to the so-called *purification of the nine nights*, which Spiegel has fully described on the basis of the

---

[1] The idea in Vd. XVIII, 67–76 and XVI, 14–16 on the one hand and that in Vd. XVI, 17 on the other seem to contradict each other. We have here probably again to do with two different views of the Vendidad (comp. *ZddmG.* vol. xxxiv, p. 415).

[2] Vd. V, 45; cf. Geldner, *K. Z.* xxv, pp. 209–210.

[3] *Frasnāiti, upasnāiti, usnāiti,* Vd. VIII, 98. Comp. Spiegel, *Av. üb.* vol. ii, p. lxxxv.

[4] Vd. V, 54; cf. Geldner, *K. Z.* xxv, p. 209; Vd. III, 14 (*ZddmG.* vol. xxxiv, p. 419).

statements contained in the ninth chapter of the Vendidad and of the traditional supplements [1] :—

'For such a purification a barren piece of ground is selected, where there is neither water nor tree, and which is distant from fire and from pure beings. Six holes are then dug in the ground, two fingers deep in summer, four fingers deep in winter, each of them a step distant from the other; afterwards three more holes are dug, which are three steps distant from the six before mentioned. Round these holes twelve circles are drawn, in such a way that three circles surround the three holes, three the six holes, three all nine, and lastly three more surround them all. The defiled person stands near the six holes inside the circles, the priest outside of them. After a short prayer is recited by the priest, and repeated by the polluted one, the latter is besprinkled by the purifier with the urine of the bullock, which is first poured into a vessel (commonly a spoon) that is fastened to a stick containing nine knots ; in this way the priest can approach the body of the defiled with the spoon, although he himself stands outside the circles. After the polluted person has cleansed his whole body with the urine, the *Ahuna-varya* is recited, and thereupon the uncleanness or, according to the notion of the Irānians, the demon of uncleanness, leaves the man. The person purified then approaches the other five holes, at each of which the priest recites the *Ahuna-varya* anew ; near the sixth hole he rubs himself fifteen times with earth, and washes himself afterwards with water near the remaining three holes. After this he has still to wait for nine nights, and to wash himself every third night; then only is he again fit to associate with other people.'

---

[1] *E.A.* vol. iii, pp. 698–699 ; (*Av. üb.* vol. ii, p. lxxxv. seq.).

[In connection with the Bareshnūm Ceremony of purification for any Zoroastrian man or woman, it would be very interesting to read Dr. West's elaborate description of the same, given in his 'Pahlavi Texts,' part ii, pp. 431–454. *Tr.*]

§ 10. *Death and Disposal of the Body.*

DEATH is regarded in the Avesta as a separation of the
body and the soul[1], as an analysis of the two constituent
parts of man, of the perishable matter and the immortal
everlasting force which had made her abode in the body
during life. The activity of the soul of man manifests itself
according to different tendencies and in different spheres.
Consequently the Avesta assumes the existence of several
faculties of the soul, which, dissimilar in their nature and
mode of operation, reside in the human body. We shall
later on make it our business to express our thoughts on
the Avesta doctrine of the soul. At present it will suffice
to prove that the soul and the vital power are not identical;
through the decay of the latter the soul is forced to quit
the body.

When death takes place, the soul does not at once depart
entirely from the body to which it once belonged, but still
remains for three days and three nights in its vicinity[2].
Death is, therefore, a kind of transitional stage, during
which, however, the soul experiences a foretaste of the
fate that awaits it. The soul of the pious man already
feels the delights and joys of Paradise, but that of the
impious man the anguish and torments of Hell.

The body of the deceased Mazdayasna falls a prey to
the powers of evil as soon as the soul has vanished from it;
yea its activity has ceased. It can never subdue and impair
the kingdom of Angra Manyu. The demons rejoice over
its death. From the Northern regions which are considered by the Eastern Irānian to be the abode of every-

---

[1] *Astascha · baodhaghascha · vi-urvishti*, Vd. VIII, 81; XIX, 7.
Designations for ' body ' are, besides *asti*, the rather irregular *azdēbīsh*
(?skeleton), *ushtāna* ('form, outward appearance,' comp. Geldner,
K.Z. xxv, p. 309, note 1), and *kehrp*. Ys. LV, 1.

[2] *Urvan*; this includes the moral and intellectual power of man
(*urvan* and *baodhagh*), as well as the guardian spirit (*fravashi*) accompanying it during life. With this description comp. Yt. XXII;
next Haug and West, 'Essays,' p. 219 seq.

thing evil—where the waterless, barren deserts extend, where the burning winds of summer and the snow-storms of winter blow, where hostile tribes dwell — comes the ghost of the corpse, the frightful DRUJ-NASUSH [1]. It takes possession of the corpse in the shape of a fly, probably because on every corpse are to be seen flies—in themselves loathsome and impure creatures. It has its chief seat in the nose, the eyes, the tongue, the jaw-bones—here by metonymy used for ears,—the sexual organs, the *clunes*,—that is at the doors of the body,—which always appear subject to pollution to a particular extent [2].

From the dead body the impurity spreads itself further in the house in which the corpse lies, and to everything that is in it. It communicates itself to survivors and relations, and does so the more the nearer they have stood in relationship to the dead. There now begin a series of ceremonies, which I have already described, for the purpose of washing away the pollution.

But the most peculiar ceremony, which is performed on the dead body itself before its disposal, is the SAGDÎD. I here confine myself to the most essential points, since this subject has been before fully and frequently treated [3].

The ceremony consists in leading a dog towards the deceased, so that his eyes may fall on the corpse. I may here mention that they ascribe to the glance of a dog the power of scaring away the Evil Being. With the same view evidently a dog is conducted over the way by which a deceased person has been carried, in order to make it again accessible for men and beasts.

The dog to be employed for the *Sagdîd* must have

---

[1] Vd. VII, 2 [so to say, the wind of putrefaction].

[2] Vd. III, 14 ; IX, 40. Comp. *supra*, p. 82.

[3] The word comes from N.P. *sag* ' dog ' + *dîd* from the infinitive *dîdan*, from rt. *dî* ' to see.' *Vide* the commandments of the Pârsee tradition respecting this custom in *Pahlavi-Vendidâd*, III, 48 ; and in *Shâyast-la-Shâyast*, II, 1–3 (West, ' Pahlavi Texts,' part i, pp. 245–246) ; comp. further Spiegel, *Av. üb.* vol. ii, p. xxxii. seq. ; ibid. *E.A.* vol. iii, 701 seq. ; Dossabhoy Framjee, ' The Parsees,' p. 93 seq.

certain special marks: he must be four-eyed—this I shall explain further on—he must be of a yellow colour or white with yellow ears [1].

A very ancient popular idea lies at the root of this entire custom, the knowledge of which, however, was wholly lost even to the Avesta people [2]. According to the old Indian legend, Yama, the god of death, has two dogs who follow him. They guard the path leading into the next world, and alarm and frighten the souls wandering therein. Or, like a hunter, Yama sends forth the dogs as his messengers, to bring home the souls who have fallen into his power.

In a funeral song of the Rig-veda they call out, therefore, to the deceased :

'Run straight past the two dogs of Saramā, the four-eyed, parti-coloured.'

Or the departed ones are recommended to the protection

---

[1] *Spānem · zairitem · chathru · chashmem · spaçtem · zairi-gaoshem*, Vd. VIII, 16.

[2] [We cannot see how the Avesta people could have been ignorant of this oriental idea regarding the power of the spiritual dogs on the Chinvat Bridge, or of what is already alluded to in the passage (Vd. XIII, 9), where the soul (*urva*) of the deceased person is represented as being (on the morning of the fourth day after death) accompanied by his conscience (*daçna*, i. e. the consciousness of his own good or bad actions), together with the two spiritual dogs (i. e. spiritual confidence and watchfulness over one's self), called in the Avesta *peshu-pāna*, or '(the dogs) that guard the bridge.' Their work is to preserve the soul, during its passage, from any evil influence of the hellish fiends (probably distrust in one's own moral behaviour), which are supposed to be haunting the Bridge of Judgment in order to drag away the pious soul into hell. We would rather presume that the old Irānian notion regarding the *Sagdīd*, as scaring away any evil influence, is quite in accordance with their conception of the *peshu-pāna* dogs. By the commandment of the *Sagdīd* and the exposition of its influence produced directly upon a dead body, the Avesta introduces, so to say, a new element in the useful characteristics of the dog's eye, viz. its magnetic power in checking the contagious impurity of a corpse. Comp. Haug and West, 'Essays,' p. 240, note 1. *Tr.*]

of the two dogs in order that they may conduct them safely to the shades :

> ' Those are thy watchers, O Yama, the two dogs,
> The four - eyed, the path - watching, men - contemplating,
> To them surrender this dead, O king,
> And grant him safety and freedom from pain !'

To this is then added the wish that he may himself be spared from the dismal companions :

> ' The two broad-nosed, soul-robbing, brown
> Messengers of Yama wander among men ;
> Those shall, to contemplate the sun,
> Grant us once again a happy life !'[1]

In order to prove the high antiquity of this myth, I shall here only mention the guard at the gate of Hades, the hell-hound Kerberos or the dog Garm, who, according to the narrative of Edda, raises his howling at the breaking of the twilight of the gods in the depth of the Genupa Hollow[2].

If, therefore, in old Irān a dog was conducted towards the dead body, it was, originally, only intended thereby to indicate in a symbolical way, that the soul of the deceased was given over to the god of death and his followers, and was at the same time recommended to their protection. The myth itself, in conformity with the unvarying character of the Avesta religion, was forgotten in course of time, but the ceremony was firmly adhered to, and the once very ingenious custom sank into an empty unintelligible form which has survived to the present day amongst the latest adherents of the Zoroastrian doctrine[3].

It is highly characteristic, how the epithet 'four-eyed' was explained in a sober rationalistic manner. Originally, in the poetical language of the myth, the great watchful-

---

[1] Rig-veda X, 14, 10–12. Comp. Max Müller, ' Lectures on the Science of Language,' vol. ii, p. 435 seq. ; Kaegi, *Der Rig-veda*, pp. 59–60, particularly note 337.

[2] *Völuspā*, 48.

[3] [*Vide* the translator's note 2 on the preceding page.]

ness of the dog was chiefly to be emphasized. Hence the precept was construed to mean that the dogs employed for the *Sagdīd* must have two black spots over their eyes that the ceremony might be efficacious[1].

After the performance of the *Sagdīd*, for which the tradition naturally gives the most detailed casuistic rules of direction, the dead body was disposed of. The disposal neither consisted in burying nor in burning, but, according to the Zoroastrian ritual, in exposing the corpse on a lonely place to be eaten by birds, dogs, and ravenous animals.

Herodotus relates that this mode of disposing of the dead was common amongst the Magi, that is, amongst the Persian priesthood. Strabo mentions it in connection with the Hyrcanians, and Cicero expressly distinguishes between the funeral customs of the Magi and those of the Persian nation[2].

Among Westerns that remarkable injunction of the Avesta regarding the treatment of the dead, which appears to us so unnatural, was also well-known. But there is no doubt that it never found acceptance throughout the whole of Irān, but was possibly confined to the North-Eastern districts and, moreover, entirely to the priesthood. The Avesta itself informs us that in *Chakhra*, that is, somewhere in the district of Meshed, the dead were burnt, and that in *Harahvati*, where people do not seem to have very strictly adhered to the Zoroastrian commandments, they were interred[3].

The exposure of the dead owed its origin, as it appears, to the natural condition of Eastern Irān. The waste lands

---

[1] In Vd. XIII, 9 the dog is also called *peshu-pāna* 'guarding the bridge, the passage (to the next world),' which reminds us of the *çvānau pathirakshī* in the Rig-veda; *chathur-aksha* is identical with *chathru-chashma* (Kuhn in *Haupt's Zeitschrift für deutsches Alterthum*, vol. vi, p. 125; Weber's *Indische Studien*, vol. ii, p. 296; *vide* Justi, *Hdb.* s. v.).

[2] Spiegel, *E.A.* vol. iii, pp. 703–704.

[3] Vd. I, 17 (*nasushpachya* 'the burning of the dead,') and 13 (*nasushpaya* 'the burying of the dead').

immediately adjoining its borders were themselves comparable to a gigantic grave. They to a great extent suggested the idea of conveying the dead thither and abandoning them to their fate. Besides, people were also compelled to do so, when anybody—and this was certainly not rare—lost his life in longer or shorter wanderings through the sand and salt-steppes.

We must also add that, considered from a strictly logical stand-point, the burning as well as the burial of the dead contravenes the whole idea, respecting the world, of the Avesta and its followers. Through both, the impure corpse, which has fallen a prey to the demons, comes in contact with the essentially sacred and pure elements, with fire and earth. Such a pollution however was to be avoided under all circumstances.

The exposure of the dead body was certainly an old custom which, though perhaps not in general use amongst the kindred Indians, was nevertheless now and then put in practice in all urgent cases. The Atharva-veda seems to us to bear witness to this fact. It distinguishes between the *manes* of such as were buried, thrown aside, burnt or exposed. We may believe that it here enumerates the different modes of disposing of the dead, with which it was familiar and which it considered to be lawful [1].

Here everybody will naturally be reminded of the Kāfirs, a very remarkable nation inhabiting the high mountain-valleys of the Hindukush, which are difficult of access and situated on the North of Cabul. With them it is a general custom to expose the dead, without interring them, in deal chests on the summits of mountains, that is, on the most elevated points [2]. If we further consider what an im-

---

[1] Atharva-veda XVIII, 2, 34. The expressions are : *nikhāta, paropta* (from rt. *vap + parā*), *dagdha, uddhita.* Comp. Zimmer, *AiL.* p. 402. We have observed that in the Avesta *uzhdāna* indeed also designated the scaffold erected for the exposure of the corpse (*Hdb.* s. v.)

[2] Masson, ' Narrative,' vol. i, p. 224 : ' It is agreed that the Siāposh place their corpses in deal boxes and, without interring them, expose them on the summits of hills.' Comp. Elphinstone, ' Kabul,' vol. ii, pp. 336–337 ; Spiegel, *E.A.* vol. i, p. 398.

placable hatred the Kāfirs cherish against the followers of
Islam, and how they have been able to preserve their freedom and independence, especially in the exercise of their
religion, in spite of all the efforts of their enemies, that
remarkable custom might lead us to recognize in the
Kāfirs descendants of the old Zoroastrians. It must, however, be taken into consideration here that, according to the
'Inquiries' of Trumpp, the Kāfirs speak an absolutely
Indian language. At all events we shall have to wait for
still fuller and surer accounts before we can form a definite
opinion regarding that nation.

In the exposure of the dead, we have, therefore, to deal
with a custom, which, due to local circumstances, was most
probably occasionally practised before the introduction of
the Zoroastrian Reform. As that custom completely corresponded to the spirit of the reform, it was accepted by its
originators and laid down as a generally binding precept.
But that, previous to the burning of corpses, this custom
was most widely spread amongst the Indians is strikingly
proved by the linguistic usage concerning it.

The place which is destined for exposure bears the
name of DAKHMA. This word originally meant, as clearly
appears from its derivation, nothing else than the place
for burning[1].

The *dakhmas* must be erected on places situated on
high, on the tops of hills or slopes. Dogs and wolves,
foxes and ravenous birds can thus easily perceive the
corpse there laid down and seize their prey. The so-called
Towers of Silence, which serve the Parsees in Bombay as
places for the disposal of their dead, crown the summit of
the magnificent Malabar Hill which rises above the city.
The view which they present is naturally most gloomy.
A body of lazy vultures, densely crowded, guard the edge
of the Tower. There they sit immovable and motionless,

---

[1] *Dakhma* comes from rt. *das* = Skr. *dah* 'to burn.' [Others
derive it from rt. *dak* = Skr. *damç* = Gr. δακ ' to bite.' Hence it may
originally mean the place where dead bodies are consumed either by
insects (in the grave), or by vultures (on the tower). *Tr.*]

save when a funeral procession approaches and the flock are filled with excitement. They fly upwards with screams, and as soon as the dead body is laid within by the bearers, they throw themselves with greedy haste upon their prey. In a few minutes the dreadful work is finished, and the birds return satiated to their place to wait for fresh food.

Originally, the *dakhmas* were certainly nothing more than natural hills or primitive elevations of sand, earth, or stones. In course of time the structure became a more elaborate one. It is a rule that the *dakhma* must be uncovered and exposed to the solar rays as well as to the rain [1].

Nor are all places suitable for the erection of *dakhmas*. Wastes and unproductive pieces of land are the most fit, for they belong already to the evil powers and are the abode of demons. But the Mazdayasna lives in a constant struggle with the desert lands themselves. Plough and hoe are the weapons with which he takes the field against them, and tries to make the land, which was before sterile, piece by piece, arable and available for 'the good creation.' Thus many *dakhmas* had to be pulled down and re-erected further off, when civilization had approached them. This explains why the closing of *dakhmas* is esteemed meritorious [2]. It is a token that another piece of land has been wrung from the evil spirits through human labour and exertion. Close to the *dakhmas* wild animals are on the watch; there dwell ghosts and demons that rejoice in death and destruction; there also, as the Irānian very well knew, are the breeding places of manifold maladies and pestilential diseases [3].

---

[1] Hence the expression *hvare-daresim · kar* 'cause that (the corpse) is looked at by the sun,' quite synonymously with 'expose the dead.'

[2] Vd. III, 9 and 13; VII, 51.

[3] Vd. VII, 58. [How Dr. Geiger could conceive this totally new aspect of the meritoriousness of pulling down the *dakhmas*, we cannot imagine. The word as it is used throughout the Avesta (Vd. III, 9, 13; V, 14, 16, 18, 51; VII, 49, 50, 51, 56, 57, 58; VIII, 2, &c.) does not mean the place for the exposure of the Irānian dead but the

The corpse, which is exposed, is laid, as it seems, on a special layer of mortar or similar material [1]. There it remains, according to the expression of the Avesta, until it is mixed with the dust, until its fatty and fleshy parts have disappeared [2]. The birds and beasts should only gnaw the flesh from the bones, the skeleton, on the contrary, remaining uninjured and complete, and for this reason the dead in the *dakhma* are weighted near the head and feet with iron chains or stones or wooden blocks. Were this not done, a wolf or a vulture could remove portions of the dead body, and with them pollute water and plants [3].

covered tomb of any person, be he Zoroastrian or non-Zoroastrian. As the Vendidad strictly orders the exposure of the dead body to the light of the sun, its consumption by vultures, and the preservation of its bones in an *astodān*, so also does it forbid closed sepulchres to the adherents of the Law, while it compels them to pull down and destroy any tomb, whereby to restore, as science has taught us but lately, the natural purity of Mother Earth, upon whom solely depends the subsistence of the animal creation. To what extent the Irānian system of exposing the dead is more beneficial to life than the practice of interment, we do not here discuss ; suffice it to listen to the remarks of Prof. Monier Williams in his ' Modern India and the Indians':

' When the Secretary had finished his defence of the Towers of Silence, I could not help thinking that however much such a system may shock our European feelings and ideas, yet our own method of interment, if regarded from a Parsi point of view, may possibly be equally revolting to Parsi sensibilities.

' The exposure of the decaying body to the assaults of innumerable worms may have no terrors for us ; but let it be borne in mind that neither are the Parsi survivors permitted to look at the swoop of the heaven-sent birds. Why, then, should we be surprised if they prefer the more rapid to the more lingering operation ? and which of the two systems, they may reasonably ask, is more defensible on sanitary grounds ?' *Vide* pp. 88–89. *Tr.*]

[1] I translate the difficult passage, Vd. VIII, 10, thus : ' Then shall two men, as strong and skilful as possible, bring it (the corpse) near naked and unclad, and shall lay it down upon a pile of clay or stone or upon a wooden scaffold [rather cement] (by which the *dakhma* is naturally meant) in mortar upon the earth.'

[2] Vd. VII, 49.

[3] Vd. VI, 46. The passage Vd. V, 3–4, only apparently militates

The skeleton requires peculiar treatment. After a certain time it is removed from the *dakhma* and brought to a place where beasts cannot enter, and where it is no longer exposed to the rain[1]. A detailed description of the charnel-house is wanting in the Avesta. The modern Parsees cause the *dakhma* to be cleaned twice every year, on which occasion the bones are thrown through a large opening in the middle of its surface, into the interior of the tower[2]. It is possible that in ancient times also an excavation was left open in the *dakhma* as a receptacle for bones. It may however be also assumed that originally the ossuary was altogether separate from the place of exposure. The skeleton also was deposited on a base of stone or mortar or on carpets. In case that could not be done, common coverings or mats, such as those which were then used for sitting and resting upon, would suffice.

The diverse mode of treatment of the whole body and of the bones remaining is grounded probably on the notion that the impurity of the corpse attaches itself above all to its perishable parts, and that, therefore, the latter must be subjected to an annihilation as speedy as possible, while the bones meet with a worthier treatment. This custom corresponds in a striking way with a statement of Justin respecting the Parthians, that they abandoned their dead to the birds and dogs, but interred the bones when stripped of the flesh[3].

It was ordered in the Avesta to convey the dead only in fine and clear weather to the *dakhma*. The sun should

---

against such an idea, for it only brings out prominently that the *man* does not become polluted by the carcass having been dragged away by dogs, wolves, birds, winds, or flies; here, on the contrary, the question is one respecting the contamination of water and plants.

[1] With the whole section compare the beginning of Vd. VIII, as well as Vd. VI, 44–46, 49–50. The twofold treatment of the whole corpse and of the skeleton in particular, according to my comprehension of the last passage, is illustrated in my *Handbuch* at the foot of page 99.

[2] Spiegel, *Av. üb.* vol. ii, p. lvi.

[3] Justin, 41, 3, in Spiegel, *E.A.* vol. iii, p. 704.

shine over them in their last journey, perhaps in accordance with the old popular idea, which compares the dying of the man with the setting of the sun in the West. In case dark and inclement weather prevailed, the exposure had to be postponed. In connection with this the Avesta expresses itself as follows:

> 'If in the house of a Mazdayasna a man or a dog die, and if it rain, or snow, or storm, or if it be dark or if it be a day, when men and animals are prevented from going out, what shall the Mazdayasna do?'

It is then prescribed, that for such cases there shall be in each village and on each farm three *katas*, 'pits or cavities.' They must be situated in a place cleared of all plants and entirely dry, where neither men nor animals pass, and which is a few steps distant from fire and water, from sacred chattels, and from the dwellings of pious men. Such a *kata* serves as a principal receptacle for the dead. It must be of a certain size, so that the corpse may not strike against the sides either above or below. Besides, the bottom must be strewed with sand or brick-dust, probably in order to prevent the corpse from touching the earth, and to keep away all moisture:

> 'Here they shall deposit the lifeless body for two or three nights long, or for a month, until the birds fly again and the plants germinate, until the waters run again towards the valley and the wind dries the earth. And afterwards, when the birds fly again and the plants grow, when the waters flow again towards the valley and the wind dries the earth: then the Mazdayasna shall (bring the dead body to the *dakhma* and) expose it to the sun[1].'

---

[1] Vd. VIII, 4–10; V, 10–13. Both of the passages treat evidently of the same subject, as it occurs frequently in the Vendidad, though in somewhat different ways. Instead of the detailed description of the weather, which is found in Vd. VIII, we have in Vd. V. only 'but when the summer has passed and the winter sets in;' the sense of course is quite the same. In Vd. VIII. the provisional pit is called *kata*, in Vd. V. *avakana*; there the *dakhma* is called *skemba* 'scaffold.' Comp. also my *Hdb.* p. 81, note 2.

If any contact whatever with a corpse caused pollution, such pollution must have fallen to a great degree upon the people who carried the dead to the *dakhma*. Hence this work was in ancient as well as in modern times performed, not by the survivors, but by corpse-bearers, specially appointed for that purpose[1], whose profession was generally held in abhorrence, its representatives being excluded from human society. . . . . .

Never can one man alone bear a corpse, as such an action would render him polluted for ever, even in the next world. There must always be two, who, after having finished their business, must undergo a special purification. This consists in the washing of the head and of the body with the urine of cows (and water). . . . . .

The dwelling of the corpse-bearer lies apart from the houses of other men, and nobody holds any intercourse or communion with him. In a barren, waste region does he live, evidently in a kind of a cavern. He is only scantily furnished with food and clothing; a poor and miserable life shall he lead until his old age. . . . . .

As soon as the corpse was laid in the *dakhma* and abandoned to wild animals, there was yet a long period of mourning for the survivors. The commandments, originating in a later period concerning the ceremonies which were performed in the name of the dead to honour his memory, I may here conveniently pass over, as they have been collected and treated of before[2]. According to the Avesta, the relatives of the deceased had to refrain for a time from all intercourse with men[3]. During that time they devoted themselves exclusively to the remembrance of their beloved

---

[1] This statement is based on Vd. III, 14–21 (besides Vd. VIII, 10), with which we should compare *ZddmG*. vol. xxxiv, pp. 419, 420. The corpse-bearer is called *nasukasha* or *iristō-kasha*, by the modern Parsees *nasāsālār*. *Vide* Spiegel, *Av. üb.* vol. ii, p. xxxiv ; Dossabhoy Framjee, ‘The Parsees,’ p. 92.

[2] Spiegel, *Av. üb.* vol. ii, p. xxxviii. seq.

[3] Vd. XII. Comp. above all Darmesteter's Vendidād, introduction to that chapter.

dead, and sent up their prayers to Ahura Mazda for him and for his eternal salvation.

The soul, however, delivered from the shackles of the body and freed from the clay of this earthly life, was borne up into higher worlds.

11. *Immortality* [1] *and Eschatology.*

THE belief in the continuation of existence after death, in a future world into which enter souls leaving their mortal

[1] [' Next to the being of a God, the doctrine of the Immortality of Man lies at the foundation of all religion, and of all the animating prospects which can cheer us in the land of our pilgrimage. Remove from the mind the belief of a future existence and the hope of immortality, and religion becomes a shadow, life a dream, and the approach of death a scene of darkness and despair. Upon this short question, " *Is man immortal, or is he not?*" depends all that is valuable in science, in morals, and in theology; and all that is most interesting to man as a social being, and as a rational and accountable intelligence. If he is destined to an eternal existence, an immense importance must attach to all his present affections, actions, and pursuits; and it must be a matter of infinite moment, that they be directed in such a channel as will tend to carry him forward in safety to the felicities of a future world. But if his whole existence be circumscribed within the circle of a few fleeting years, man appears an enigma, an inexplicable phenomenon in the universe, human life a mystery, the world a scene of confusion, virtue a mere phantom, the Creator a capricious Being, and his plans and arrangements an inextricable maze.

' Since it appears that the desire of immortality is common to mankind, that the soul is incessantly looking forward to the enjoyment of some future good, and that this desire has been the spring of actions the most beneficent and heroic, on what principle is it to be accounted for?

' Whence springs this pleasing hope, this fond desire,
This longing after immortality?
Or, whence this secret dread, and inward horror,
Of falling into nought? Why shrinks the soul
Back on herself, and startles at destruction?'—*Addison.*]

frame, in a judgment and recompense in that world, is found amongst the most diverse nations on our globe, in a form sometimes more and sometimes less distinct and definite.

Among the Indo-Germanic races this belief was evidently deep-rooted, and formed an essential portion of their doctrine.

According to the Rig-veda, the spirits of the dying follow *Father Yama*, the primeval sun-god, into his distant realm, on the path which he has trodden before them. There the '*Fathers*' assemble round him, in order to enjoy convivial feasting in the middle of heaven under the dense foliage of trees:

'Where light is, which never becomes extinct,
And where the heavenly radiance glitters,
There, into the immortality,
The eternal, carry me, Soma!

'Where king is Vaivasvata
And where the innermost region of heaven is,
Where those eternal waters are—
O Soma, make me immortal!

'Where one, according to wish, stirs or moves,
In the third stage of the kingdom of heaven,
Where all the rooms are resplendent—
O Soma, make me immortal!

'Where wish and aspiration are gratified,
At the highest point in the sun's rotation,
Where desire and gratification exist together,
O Soma, make me immortal!

'Where pleasure and mirth and gaiety
And delight reside, where the will
Of the willing is attained—
O Soma, make me immortal!'[1]

In the Homeric poems a two-fold conception prevails regarding the next world, which is looked for at the confines of the world, in the remote part of the West, or in the

---

[1] Rig-veda, IX, 113, 7 seq.; Geldner and Kaegi, *Siebenzig Lieder des Rig-veda*, p. 111; Zimmer, *AiL.* p. 408 seq.

depths of the earth. It is a dismal and foggy land, hateful
alike to men and gods, in which the souls of the departed
lead a visionary and fantastic life. Besides this there is
also found the milder and more agreeable picture of the
Elysian fields, where the fair Rhadamanthus reigns, and
where there is neither snow, nor storms, nor even showers
of rain, but where a cool west wind blowing from the ocean
refreshes men. Indeed these blessed fields are at first only
the paradise of specially favoured men, who, without under-
going death, are carried thither by the gods[1]. I believe,
however, that these descriptions have their foundation in
old legends of a more beautiful and better future world.
In fact in a later period only *one* Hades is mentioned, in
which the good and the bad both find a place, the former
in the fields of the blessed, the latter in the space set apart
for the damned.

A very striking analogy to the views of the Greeks is
presented by those of the old Germans. Those men who
perish fighting and remain on the field in the heat of battle
are conveyed into the illuminated hall of the *Walhalla*,
where they, together with Odin, the war-father, enjoy merry
war-games and jovial feasting. However all other men,
good and evil, wander into *Hel*, which is represented as a
dismal, misty region like the Hades in Homer[2].

But nowhere, I think, does the belief in the future life
after death stand out more prominently, nowhere are the
ideas respecting it expressed more decidedly and carried out
in all their details more fully, than among the Avesta people.

Here the doctrine of immortality and of compensating
justice in the next world forms a fundamental dogma of the
whole system. Without it the Zoroastrian religion is in
fact unintelligible. If all the powers which contend upon

---

[1] Odyssey, bk. XI, l. 15 seq., l. 155 seq., ll. 474-476, ll. 489-
491 ; Iliad, bk. XXII, l. 482 ; bk. XX, l. 61 seq. ; Od. bk. IV, l.
561 seq.

[2] Hence the names *Niflheimr* 'land of mists' and *Niflhel* 'misty
hollow.' Comp. Gylfaginning, p. 49 (Simrock, *Edda übersetzt*, p.
319); on Walhalla comp. Grimnismal, 8, 23 ; Gylf. 38–41 (idem 15.
303–305).

earth for the kingdom of light were lost, the conviction of divine justice would have to be abandoned.

So far as we are able to follow up the Mazda doctrine, we find that, even in the first period of its foundation, the belief in immortality is strong and active. For who in that age would have fixed his choice upon a new religion, if the hope of a better life after death had not been held out to him as the reward of all the troubles and hardships to be endured for its sake?

Accordingly, the first proclaimers of the Mazda religion in their teaching and preaching speak directly of the next world as being the greatest of all possessions, of the eternal beatitude of the pious, and of the eternal damnation of the impious. The believer belongs to the spiritual world, he shall enter into it ; the corporeal world is only the transitory scene of his activity, his battles, and his trials.

> 'Whosoever in righteousness shows to me
> The genuine good actions, to me, who am Zara-
> thushtra :
> Him may they (the divine beings) grant, as a reward,
> the next world,
> Which is more desirable than all others[1].'

> 'That man may attain the best of all good,
> Who exhibits to us the direct path of bliss
> In this corporeal world, and in that of the spirit,
> Towards the pious people with whom Ahura dwells :
> It is he, the Singer, who surrenders himself to Thee,
> O Mazda! Who art wise and blissful[2]!'

According to the Hellenic belief, the souls wandering in

---

[1] Ys. XLVI, 19. *Vasnā frashotemem* at the end of the second verse literally means ' standing in the uppermost place with a wish (a desirableness),' and refers, I believe, to *parāhum* (*vide* Haug, *Gāthās*, vol. ii, p. 154; Spiegel and C. de Harlez differ). This expression is the same as the otherwise written *parō-asna · aghu*. *Hanenti* may be translated ' they may grant.'

[2] Ys. XLIII, 3. *Vaghēush · vahyō* is literally 'what is better than the good.' The *hvō · nā* in the beginning is to be taken with *aredrō* of the last verse (*vide* Haug, *Gāthās*, vol. ii, pp. 65–66).

the next world must either pass over the ocean or be allowed to cross over the rivers of the nether regions in the boat of Charon.   The northern legends of the Edda make mention of a bridge, the Gioell Bridge, by which the dead enter *Hel.*   The people on the western coast of Gaul believed that their dead were carried by mariners over the sea to the foggy and gloomy Britannia [1].

According to the Rig-veda also the departing soul has to pass immense oceans before it reaches the next world.   At one time it is a boat, at other times a bridge, 'the Bridge of Happiness,' by means of which it crosses [2].

On such ideal conceptions also rests the doctrine of the Avesta regarding the *Chinvat Bridge,* more probably 'the Bridge of Retribution,' upon which justice is administered to the departing souls [3].   The bridge was believed, I think, to have been built over a wide expanse of water, which separates Paradise from this world.   Only he who is found pious and good before the holy tribunal is entitled to cross this bridge, but the wicked one is thrown into outer darkness and hell.

Thus it is said in the Gāthās :

'What man or what woman, O Ahura Mazda !
Achieves for me in this life the best actions that Thou knowest,
(That bring) blessing for the pious, and power by means of the Good Sense,
And those, whom I call to follow me in your praise :
With all these will I cross over the Chinvat Bridge !'

'But with the princes the idol-worshippers and the false priests unite themselves,

---

[1] Procopius, *De bello Gothico,* 4, 20 ; *vide* Grimm, *Deutsche Mythologie,* 2⁴, 694–695.

[2] Rv. IX, 41. 2, *suvitasya manāmahē 'ti setum.*   Comp. Zimmer, *AiL.* p. 409.

[3] *Chinvatō · peretu* is probably not the 'Bridge of the Assembler,' as I have previously rendered it, but the word *Chinvat* should be derived from the root *chi* 'to suffer, to punish.'   Cf. *chitha.*   In Vend. XIX, 30, the bridge *Chinva*t is explained by *haetu · mainyavanām · yazatanām.*

To destroy human life by means of evil deeds.
The former will greatly distress their own souls and
    their own conscience,
When they arrive there where the Bridge of Retri-
    bution is ;
For all eternity do their bodies belong to the habitation
    of the devils!'[1]

The region into which the pious departed enter is the
Garō nmāna, 'the abode of hymns,' as the name may be
well translated.   Here all is light, splendour, and glory,
here reigns Ahura Mazda with all the angels, praised by the
anthems of the blessed.

Opposite to Paradise lies the abode of the condemned,
Hell or 'the dwelling of the demons[2].'   Here eternal night
and darkness reign, and the scorn of the demons further
enhances the pains and torments, which the fallen soul,
doomed to eternal damnation, has to endure.

To the pious the Bard says:

'Whatsoever reward Zarathushtra before conferred upon
    the truly faithful,
(Saying), "In the *Garō nmāna* Ahura Mazda is first
    of all perceived,"—
Would be conferred upon you, together with happiness,
    on account of your good mind and piety[3].'

On the contrary the following threat is pronounced against
the impious, who oppose the new doctrine :

'Whoso brings about that the pious man is defrauded,
    his dwelling is finally
For a long time in darkness, and vile food and irony
    (shall fall to his lot).
Towards this region, O ye vicious! your souls will
    conduct you on account of your actions[4].'

---

[1] Ys. XLVI, 10–11.   I take *astayō* in 11 as nom. plur. of *asti*
'*corpus*, body ;' comp. Ys. XLIX, 11, Spiegel, *Comm.* vol. ii, p. 375.
[2] For another use of this expression, *vide* Yt. X, 86, *supra*, p. 30.
[3] Ys. LI, 15.   I believe the meaning to be as follows : Ahura
Mazda has first entered into Paradise ; thither the pious and the
faithful will follow Him according to the promise of Zarathushtra.
[4] Ys. XXXI, 20.   *Dāya*t is to be read in the first line (Bartholo-

'The wicked rulers, offenders and liars,
The unbelieving, who are of evil mind and wicked,
Do the souls come to meet with vile food (in Hell).
In truth their bodies will remain in the dwelling of the
demons (*Drujas*)!'[1]

The ideas of the later Avesta harmonize entirely with those of the Gāthās. Thus the doctrine of immortality and of eternal judgment was firmly established in the earliest period of the Mazda religion as an essential dogma, and naturally remained so throughout the whole period.

Mention is very often made of the two worlds, the present and the future, the earthly and the heavenly[2]. The idea which was in the oldest ages only incipient, existing as it were only in embryo, became more and more perfect with the development of this religion, and was more and more worked out in all its details.

An exact description of the fate of the soul after death is found in Yasht XXII. Unfortunately it is incomplete. But as the Minokhired treats of the same subject, and agrees entirely with the Avesta text, so far as that text is preserved, we may be allowed to utilize it to supply the deficiency[3].

The soul of the pious man, as I have already remarked, remains near the head of the corpse, for three days and three nights, after death has taken place. During this time the soul experiences, as a foretaste of the joys of Paradise, greater delight and happiness than it ever enjoyed during its entire life upon earth.

On the beginning of the fourth day, with the appearance of Aurora, when the gates of the heavens are opened, the soul passes over the Chinvat Bridge. Here justice is

---

mae, *Gāthās*, XXXI); I would insert *chā* after *avaḍtās* in the second line.

[1] Ys. XLIX, 11.

[2] *Ubōibyā · ahubyā*, Ys. XXXV, 3; *uvaḍibya · ahubya*, Ys. LVII, 25; *ahmāichā ahuyē · manahyāichā*, Ys. XL, 2; *parō-asnāi · aǧuhē*, Ys. LV, 2. Haug and West, 'Essays,' p. 310 seq.

[3] Yt. XXII; *Minokhired*, 2, p. 114 seq. (West, *Mkh.* 9, 69, 133); comp. Vd. XIX, 27–32. Haug and West, 'Essays,' p. 219 seq., 254–255; Spiegel, *E.A.* vol. ii, pp. 149–151.

administered to it [1]. Angels like Srausha, Verthraghna, and the Good Vayu, stand by and support it. Demons, especially the death-bringing Astōvidhōtu and the Wicked Vayu, bearing ill-will towards it, endeavour to secure it for themselves.

Rashnu the Just holds in his hands the scales in which good and evil deeds are weighed against each other—he, who does not yield even a hair's breadth, before whom kings and princes prevail no more than the most indigent and base among men.

Mithra and Srausha intercede on behalf of the soul, evil spirits raise accusations against it. If its pious deeds outweigh the evil ones, it is allowed to pass over the bridge into Paradise.

Under certain conditions it also appears to have been permitted to a particularly pious soul with a surplus of good deeds to render assistance to another that was deficient therein—which would at all events be remarkably analogous to the Catholic belief in saints in many countries. The surplus good works were preserved in a proper region, the *Misvāna*[2].

The Chinvat Bridge appears to the pious soul 'a *farsang* in breadth.' The soul on passing over it meets a most fragrant wind blowing from the southern regions of heaven. It is the breeze wafted from Paradise. And in this wind there appears to the Soul 'its own conscience' in the shape of a charming maiden [3]—a pretty symbolical impersonation of the inner peace and quietness of soul, which the righteous man enjoys.

---

[1] *Chinvat-perethum · Mazdadhātām · baodhascha · urvānemcha · yātem · gaēthanām · paiti-jaidhyēiñti · dātem · astvaiti · aŋhvō,* 'the bridge *Chinvat*, created by Mazda, where they question the spirit and the soul regarding their behaviour on earth, which they practised during their existence in the body,' Vd. XIX, 29.

[2] *Vide* Justi, *Hdb.* sub voce *miçvāna.* The Misvāna cannot be compared with the *hamēstagān* of the later Pārsi books (*vide* West, *Mkh. Glossary* s.v.).

[3] *Hava · daēna* Yt. XXII, 9. The *Minokhired* has a more indefinite expression, *ā i hvēsh kuneshn nīk.*

With astonishment does the soul ask : 'Who art thou, O Maiden, that seemest to me more beautiful and fair than ever a maiden of earth ?' Its conscience replies:— I am thy own doing and acting, I am the embodiment of thy good thoughts, words and works, and of thy pious faith,' and then it recounts all the good works which the soul accomplished during its earthly career.

Now the soul enters, at the first step, into Paradise, *Humata*, the place of good thoughts; at the second into that of good words, *Hūkhta*; and at the third into that of good works, *Huvarshta*. Just as all righteousness on earth is divided into the three heads of thought, word, and deed, so also is Paradise, the reward of piety, divided into three regions.

At the fourth step the soul finally attains the region of imperishable splendour, that delightful Paradise, where Ahura Mazda dwells together with angels and the blessed spirits of the earlier pious dead [1].

Vohu Manō, the greatest of the Amesha Spentas after Ahura Mazda, and all the Yazatas rise from their golden seats and question it : ' How comest thou here from the world of mortality and misery to this world of eternity and enjoyment?' But Ahura Mazda says; 'Question it not; it cometh on the awful path of separation of the body and the soul.' Therewith the soul is received into the number of in-mates of Paradise; it is conducted to the gold-adorned throne destined for it, and entertained with the most costly of viands.

The fate of the souls of the impious is in all respects the opposite to that of the souls of the pious.

In helpless and despairing anguish the wicked soul wanders about near the corpse for three days and three

---

[1] The names of the particular regions of Paradise, viz. *Humata*, *Hūkhta*, *Huvarshta*, and *Anaghra-raochāo* are contained in Yt. XXII, 15. Other designations are *tem · ahūm · yim · ashaonãm* ' the world of the pious,' Vd. XVIII, 76; *vahishtem · ahūm · ashaonãm · vīspōqāthrem, maęthanem · Ahurahę · Mazdāo, maęthanem · Amesh-anãm Speñtanãm, maęthanem · anyaęshãm · ashaonãm*, Vd. XIX, 36. From Av. *vahishta* is derived the N.P. *bihisht* 'Paradise.' On *Garo-nmãna, vide* Yt. X, 123 ; III, 4.

nights. Even now it feels the weight of all the torments and horrors which await it in Hell. The demon of Death drags it forth in fetters, and when near the Chinvat Bridge the formidable sentence has been pronounced over it,—' Thou art weighed and found wanting,'—it passes towards the region of the condemned.

A foul wind coming from the North meets it, and in that wind it perceives its own conscience in the shape of an ugly hag—the embodiment of all the torments of soul which it feels. Shuddering the Soul asks: 'What art thou, O maiden, that appearest to me more ugly than ever an earthly maiden?' And it receives its reply as follows: ' I am thy own doing and acting, the embodiment of thy evil thoughts, words and works, and of thy false belief!'

As the soul of the pious enters Paradise, the soul of the damned now enters into Hell; first into the place of evil thoughts, next into that of evil words, thence into that of evil works, and lastly into the region of eternal darkness, into the terrible dismal hell full of suffering [1], which is the abode of Angro Manyu and his followers. Here it is received by the demons with scorn and mockery, and the prince of hell causes it to be furnished with the most foul and nauseous of eatables, loathsome to the taste of men [2].

The doctrine of the Avesta regarding the fate of the soul after its departure from this world is directly followed by Eschatology, the doctrine of the last things and of the end of the world.

The visible world is the scene of contest between Ahura Mazda and Angro Manyu, between the good genii and the demons, between the pious and the impious. But this conflict is not an everlasting one, it will end in the complete triumph of the good cause. As, moreover,

---

[1] Hell is called *duzhaĝh* or *daozhaĝha*, Yt. XIX, 44, Vd. XIX, 47; comp. the epithets *ereghat*, *temaĝha*, *temaschithra*, Vd. III, 35, V, 62.

[2] 'Mockery and foul eatables' are even mentioned in the Gāthās as punishments of Hell. *Vide supra* p. 101.

the earth, by the invasion of the evil spirits, is much disturbed and deformed, its transformation and renovation goes hand in hand with this triumph.

Already in the old hymns the ' dissolution of the world ' is spoken of, when the wicked will receive their punishment, and the good their reward :

> ' I thought of Thee as the blissful, O Mazda Ahura,
>   Because I saw Thee as the first one in the be-
>   ginning of the world,
>   Because Thou didst first commence the work (of
>   sacrifice) and the speech, promising reward ;
>   Namely, evil for the bad, but good blessing for the
>   pious,
>   By means of Thy Glory at the final dissolution of
>   creation [1].'

If by this a complete annihilation of the world be indicated, the passage seems entirely isolated. However it probably refers, in accordance with the general doctrine of the Avesta, only to a regeneration and renovation of the world, which is of course preceded by manifold conflicts, and especially by the extirpation of all evil.

At all events it is important to note that the everlasting destiny of the good and the wicked is, according to that passage, sealed by the end of the world.

A final judgment also is coupled with the end of this world.

This idea stands only in apparent contradiction to what is said above, when, consistently with the notion of the Avesta, judgment is pronounced upon the soul immediately after its departure from this world, and the soul in accordance with that decree finds admission either into Paradise or into Hell. Here the soul alone is concerned. But at the end of the world the bodies of the dead will also rise and will share thenceforward the fate of the soul for all eternity.

In the Christian doctrine, which in its very eschatology

---

[1] Ys. XLIII, 5 : *dāmōi*sh · *urvaęsę̄* · *apēmę̄*, which is apparently contrasted with *aġhēu*sh · *zāthōi* in verse 2.

shows the most curious analogy to that of the Parsees, we meet with the same seeming dilemma. On the one hand, it is indeed believed that the spirit of the dead goes forthwith towards God, or towards the place where it suffers the torments of those separated from Him. On the other hand, the Christian Church teaches that the solemn judgment of the world will only take place on the last day and at the return of Christ.

The dogma of the resurrection of the body belongs, according to my view, already to the Gāthā period, thus to the oldest period of the Zoroastrian religion[1]. The

---

[1] [Dr. Ferdinand Justi in his discourse upon Dr. Geiger's *Ostiranische Kultur* (*vide Deutsche Litteraturzeitung*, 1883) seems to view the matter thus :—The belief in the Immortality of the Soul is in the Zoroastrian doctrine original, but the faith in the Resurrection of the Body could not have originated with the Zoroastrians since they immediately consign the body to destruction. It must have originated from a country where people indicated their belief in a future existence of the body also externally (i. e. by interment in sepulchres or by embalmment of the corpse). Thus it was introduced from Anterior Asia into the land of the Avesta people.—In the first place, it should be observed that from the Avesta precept that the dead body shall be consumed by carcass-eating birds, we must not infer that the Zoroastrian religion does not at all inculcate its preservation. Along with the precept regarding the immediate consumption of the corpse, there is also a strict commandment for erecting an *astōdān* (charnel-hollow) for the preservation of its bones (*vide* Fargard VI, at the end). It is only for the fleshy and fluid portions of the human body, which, after death has taken place, are subject to putrefaction and consequently exercise a destructive influence on the living, that the Vendidād explicitly orders its annihilation, while at the same time it commands the proper preservation of the bones. Moreover, the violation of this command is liable to heavy penalties set down in the law. In the second place, the passages referring to the *Frashōkereti* ' the advancement or new formation' in the Gāthās, as well as the description of the Resurrection given in the *Jamyād Yasht*, as interpreted by the author in the text, clearly prove that the resurrection-theory was established in Eastern Irān long before it was propounded by any other monotheistic religion of the civilized world. That Spitama Zarathushtra was the first known prophet by whom this doctrine was revealed to

bodies of the wicked, as it is said in the Avesta, pass into Hell ; where they are condemned to corporeal punish-

man is confirmed by several Christian writers, amongst whom I would here quote the view of an American author upon this question (*vide* 'History of the Doctrine of Future Life,' by W. R. Alger, Boston, 1880, pp. 140–141):—

' The doctrine of a general resurrection is literally stated in the Vendidād, and in many other places in the Avesta, where it has not yet been shown to be an interpolation, but only supposed so by very questionable constructive inferences. The consent of intrinsic adjustment and of historical evidence, therefore, lead to the conclusion that this was an old Zoroastrian dogma. In disproof of this conclusion we believe there is no direct positive evidence whatever, and no inferential argument cogent enough to produce conviction.

' There are sufficient reasons for the belief that the doctrine of a resurrection was quite early adopted from the Persians by the Jews, not borrowed at a much later time from the Jews by the Parsees. The conception Ahriman, the evil serpent bearing death (*Die Schlange Angramainyus der voll Tod ist*), is interwrought from the first throughout the Zoroastrian scheme. In the Hebrew records, on the contrary, such an idea appears but incidentally, briefly, rarely and only in the later books. The account of the introduction of sin and death by the serpent in the garden of Eden dates from a time subsequent to the commencement of the Captivity. Von Bohlen, in his Introduction to the Book of Genesis, says the narrative was drawn from the Zend-Avesta. Rosenmüller, in his commentary on the passage, says the narrator had in view the Zoroastrian notions of the serpent Ahriman and his deeds. Dr. Martin Haug—an acute and learned writer, whose opinion is entitled to great weight, as he is the freshest scholar acquainted with this whole field in the light of all that others have done—thinks it certain that Zoroaster lived in a remote antiquity from fifteen hundred to two thousand years before Christ. He says that Judaism after the exile—and, through Judaism, Christianity afterwards—received an important influence from Zoroastrianism, an influence which, in regard to the doctrine of angels, Satan, and the resurrection of the dead, cannot be mistaken. The Hebrew theology had no demonology, no Satan, until after the residence at Babylon. This is admitted. Well, is not the resurrection a pendant to the doctrine of Satan ? Without the idea of a Satan, there would be no idea of a retributive banishment of souls into hell, and of course no occasion for a vindicative restoration of them thence to a former or a superior state. . . .

ment[1]. In the later Avesta this dogma is fully expressed in clear words and the resurrection is brought into connection withthe regeneration of this world[2].

The Bundehesh contains a distinct chapter on the end of things. It cannot be my task here to repeat its contents[3]. I will rather enter into those points of Parsee eschatology which are found already in the Avesta, and I will also refer as much as possible to the age and primitive form of these different dogmas.

The end of the world consisted in a regeneration of creation. This is evident from the expression by which that event is constantly referred to in the Avesta[4]. This expression, moreover, is even used in the more ancient Gāthās, where the poet desires for himself and his friends that they may be included among those who will help to renovate the world[5].

As is well known, the idea of the return of Christ, and the hope in the same, were especially lively among the primitive Christians. As it appears, the end of the world was also believed, in the very first period of the Zoroastrian community, to be closely impending. Or can this doctrine, which later on appears in the Parsee writings, have been in force at that time, according to which a small number of

---

'In view of the whole case as it stands, until further researches either strengthen it or put a different aspect upon it, we feel forced to think that *the doctrine of a general resurrection was a component element in the ancient Avestan religion.*' Tr. note.]

[1] Ys. XLVI, 11 ; *vide supra*, pp. 100–102.

[2] Yt. XIX, 11 and 89 : *yat · irista · paiti · usehishtā.* Comp. also Vd. XVIII, 51. . . . .

[3] *Bundehesh*, chap. 30. West, 'Pahlavi Texts,' part i, p. 120 seq. Comp. on the whole Hübschmann, ' *Die parsische Lehre von Jenseits und jüngsten Gericht* in the *Jahrbücher für prot. Theol.* 1879, pp. 203 –245 ; Windischmann, *Z. St.* p. 231 seq.; Spiegel, *E. A.* vol. ii, p. 158 seq.

[4] *Frashō-kereti* ' the advancement, extension and new formation.' Verbal form *frashem · kar.*

[5] *Atcha tōi vaęm hyāmā, yōi īm frashēm kerenaon ahūm,* Ys. XXX, 9.

chosen pious men are to be preserved in order to help the 'Saviour' in the renovation of the world? But in whatever manner we may understand it, so much is certain, that at least the fundamental features of the Parsee eschatology reach back to the earliest period of the existence of their community, and belong to the oldest and most original doctrines of their system.

If we enter into details, we are really obliged to adduce our quotations from the more modern Avesta for the sake of proof. But still we cannot hence infer in any way that the dogmas contained therein were foreign to the Gâthâ period.

The day of doom is preceded by the appearance of three great prophets. Every one of these appears after the expiration of a certain period, every one is regarded as a supernaturally-begotten son of Zarathusthra . . . .

The three prophets are called *Ukhshyat-erta* 'growing piety,' *Ukhshyat-nema* 'growing prayer,' and finally *Astvat-erta* 'embodied piety[1].' The last one is plainly the 'Saviour,' the Redeemer of the world, whom the faithful people expect and long for[2]. His mother is *Erdhat-fedhri*. She bears also the name *Vispa-tarvi* 'the all-conquering,' since he who will be born of her will overcome all torments which originate from men or demons[3].

It is also said, that the *Astvat-erta* shall come from

---

[1] Yt. XIII, 128. The meaning of the name is explained by Hübschmann, *ZddmG*. vol. xxxv, p. 180.

[2] Yt. XIII, 129 : 'Who will be the victorious saviour with the name of *Astvat-erta* "embodied piety." He is called the saviour, because he will be the safety of the whole world ; he is called embodied piety, since he, as a corporeal being of flesh and blood, (*astvão hã ushtanavão*), is opposed to the annihilation of corporeal existence.' —*Saoshyâs*, plural *saoshyañtõ* from root *su* 'to help, to rescue,' serves as a designation for a saviour or prophet. Even in the Gâthâs *saoshkyañtõ* or *saoshyañtõ* occurs frequently (the singular form also once); however, I doubt whether it has even here the dogmatical import of the later Avesta. It appears to me better to designate thereby chiefly the teachers and preachers of the Mazdayasnān Community.

[3] Yt. XIII, 139; cf. Yt. XIX, 92 ; *Vispa-taurvayão puthrõ*.

the lake *Kansu* far distant in (?) the East [1], the original
fountain and abode of light.   It is his task to carry out the
renovation of the world.   He makes the living immortal,
the dead he awakens from their sleep.   Age, death, and
decay he brings to an end.   Eternal life, eternal happiness,
and the fulfilment of all desires he bestows upon the
pious [2].

But as, according to the German mythology, in the 'twilight of gods' the new earth emerges out of the turmoil
of the world's conflagration and of the general battle of
gods and giants, so also, according to the ideas of the
Zoroastrians, a mighty combat precedes the end of the
world.

The demons and their adherents [3] rise once more with all
their might to annihilate the *Astvat-erta* and his companions,
who are helping him in the execution of his great work.
The last decisive battle takes place between the powers of
light and those of darkness.   Every genius finds his special
opponent among the demons.   *Vohu Manō*, the spirit of the
Good Mind, fights against *Akem Manō*, the spirit of the Bad
Mind ; *Haurvatāt* and *Amertāt* against Hunger and Thirst ;
the genius of Truth against the genius of Falsehood ; and,
finally, *Ahura Mazda* himself against *Angra Manyu*, the
Prince of Hell.

But *Astvat-erta*, with the help of the good genii, emerges
victorious.   The demons are vanquished, evil itself is ex-
tirpated.   And since all evil originates from the demons,
a state of undisturbed bliss is now established, in which the
spirits of the pious, no longer injured and attacked by any
hostile power, live together with Ahura Mazda and the
other genii.

---

[1] Vd. XIX, 5; Yt. XIX, 92.   [2] Yt. XIX, 11–12, and 89 seq.
[3] According to Yt. XIX, at the end.

§ 12. *The Cult of the Manes.*

WITH the belief in the immortality of the soul the veneration of departed spirits is naturally connected.

Delivered from the care and misery of this world, the soul
has departed to the next. There it now dwells, where also
the Deity dwells—in a better and more beautiful land.
Manifestly it cannot have lost in strength and faculties, but
it can only have gained. People, therefore, began to ascribe
to it qualities which otherwise plainly describe the divine
nature.

If the soul still really exists, there is no cogent ground
for considering all intercourse with it as suspended. Pious
remembrance, besides, yearns to maintain that communication, and clings to the hope that the body alone may fall
a prey to death, but that the soul, invisibly yet perceptibly,
may hover over those that remain behind.

It has been known of many a man that anxiety on
account of a wife, a child, or a relation, has rendered death
so painful to him, that in his last moments he feared for
his hereafter and the welfare of those belonging to him.
Should all this solicitude and love terminate with his
death? Should the soul now suddenly forget all those
for whom it has restlessly worked and provided during its
life-time? That would be inconceivable, if the spirits of
the dead were regarded as higher, more perfect, and more
mighty beings than the souls of the living.

So, next to love and reverence for them, personal interest
made it desirable to be in communication with departed
souls. In them were to be found affectionate advocates
near God. In direct proximity to the Deity there were
beings with whom men had once been linked by ties of
blood, and in whom they could also presuppose a special
sympathy for their own good-fortune and welfare, a particular understanding of their special wishes and needs.

From the wish to the belief, however, is only a step.

The Avesta people speak of the *manes* of the dead as the *Fravashis*. Taken strictly, we must understand by the Fravashi, that divine part in men which, existing from eternity to eternity, unites itself only for a limited time with the body. Consequently there are Fravashis of such as are dead, of such as are at this time living, and of such as are yet unborn[1]. As regards the veneration of the *manes*, naturally those of the first class only are meant.

The worship of the *manes* was a family rite among all Indo-Germanic races. Every one cherished most the memory of those who had when living been nearest and dearest to him. From such could also be expected the readiest help and support in all need and danger. Furthermore, the closer the ties of blood and relationship were considered to be, and the greater the consciousness which men felt, as belonging to this or that family, this or that clan, the more would that family rite develop and command respect.

I have already alluded several times to the fact that the family pride of the Eastern Irānian people was extremely vigorous. In consequence of this also does the religious veneration of the *manes* play a very important part in their system.

The nation[2] is based upon the family, which developes itself into the clan, the clan growing into the tribe. There were also Fravashis of the family, of the clan, of the tribe, of the country[3], spirits of the deceased relations of the family, and spirits of the members of the clan, tribe, or country. They had all more or less claim to honourable commemoration, and in a certain measure to a special worship. But in preference to all others, offerings were

---

[1] *Mat vīspåbyō ashaonibyō fravashibyō, yāo iririthushām ashaonām, yāoscha jvañtām ashaonām, yāoscha narām azātanām (frasho-charethrām saoshyantām),* Yt. XXVI, 6. The last words are used as an epithet of a *diaskeust*, who in this passage would recognize, as we may often observe, a reference to the end of this world.

[2] Lit. country.

[3] *Fravashayō . . . nmānyāo, vīsyāo, zañtumāo, daqyumāo,* Yt. XIII, 21; cf. Yt. XIII, 150–151; Ys. XXVI, 1.

made to the Fravashis of the next-of-kin, to those who had belonged to one's own family. Hence such Fravashis also form for themselves a particular category, having a distinct appellation[1].

The Fravashis of the original members of the tribe or country must have been invoked in general only during offerings and prayer. Reverence may also have been paid to individuals of special eminence, namely, such as had lived in ancient days, and had been glorified by myth and legend. Individual families or clans paid homage probably to their common ancestor, whole tribes to their founders and the establishers of their power. Thus the veneration of the *manes* is accompanied with a cult of heroes.

As the Fravashis are revered within the family, so also do they on their part render to every one of their family or their race help and protection. At the time of the *Hamaspatmaidhaya* festival, when the earth awakens from her winter-sleep and when nature begins to stir with new life, the souls come back from the next world to the earth. For several days they dwell among men ; and if they find that their memory still survives among their relatives or descendants, and that their service is neither forgotten nor neglected, then they support them, bestow upon them plenty, prosperity and blessings, pour out in abundance water that moistens their fields, and protect them against the assaults of their enemies.

'They, the spirits, fly towards their village at the time of *Hamaspatmaidhaya*, and go round about here for ten nights long. They wish for such help, observing : Who will praise us, who will offer to us?'[2]

'They deal out water, each to his own relations, his house, his village, his community, and his country, also saying : "Our own country shall increase in wealth and prosperity!"'

'They fight in the combat, each for his land and his

---

[1] *Fravashayō · nabānazdishtanām*, Ys. XXIII, 4 ; XXVI, 6, &c.

[2] Yt. XIII, 49 ; *visādha* must be read in the first line, for in the second it would disturb the metre.

district, as if some land and house have been fixed for them as their dwelling[1].'

In war and battle especially the *manes* manifest their powerful help ; and here I believe we directly touch upon a sphere of primitive ideas. They continually make their appearance as powerful and well-armed combatants. In the heat of battle their assistance is invoked. Here they stand by the side of the pious, and help them to gain the victory :—

'They, the Fravashis of pious people, convey their utmost assistance in fierce battles[2].'

'They form many armies, and carry hundreds of weapons; they bear banners, the radiant, who in hot fighting hurriedly descend, who vigorously and rapidly give battle to the Dānūs ; ye have subdued the opposition of the Tūrānian enemies[3].'

The antiquity of these ideas is attested by the fact that we find in the Rig-veda quite similar invocations and prayers, which the old Indian addresses to the *manes*, the *Fathers.*' Here, also, they are chiefly esteemed as mighty warriors and as helpers in battle[4].

'Lovely sit together our *Fathers*, dispensing vitality, exposing themselves to peril, full of strength, inexhaustible, with glistening spears, powerful arrows, not lingering, real heroes, ruling far and wide, subduing entire armies :'

'The priestly *Fathers*, loving the Soma-drink, and the

---

[1] Yt. XIII, 66–67. We should read *dādhara.* Comp. Skr. *dhṛ*, which is perhaps construed with the acc. and dat.: 'to persuade anybody to do anything.'

[2] Yt. XIII, 17. *Dāhishta* is derived from *dāha*, formed from root *dā* ' to give.' Comp. Skr. *dāsvat, sudās.*

[3] Yt. XIII, 37–38. *Khshtāvi* might be translated by 'a chariot-warrior,' and referred for confirmation to Skr. *sthātṛ.* However, *khshtāvi* probably means simply 'active, stout, hero ' (like *takhma, aurva*), to which we would compare *khshtāvant*, an epithet of the moon, perhaps 'the wandering, speedy,' just as *shtum* and *khtūm* ' a hare=the swift one' in the Pāmir dialects (Tomaschek, p. 31).

[4] Kaegi, *Der Rig-veda*, p. 61, notes 346 and 347.

salutary heaven and earth, who have not their equal, and Pushan shall protect us against misfortune. O ye Increasers of Holiness! no malevolent demon shall obtain power over us[1].'

As to the Zoroastrians, however, closer or more remote relationship was not their sole guide in the veneration of departed spirits. They also took into account the attitude, hostile or friendly, which the dead had assumed during their lifetime with respect to the Mazda-religion.

First of all 'the Fravashis of pious men and women' form *one* principal category, and are invoked as such very frequently. This form of invocation alone goes to prove that the unbelieving also owned their Fravashis; yet neither adoration nor offering was ever vouchsafed to them. However, we may admit that they constituted the other principal category.

Among the spirits of the pious, the Fravashis of those that lived and died before the coming of Zarathushtra, and before the announcement of his doctrine[2], form a separate group. I have already observed that reverence for the *manes* naturally leads also to hero-worship. Such religious observances in honour of the heads of tribes or other heroes of antiquity probably existed of old among the different Eastern Irānian families and races, when the reform movement began, which is connected in history with the name of Zarathushtra. It was impossible to eradicate them, because the people strictly adhered to such family customs with singular pertinacity. Nor were these customs even begrudged a place amongst the new doctrines, where room was found for them by regarding those heroes as the

---

[1] Rig-veda, VI, 75, 9–10.

[2] These are the *fravashayō paoiryō-tkaęshanăm* 'the souls of those who belonged to the first (pre-Zarathushtrian) religion.' A distinction is also to be observed between *tkaęsha* and *daęna*!—Yt. XIII, 150 : *paoiryăn tkaęshę yazamaidę ; nmānanămcha vīsămcha zańtunămcha daqyunămcha yōi āoġhare paoiryę tkaęshę yazamaidę* 'the earlier pious we revere; those, who were the earlier pious in family, race, tribe or country, we revere.'

followers of an ancient and venerable religion, which preceded Zoroastrism, and to a certain extent paved the way
for it.

Moreover, later on a distinct position was held by the
Fravashis of those pious persons who had been thought
worthy to behold the prophet face to face, to hear his doctrine from his own lips, and to receive it from himself.
These are the Fravashis of the contemporaries and first
adherents of Zarathushtra [1]. They are followed by the great
multitude of the Fravashis of those in general who belonged
to the Mazdayasnian community, and paid allegiance to the
religion of Ahura.

The sphere within which the Fravashis were supposed to
have power was a very elastic one. It seems that people
always ascribed to them, as time went on, more and more
influence and higher faculties. When the souls of the pious,
departing in countless multitudes, occupied the apartments
of Heaven, their influence was to be felt everywhere. Thus
they become at last the supporters and preservers of the
whole world, with whose help Ahura Mazda rules over earth
and heaven :

'Through their power and their glory I uphold firmly
the firmament, O Zarathushtra ! which, blazing on
high, surrounds this earth far away from its side and
in a circle [2].'

It is the Fravashis that keep up the sacred stream Ardvi-
sūra, in order that it may flow on with great force and
volume. They make the sun, moon, and stars follow their
paths [3]; it is they that support the fastnesses of the earth.

'Through their power and their glory, O Zarathushtra !
I support the wide Earth, created by Ahura, the
great, broad one, who is the bearer of much beauty,
who bears the whole corporeal world, living and

---

[1] *Fravashayō paoiryanãm sāsnō-gūshãm*, 'the Fravashis of the
first ones, who listened to the doctrine.' Yt. XIII, 149.

[2] Yt. XIII, 2. The second *yō* is to be extended in order to preserve the metre.

[3] Yt. XIII, 4–8, 16, 57.

dead, and the high mountains, which abound in pastures and fountains[1].'

We have to thank the Fravashis, when children are preserved in the mother's womb, when women are easily delivered, and when excellent sons, who 'are active in council and whose words are heard with pleasure,' rejoice them[2].

And not only does the Ardvi-sūra stand under their protection. It is their principal charge that the precious element of water, the fundamental importance of which for life and cultivation was so very clearly impressed upon the Eastern Irānians, may be well spread over their country; and they also support the other genii, who are entrusted with that work. Hence it is also they who cause the plants to germinate and sprout for the nourishment of men and beasts.

'Through their power and their glory the waters gush forth impetuously from inexhaustible sources. Through their power and their glory plants spring up from the earth from inexhaustible sources. Through their power and their glory winds chasing away clouds blow from inexhaustible sources[3].'

'They can travel to the star *Satavaisa* (*posted*) between earth and heaven, who causes waters to flow, granting prayers, who causes waters to run and plants to germinate for the nourishment of beasts and men, for the maintenance of the Arian countries, for the nourishment of the five kinds of cattle, for the protection of pious men[4].'

In conclusion I must notice yet one point more.

It has been observed that the cult of the Fravashis stands in close connection with the stars and the veneration paid

[1] Yt. XIII, 9. Cf. Geldner, *Metrik*, § 120.
[2] Yt. XIII, 11, 15, 16; Geldner, *Metrik*, § 109.
[3] Yt. XIII, 14.
[4] Yt. XIII, 43. Regarding the star *Satavaisa, vide infra.* It is better to read *pañchō-hayayāo* instead of *pañchō-hyayāo* (cf. the variants in Westergaard) and to trace the word *haya* from rt. *hi* = Skr. *si*.

to them[1]. We have already heard that the stars are under the special protection of the Fravashis. Even the latter are themselves undoubtedly identified with the stars, when it is said of them that, led along the celestial path, they travel on the heights of the firmament[2].

The true home of star-worship is really Mesopotamia ; nevertheless I would not suppose that the notion of the Fravashis being stars is due to any Semitic influence. We very often meet with analogies between two different nations in morals, culture, and religion ; yet I do not consider it fair to regard such a conformity as the result of borrowing or external influence when no other grounds for such a supposition can be adduced. How easily may such resemblances present themselves in different countries having no mutual dependence on each other, provided that analogous conditions are found to pre-exist in history and nature![3] I mean that the assumption of a borrowing is an explanation which the writer of the history of civilization should adopt very sparingly. So long as we are able to interpret a phenomenon as one produced in an organic manner, we may rest content with the above explanation.

So with the Irānians and Semites. The idea of identifying the souls, that have passed into the heavenly kingdom, with the numberless stars shining and blazing in the firmament is by no means foreign to human nature. A somewhat vivid fancy can take this turn precisely as well in Central Asia as in Asia Minor.

The heavens and stars have certainly not occupied the human mind in Mesopotamia alone. Why should the eyes

---

[1] Spiegel, *E.A.* vol. ii, p. 98.

[2] Yt. XIII, 42 : *mainyu-shūtāo frashūseñti * bareshnavō avañhę ashnō.*

[3] The idea which I would thereby convey is this, that according to my conviction the Avesta religion must be interpreted wholly from its own teaching. I do not believe that it has borrowed anything from the Semites. It is the special property of the Eastern Irānian nation. Even where apparent or real similarities strike us, we ought to assume them to be a mere accidental coincidence.

of the Arian not have been directed towards them in the
low plains near the Oxus and the Jaxartes, where, moreover,
the stars glitter with a peculiarly bright lustre through the
clear atmosphere of the desert? Why should he not have
guessed at the unknown land behind the mysterious space
of heaven, wherein the departing soul wanders, and where
it shines in the form of a star?

Here I may even call to mind the well-known popular
belief of the Germans, according to which the soul, particularly the soul of a child, on separating from the body, is
transformed into a star. Finally I may also observe that,
according to the Indian idea, the '*Fathers*' are connected
with the stars. The '*Fathers*,' says the Rig-veda, 'adorned
heaven with stars, as a black horse with pearls[1].'

---

[1] Rv. X, 68, 11 ; Justi, *Hdb.* s. v. *fravashi*; Kaegi, *Der Rig-veda*,
p. 62, note 348.

CHAPTER III [1].

MENTAL AND MORAL CULTURE.

§ 13. *Man in Relation to his Body and Soul.*

THE mental and moral gifts of a people, the extent of their general knowledge and their ethics, are an essential constituent of their culture. They are not of less importance for the right understanding of the stage of civilization, which they have reached, than perhaps their social and political institutions. We must, therefore, also briefly discuss those features of Eastern Irānian life.

The spiritual horizon of the Avesta people is naturally still comparatively narrow. Their knowledge is empiric, the sum total of many more or less accidental experiences and observations. An investigation, conscious of its aim, which had for its object the deliverance of the human mind from the fetters of error, we can hardly presuppose.

It is, however, interesting to see how the old Irānian observed with a clear eye and mind the world and its phenomena, and endeavoured to bring into an organized system the observations made regarding the earth and the heavens. Not all the knowledge which we find amongst the Avesta people is self-acquired. We cannot consider as an age of rude unrefinement and ignorance the Arian epoch in which the Indians and the Irānians, still united, formed one and the same nation. From them the Avesta people inherited a great deal, and employed their inherited talents to the greatest advantage. In many cases the very first germs and rudiments of some branch of knowledge may be traced back to the primitive Arian age, but their further cultivation and development belong to the separate history of both the tribes.

---

[1] Chapter V, § 35, *Ostirānische Kultur.*

Hence it is not easy always to distinguish the old property from the newly-acquired possessions. This is, however, so much the less to be regretted, as it most concerns us to indicate the degree of spiritual culture to which the Avesta people had attained, and to fix to a certain extent the limits of their knowledge.

I now commence with the observations which the old Irānian made regarding man himself.

Man consists of body and soul. The body is composed of numerous constituents and members, several of which have their special names [1]. It is, however, to be observed

---

[1] Body : *kehrpa* ; Skr. *krp* 'a handsome look'—*tanu* = Skr. *tanū.*
Bone : *astan, asti* = Skr. *ȧsthan, asthi.*
Skin : *pāsta* (Tomaschek, *Pamirdialekte*, p. 45.)
Flesh appears to be *kehrpa* ; comp. *kerefsh-hvara.*
Marrow, brain : *mazga* = Skr. *majja.*
Blood : *vohuni* = Skr. *vasā.*
Fat : *ūtha* (?)—*pīvagh* (?)
Head : *sara*=Skr. *çiras* ; further, Ir. *kameredha, vaghdhana.*
Hair : *varesa* (N. Pers. *gurs*) ;—? *gaęsa* (*Hdb. sub voce*).
Beard : *raęsha* (cf. Tomaschek, p. 47).
Face and forehead : *ainika* = Skr. *anīka.*
Eye : *akhshi, chashman, dōithra* ; Skr. *akshi, chakshman.*
Eyebrows : *brvat* = Skr. *bhrū.*
Nose : *nāogha* and *nāoghan* ; Skr. *nāsā.*
Mouth : *āogha* = Skr. *ās.*
Tooth : *dañtan* = Skr. *dantan.*
Tongue : *hizva* = Skr. *jihvā.*
Jaw, cheek : *paitish-qarena* (*ZddmG.* vol. xxxiv, p. 419).
Ear : *gaosha* (also *ghūsh, ghokh, ghaul,* and *ghowar* are found in Tomaschek's *Pāmirdialekte*, p. 50) corresponds to the Skr. *karna*, Ir. *karena,* 'deaf' (just as in Tomaschek's *Pāmirdia-lekte*, p. 83).
Neck : *grīva* = Skr. *grīvā.*
Back : *parshti* = Skr. *prshthā.*
Shoulder : *supti* = Skr. *çupti.*
Shoulder, arm-pit : *kasha* = Skr. *kaksha* 'waist.'
Breast : *vara* and *uragh* = Skr. *uras* ; *paitivara* the upper-chest, collar-bone ;—*fshtāna* ('nipple' Vd. IX, 19) also for the female-breast, = Skr. *stana.*

that most of these names were not first invented by the Iranians, but are actually of Arian origin. A collection of such names might not be without interest. The Avesta contains particular designations for flesh, skin, and bone, blood, marrow, and fat. Of the bodily parts the following are recognized : the head (including hair and beard), face, and forehead, eye, eyebrows, nose, mouth (with teeth and tongue), chin, cheek, and ear. After these follow: the neck, back, shoulder, armpit, and chest. The female breast is particularly distinguished. Further, the ribs, waist, abdomen, navel, hips, thighs, male and female sexual parts ; the arm, elbow, hand, finger, fist ; the

---

Ribs: *peresu* = Skr. *pārçva.*

Waist, the middle part of the body : *maidhya* = Skr. *madhya* (Tomaschek, p. 44).

Belly, abdomen : *kushi* = Skr. *kukshi* (Tomaschek, p. 55).

Navel: *nabi* = Skr. *nābhi.*

Hips : *sraoni* = Skr. *çroṇi* (*clunes*); also probably *pudenda*. Comp. .*perethu-sraoni* = *pṛthu-çroṇi.*

Thighs : *hakhti* = Skr. *sakthi* and *sakthan*, also translated ' shame.'

Pudenda: (a) female : *upasta, yaona* = Skr. *upastha, yoni.* (b) male: *fravākhsha*, an euphemism for the *membrum virile*, perhaps 'a branch, a sprout,' *ZddmG.* vol. xxxiv, p. 419 ; like German ' Rute ' and Indian *vaitasa* ' reed.'

Arm : *bāsu* = Skr. *bāhu* ; *arema* (Tomaschek, p. 53).

Hand : *zasta* = Skr. *hasta.*

Elbows: *bareshti* (Tomaschek, p. 53).

Finger : *erezu* ' straight'; *tbishi* 'finger-joint';—*angushta* ' thumb' = Skr. *angushtha.*

Fist: *mushti* = Skr. *mushti.*

Right and left: *dashina*, havya=Skr. *dakshiṇa, savya.*

The bone from the thigh up to the knee : *rāna.*

Knee : *zhnu*—Skr. *jānu.*

The calf of the leg : *aschu.*

The shinbone: *zañga*—Skr. *jañghā.*

Foot : *pādha*=Skr. *pāda.*

The instep : *frabda*=Skr. *prapada.*

The sole : *hakha.*

The heel : *pāshna*=Skr. *pārshṇi.*

Heart: *zaredhaya*=Skr. *hṛdaya.*

Lungs: *sushi* (Tomaschek, p. 54).

upper-thigh, knee, calf of the leg, shinbone, foot, the instep, the sole, and heel. Besides, I remark the distinction between right and left; and lastly, the names of the two internal organs, the heart and the lungs.

The Doctrine of the Soul in the Avesta, is not to be called quite simple and wholly primitive. At all events it presupposes a certain amount of philosophical speculation. It rests upon the observation that the spiritual activity of man expresses itself in manifold ways[1], and upon the conclusion thence inferred, that in man a multiplicity of forces exist, of which each one has its own well-defined sphere of action. Besides, it is a specific production of the Irānian mind, and hardly admits, in its very essence, of any connection with pre-existing ideas and doctrines.

There are generally five, less frequently four, spiritual faculties, which are supposed to be innate in the human body. They are, according to their nature and efficacy, entirely different from one another, partly without beginning and without end, partly transitory, partly not existing from eternity, yet certainly continuing for ever. They are called (1) *Conscience*, (2) *Vital Force*, (3) *Soul* as a moral power, (4) *Spirit*, in the sense of consciousness and intelligence, and (5) '*Fravashi.*' Instead of the two first names there is also now and then used a special expression, which, however, does not probably denote anything more than the principle of life[2].

---

[1] *Vide supra* p. 84.

[2] The Avesta expressions are *daǫna, aĝhu, urvan, baodhaĝh, fravashi*, Ys. XXVI, 4 and 6; Yt. XIII, 149. Instead of *daǫna* and *aĝhu* there stands in Ys. LV, 1. *tēvishi* from the root *tu* 'to be strong.' Besides, it is probably only a synonym for *aĝhu* and *daǫna* 'conscience,' which does not mean a force peculiarly belonging to man, but rather a force working upon him from without, and is in fact omitted in the passage concerned. In later times the well-known passage of the Sadder-Bundehesh (in Spiegel's *Trad. Lit.* pp. 172–176), which discusses the Parsee doctrine of the soul and harmonizes most completely with the ideas of the Avesta, was naturally and especially made use of to represent this idea. In this passage are enumerated the five faculties, *jān, akhō, rvān, bōi* and *frōhar*. The

Conscience is a divine power, which exists from eternity to eternity independently of the mortal body, an inherent voice which tells man immediately after every action, whether that action was good or bad, and accordingly it praises or accuses him. Its purity and sanctity cannot be affected by the sins of man, since it has no part in them. As long as it is possible, conscience restrains man from guilt and sin ; when it is no longer able to do so, it sorrowfully abandons him and returns to heaven. This doctrine is based undoubtedly on the experience that man is able, in course of time, to drown the warning voice within and to lose his conscience.

Of course the continuance of its existence is by no means prejudiced by the death of man. It is a characteristic of its nature that, according to the Avesta, it still exercises its influence after death on the soul wandering into the next world. To the soul of the pious man it appears personified in the form of a charming maiden, who hails him as happy on account of good actions done during life ; but to that of the impious man it appears in the form of an ugly hag, who upbraids him with reproachful words for all his sins, and bitterly accuses him on account of them [1].

By this it is not meant that conscience is not unchanging, but only that it appears in one form to the one and in another form to the other. It terrifies, torments and alarms the wicked, but on the good it confers joyfulness and peaceful serenity.

To the *Vital Power* it is appointed to find and watch over the corporeal functions of man. It originates only with the body and perishes with the matter [2]. It has

---

last three correspond with the last three soul-powers of the Avesta, not merely in name, as the description which follows in the Sadder proves, but in their essence ; *jān* is, however, undoubtedly parallel to Av. *ağhu,* and *akhō* to *daęna.*

[1] *Vide supra* pp. 102, 104–105.

[2] [The Avesta does not say anything with reference to the non-existence of *ağhu* after death. On the contrary we praise the *ağhu* of every pious Mazdayasna after his departure from this world. Comp. Ys. XXVI, 4. *Vide* my paper in the *Bombay Gazette* of

therefore a beginning as well as an end, and occupies in consequence the lowest rank among the faculties of the soul.

The *Spirit* is the intellectual power in man : his consciousness, intelligence and reason [1]. If death be regarded as a separation of the body and the spirit, the latter must have a somewhat general signification. The business of the spirit is to rule over the memory, understanding and judgment, in order that each may perform its duty and co-operate for the welfare of the body. It appears to come into being first with the body, but after death to unite with the soul and the Fravashi, and to accompany them into the next world.

The *Soul* has to choose for itself between good and evil. It has a moral power by virtue of which man possesses a moral freedom of election. It *should* of course make choice of what is good, it *can*, however, turn also towards evil. For this reason it must account after death, together with the spirit, for its behaviour on earth [2], and, according to the result of the judgment, it receives either eternal bliss or

---

Nov. 3, 1882, on the 'Avesta Doctrine regarding the Body and Soul.'

With reference to this note Dr. E. W. West remarks in a letter to Dastur Peshutonji :—' As to *anghu* your son rightly corrects Dr. Geiger, as the word evidently means both bodily and spiritual life.—What life is we do not know, but even in its common acceptation it seems to be some spiritual property that becomes manifest in the body ; whether it begins and ends with the body we do not yet know, as hitherto we have found no means of maintaining the sensible existence of the one without the other, but we can conceive that such is possible. These, however, are matters of speculation in which I do not often indulge ; but I am fully persuaded that if mankind ever discover anything certain about the spiritual world, by means of their own researches, they will have to change all their past notions regarding psychology and philosophy.']

[1] Hence *baodhō-varshta* is an act perpetrated with consciousness and deliberation (Vd. VII, 38). Comp. also *baodhō-vīdhvāo · chichithwāo baodhaghailīm vīthushīm* (Vd. XVIII, 67).—A wound which deprives one of consciousness (not of life, as Justi understands), is called *snatha · frazā-baodhagh* (Vd. IV, 40, &c).

[2] Vd. XIX, 29 ; *vide supra* pp. 102, 104, 105.

damnation. Frequently, 'soul' is the designation for all the immortal powers of man that have passed into the other world.

Lastly, with the spirit and the soul is united after death the *Fravashi*, in order to form from that time an indivisible whole. The Fravashi, however, appears to be by its nature not only imperishable like the conscience, but also without beginning. It would be best to consider it as a tutelary spirit that watches over man and protects him. Hence the Fravashis and the *manes* or spirits of the dead are almost identical; for that reason there are also Fravashis of those who are yet unborn[1]. It is only for the time during which a man lives that the guardian spirit descends from heaven on this earth and accompanies him on his way . . . .

§ 14. *The World.*

THIS section will treat of the knowledge and ideas which the Avesta people had of this visible world, its structure and organization. We may begin by quoting a few strophes of an old hymn which we cannot but think one of the most poetical passages in the Gāthās. They show us that the pious mind of the old Irānian beheld in all the phenomena and wonders of nature the ever-working power of the Deity:

'That I ask of Thee, give me truly answer, O Ahura :
Who was the progenitor and father of order from the
beginning?
Who made their courses to the Sun and Stars?
Who made it that the moon waxes and wanes, who
but Thee?
This, O Mazda, and other things I long to know!'
'That I ask of Thee, give me truly answer, O Ahura :
Who then kept the earth and the clouds above,
That they fall not? Who made the water and the
plants?

---

[1] *Vide supra* p. 113.

Who gave their swiftness to the wind and the fogs?
Who is, O Mazda, the creator of the pious mind?'
'That I ask of Thee, give me truly answer, O Ahura :
Who is the artificer that made light and darkness?
Who is the artist that made sleep and wakefulness?
Who made the dawns, the mid-days and the evenings,
Which remind the careful of their duties [1] ?'

The earth, with which I begin, is the dwelling-place
of man and the other animals : bearing and feeding everything, she is the great mother, the bounteous one from
whose lap trees and herbs grow up to give nourishment
to all creatures [2].

As to its shape, it was thought, it seems, to be a large
disc. That is meant, in my opinion, by the epithets
' wide,' ' broad,' ' round,' ' far-limited [3].' In old Indian the
earth is likewise called ' the wide.'

The special guardianship of the earth is confided to
Spentā Ārmati, a female genius of temperate and devout

---

[1] Ys. XLIV, 3–5.

    *Tat · thwā · peresā · er*esh · *mōi · vaochā · Ahurā :*
Kasnā · zāthā · patā · ashahyā · paouruyō ?
Kasnā · qeñg · staremchā · dāt · advānem ?
*Ke · yā · māo · ukhshyēiti · nerefsaiti · thwa*t ?
*Tā · chi*t · *Mazdā · vasemī · anyāchā · vīduyẹ !*
    *Tat · thwā · peresā · er*esh · *mōi · vaochā · Ahurā :*
Kasnā · deretā · zāmchā · adenabāoschā ·
*Avapastōi*sh *? ke · apō · urvarāoschā ·*
*Ke · vātāi*sh · *dvānmaibyaschā · yaoget · āsü ?*
*Kasnā · vaḡheu*sh · *Mazdā · dāmi*sh · *managh̄ō ?*
    *Tat · thwā · peresā · er*esh · *mōi · vaochā · Ahurā :*
*Ke · hvāpāo · raochāoschā · dā*t · *temāoschā ?*
Ke · hvāpāo · qafnemchā · dāt · zaẹmāchā ?
Ke · yā · ushāo · arem-pithwā · khshapāchā ·
*Yā · manōthrī*sh · *chazdoḡhvañtem · arethahyā ?*

[2] *Yā · nāo baraiti* 'which bears (feeds) us,' Ys. XIII, 1 (cf. the
significations 'to feed,' 'to foment,' 'to keep up,' for Skr. *bhar*);
berethri 'bearer,' 'mother,'= Skr. *bhartṛ.—Zām · hudhāoḡhem* (= Skr.
sudās) yazamaidẹ, Ys. XVI, 6.

[3] *Perethu* (cf. Skr. *pṛthivi* ' earth '), *pathana, skarena* (in the Pamir
dialects *kard* and *cherd* mean ' curved,') and *düraṭ-pāra*.

mind [1]. What kind of connection there existed between the moral and material functions of Ārmati cannot easily be stated.

Certainly, she is the genius of the earth, whenever she is called the dwelling-place and home of mankind [2]. It is to her that Yima applies, as the earth, which he inhabits, has no longer sufficient space for man and beasts, praying:

'For love's sake, O Spentā Ārmati, widen and extend thyself, thou mother of flocks and herds and human-kind!'

And Yima extended the earth, so that it was larger by one-third than before, and there spread over it flocks and herds and men to their pleasure, as fully as they listed [3].

The first attempts at dividing and classifying the surface of the earth, according to certain principles, are to be sought for in an ante-Irānian period. In the Avesta the earth is considered either tripartite or septempartite. Both methods of division are met with also amongst the Indians, although there exist several discrepancies in the details [4].

If the Avesta speaks of the three thirds of the earth, the fact recalls vividly to our minds the 'three earths' of the Rig-veda, the superior, the intermediate, and the inferior [5]. Three strata or layers, one lying above the other, are said to be meant by this. That is certainly not the meaning of the Avesta. In my opinion it means nothing more than a quite primitive division of the earth into three zones;

---

[1] The opposite of *ārmaiti* (from *aram*=Skr. *alam*,+*maiti* from the rt. *man* 'to think') is, (Ys. LX, 5), *taromaiti* 'intemperate thinking, pride, haughtiness.' In like manner in Ys. XLV, 11 *tarēm · māsta* and *arēm · mainyālā* are opposed to each other. The reader may compare also *taramaiti*sh *qaēlēu*sh 'disregard of relationship.' In the Gāthās *āramaiti*sh (=Skr. *aramati*) is tetrasyllabic.

[2] Ys. XVI, 10; *yazamaidē thwām matthanem yām ārmaitim: spen-tām.*

[3] Vd. II, 10 seq.

[4] Spiegel, *E.A.* vol. i, p. 88 seq; Justi, *Beiträge*, at the beginning; Justi, *Bundehesh*, Glossary, s. v. *Kēshvar.*

[5] Zimmer, *AiL.* p. 357.

such a division might easily be suggested or occasioned by the nature of the country.

The intermediate zone of the earth is that in which the Avesta people live. Here they wage their wars against the hereditary enemies of their tribe, the Tūrānians[1]. To the North of them extend the inaccessible deserts and steppes near the Aral and Caspian Seas, from which those Tūrānians burst forth to devastate the Arian countries in their inroads. They may be supposed to form the second, or Northern, third of the earth. South of the Irānian territory are situated the hot sand and salt steppes of Central Persia, of Baluchistān, and the unknown India—the last third, or the Southern zone.

A more complicated division of the earth is that into seven *Karshvars*, since it seems to be in contradiction with what we have just mentioned. It is certainly very old, for the Gāthās already speak of the 'septempartite earth[2].' According to the statements of later Parsee Scriptures, the seven Kēshvars are to be considered as completely disconnected parts of the earth. Between them there flows the ocean, so that it is impossible, as stated in several passages, to pass from one Kēshvar to another[3]. Mythological explanations of the origin of the Kēshvars are not wanting.

The coincidence of this doctrine with the Indian one touching the seven *Dvipas*, as met with in the *Purānas*, is self-evident. It did not also escape the notice of the Parsees, as we may see from traditional Sanskrit translations of Zoroastrian documents[4].

But incongruities are not wanting. The Dvipas form concentric rings, which, separated by the ocean, surround Jambu Dvipa, which is situated in the centre. According

---

[1] Ys. XI, 7 : 'May not Hauma fetter thee, as he fettered the pernicious Frangrasyan of Tūrān, the iron-clad, in the middle third of the earth.'

[2] Ys. XXXII, 3 : *būmi · haptāiti.*

[3] Cf. e. g.   Vd. I, 4 of the Pahlavi Translation ; Bdh. XXI, 2–3.

[4] Neriosengh, the translator of the Yasna, consistently renders *Karshvare* by *Dvīpa*, and especially *Qaniratha* by *Jambudvīpa* (cf. also West, *Mkh. s. v. Kēshvar.*

to the Irānian view, the *Karshvar Qaniratha* is likewise situated in the centre of the rest. They form no concentric circles, but each of them is a peculiar, individual space, and so they group themselves round Qaniratha. Two, *Voru-barshti* and *Voru-zarshti*, lie in the North; two, *Vidadhafshu* and *Fradadhafshu*, in the South; *Savahi* and *Arzahi* in the East and West.

We shall, I think, arrive at a rather accurate notion of the original conception by looking upon it in the simplest possible light. Perhaps it was remodelled under the actual influence of India and did not receive the shape which appears in the later Scriptures of the Parsees, save by contact with the doctrine of the Dvipas. In the Avesta the Karshvars certainly were nothing but a progression and differentiation of the tripartite division of the earth. The intermediate Karshvar Qaniratha coincides more or less with the intermediate zone, and is reputed to be the home of Irānian human-kind[1]. The Northern and the Southern zones are each separated into two halves; the Karshvar in the East and that in the West are new additions. By this I do not mean to say that the tripartition is an older, the septempartition a later notion; both may have grown up together, and both form more or less definite conceptions of the same object.

In the Avesta the expression, 'the seven Karshvars,' is nothing but a comprehensive view of the whole earth, in the same way as the three thirds[2]. It seems also to pre-suppose the possibility of communication between the single parts of the earth. At least utterance is given to the desire that the religion of Zarathushtra may spread over the seven Karshvars of the earth[3]. It would be necessary to take refuge in a rather artificial interpretation,

---

[1] Hence *Qaniratha* alone is combined with *imat* 'this,' while all other *Karshvars* with *avat* 'that;' Vd. XIX, 39.

[2] Cf. e. g. Yt. X, 15–16.

[3] Yt. XIII, 94: *idha · apām · vījasaiti* vaĝhvi · daēna · Māzda-yasnish* (vīspāish) avi karshvān yāish hapta. Vide* Geldner, *Metrik,* § 131.

K 2

were we to think of any other mode of propagation of the
Zoroastrian doctrine than that by the natural means of
the proselytizing labour of believing priests.

I therefore think that by Qaniratha is meant the
country inhabited by the Irānian tribes, and, by the other
names, the adjacent territories of foreign nations in the
North, South, West, and East.

Above the three thirds of the earth spreads the *firmament* or *sky*, the dwelling-place of the clouds and fogs, and
above these *heaven* properly so called. It is propped up
by the Fravashis, to whose care the order of the world is
confided, that it may not break in pieces[1]. It is the home
of the divine beings, as the earth is the home of men.
Here we must suppose the regions of Paradise must be
looked for, the highest of which is the *Garō-nmāna*, the
resplendent mansion of Ahura Mazda and of the other
genii and happy spirits.

Heaven, as its name in the Avesta implies, was thought
to be made of stone. It is also called 'the swift,' on account
of the rapid rotation and revolution of the firmament[2].
The later Scriptures of the Parsees make a difference
between an inner and an outer Heaven. The latter is a
wall built of blue stone, and serves to keep off the evil
spirits. To the former, which is in continual motion, the
stars are fixed[3].

A distinction of the different points of the compass was
not unknown to the Avesta people. The Eastern Irānians
named them entirely as the Indians did, facing the rising
sun. So the East is called the anterior, the West the
posterior region; the South is the region on the right,
the North that on the left hand[4]. According to another

---

[1] Yt. XIII, 2–3 ; see above, p. 117.

[2] *Asman* 'stone' and *thwāsha* 'swift,' from rt. *thwakhsh* 'to
hasten.'

[3] I do not know whether this difference between *asman* and
thwāsha, an outer and inner heaven, can be recognized as early as
in the Avesta. It must be observed that here the former also is
said to be star-covered, which certainly contradicts the later belief.

[4] 'South-wind' *dashināt · hacha* Vd. III, 42; 'North-west wind'

terminology, the Avesta people designated the East as the region of the 'rising (sun),' the West as that of the 'setting (sun),' the North, which is regarded as the dómain of all evil and hurtful powers, as the 'starless region,' and the South, like the peoples of the Occident, as 'mid-day [1].' Among the celestial orbs, the Sun[2], the day-star, is venerated most. The Iränian beholds in light the symbol of moral purity and the peculiar sphere for celestial genii to work in. The Sun, therefore, as the bearer of light, is to be regarded as a prominently powerful champion against demons.

'If the sun does not rise, then the demons would destroy all things that exist in the seven parts of the earth ; nor are the heavenly spirits in this visible world able to find means of defence or resistance [3].'

As the eye is the light of the human body, so is the sun the light of heaven or its eye. But the bright clear heaven (or sky) was in the old popular religion personified in the Highest God, Ahura Mazda. Therefore, in the Avesta the sun is called His eye[4]. Such symbols of nature are rare in the Avesta religion, by far rarer, without doubt, than in the Vedic. It is, therefore, the more gratifying to find both agreeing in this respect. But in the Rig-veda the sun is called the eye of Varuna, and this proves to us,

---

aparō (lying behind)-*apākhtarō* (northern)-*vātō* Yt. III, 17 ; *vide* p. 141 of *OKA*. note 3. Similarly *pouru-apākhtara*. Hence Mithra, the yazata of light, closely connected with the wandering sun, is said to drive along the right side of the earth, that is to say, on the southern part of the sky. Yt. X, 99.

[1] *Ushastara* (from *ushaĝh*=Skr.*ushas*); *daoshatara* (from *daosha*= *doshā* 'evening'); *apākhtara* (from *apa*+*akhtara* 'star'); *rapithwa* Vd. II, 10 (*rapithwitara* · *naēma* Afr. III, 6 ; Yt. XXII, 7).

[2] *Hvare* = Skr. *svar*, *sūrya* ; *hvare-khshaētem*=N. Pers. *khur-shēd*. Spiegel, *E.A.* vol. ii, p. 66.

[3] Ys. VI, 3. In the last line of this verse, I think, *naēdha · pait-ishtām · vidhenti* must be read.

[4] Ys. I, 11, *hvarecha · khshaētahē · aurvat-aspahē · dōithrahē · Ahurahē Mazdāo.*

amongst other things, the fact that at least substantially
Ahura and Varuna correspond with each other, and both
originate from the same deity of the Arian period[1].
The sun is also called the body of Ahura Mazda. God
is essentially light itself. Him the human eye cannot
perceive, but it can see the sun, in which the light is
embodied[2]. No special explanation is necessary wherever
the sun appears as the enemy of thieves and heretics,
and similar wicked beings, that love deeds of gloom and
darkness[3].

The daily journey of the sun round about the heavenly
vault from East to West made of course a deep impression on the minds of the old Irānians. It was a superhuman, a divine operation. He was, therefore, thought,
especially among the common people, to be a bright-
sparkling chariot, drawn by heavenly horses[4].

Mithra also, the *yazata* of the rising daylight, rides on
horses and chariots. Four bright horses are yoked to his
car. So he mounts over the bordering eastern mountain
ranges, the *Hara-berzati*, and first embracing with his light
the highest summits, he irradiates the whole Arian land.

The notion that the *yazatas* of the sun and light drive in
chariots, must be traced to the remotest antiquity. I will
only mention Eos and Helios, and will recall to your minds
the Indian myths. Both Açvins, the light-bearers of the
morning, the sons of heaven, ride on horses. A splendidly
decorated car drawn by white horses and oxen carries up
to heaven the Ushas, or Dawn, until at length the Sūrya, the
flaming god of the sun, appears himself every day driving
his light-coloured horses along the wide vault of heaven[5].

A friendship, a closer connection, exists between the Sun
and the Moon[6]. If that is the star of the day, this is the

---

[1] *Rv.* I, 50, 6; I, 115, 1; VI, 51, 1; VII, 63, 1.—Darmesteter,
Ormazd et Ahriman, p. 43 seq., particularly p. 50.

[2] Ys. XXXVI, 6; LVIII, 8.   [3] Yt. VI, 4.

[4] Hence the epithet *aurvat-aspa* 'with swift horses,' Vd. XXI, 5;
Ys. XVI, 4; Yt. VI, 1, XII, 34.

[5] *Kaegi, Der Rig-veda* p. 35 seq.

[6] Moon *maogh;—yazāi · hakhedhremcha · yat · asti · hakhedhranām ·

luminary of the night. Her waxing and waning is the most striking phenomenon connected with the moon. Fifteen days, it is said, the moon grows, and fifteen days she diminishes[1]. Speaking correctly, the time from one phase of the moon to the return of the same phase is known to amount to twenty-nine days and twelve and three-quarter hours (the synodical month). The Avesta, therefore, distinguishes between full-moon and new-moon[2]. That is certainly the most primitive form of chronology, which combines the calculation by days with the calculation by the changes of the moon. The time which elapses between two consecutive full-moon or new-moon days is fixed at thirty days in round numbers and divided into two halves, the period of increasing and that of decreasing.

A mysterious influence on the growth of plants was ascribed to the moon. When her mild light is shining in spring, gold-coloured herbs grow up from the earth[3]. It may be that the epithet 'containing cattle-seed[4],' which is often applied to the moon, denotes an analogous influence on the fertility and increase of herds. The later tradition, it is true, explains the name in a rationalistic way by relating that, after the death of the primeval ox, the moon preserved his seed and procreated by means of it the different kinds of cattle.

The Stars in their regular unchangeable course are the very prototype of cosmic order. For this reason they are said to be the garment of Asha-vahishta, the genius of the order of the world[5].

The planets are reputed wicked hurtful stars, since they seem to mar the cosmic order. The army of fixed stars is arrayed in the sky to fight them. That the spirits of dead men were brought into contact with the stars has been stated already before.

---

*vahi*shtem · *añtare* · *māoğhemcha* · *hvarecha*—Yt. VI, 5. About the veneration of the moon *vide* Spiegel, *E. A.* vol. ii, p. 70.

[1] Yt. VII, 2.

[2] *Añtare-māoğhāoscha* · *perenō-māoğhāoscha*, Yt. VII, 4.

[3] Yt. VII, 4.

[4] *Gao-chithra*, Yt. VII, 1, 3, &c.   [5] Yt. III, 1.

The most important and powerful stars or constellations
are Tishtrya, Satavaisa, the Pleiades, and the star Vanat
'the victorious.' The first is reckoned lord of the Eastern
quarter of the heavens, the second lord of the West, the
third of the North, and the fourth of the South. The
Pleiades are seldom mentioned in the Avesta[1]; in the
later Scriptures of the Parsees they appear as the noblest
and first of all constellations[2]. Corresponding with them
is the Vanat, that dominates the southern sky. I take it
to be Fomalhaut in the constellation Pisces. It is believed
to be the chief enemy of the Khrafstra, the whole vermin-
kind, which were created by the Evil Spirit for the punishment of man[3].

Tishtrya is, beyond all doubt, Sirius, the dog-star.
Plutarch bears testimony that it was held in high veneration by the Persians[4]. It is the 'first' of all constellations[5], the brilliant, bright star, that does not remain
visible to the eye during the whole year. We shall best
understand the Tishtrya-myths by calling to mind the
times at which Sirius rises and sets.

In latitude 38° North—approximately the latitude of
Moru (Merv)—the following are the results obtained for
Sirius in the year 1000 before Christ[6]:

1st May, rises: 8h. 50m. forenoon; sets: 6h. 54m. evening.

1st June	„	6h. 50m.	„	„	4h. 54m. afternoon.
1st July	„	4h. 50m.	„	„	2h. 54m.	„
1st Aug.	„	2h. 50m. night;		„	12h. 54m. mid-day.
1st Sept.	„	12h. 50m.	„	„	10h.54m.forenoon&c.

Thus Sirius rises, between June and July, at the same

---

[1] Yt. XII, 28, XIII, 60: *hapto-iriṅga*=(*sapta*) ṛkshāḥ in the
Rig-veda.

[2] So in *Mkh.*; cf. also Spiegel, *E.A*, vol. ii, p. 74, note 1.

[3] Cf. Yt. 20.

[4] *De Iside* 47; ἕνα δ᾽ ἀστέρα οἶον φύλακα καὶ προόπτην ἐγκατέστησε
τὸν Σείριον. I here renounce the quite erroneous identification of
Tishtrya with the morning-star (*vide* my *Handbuch*, p. 134).

[5] *Poirya*—Yt. VIII, 12, if this does not designate a peculiar star.

[6] I owe these calculations to the kindness of Professor Noether.
of Erlangen.

time with the sun, becomes first visible in the morning sky towards the end of July, appears in August before sunrise in full brightness, and remains visible the whole night during November.

Quite similar results appear at the same latitude for the year 650 before Christ; but Sirius stays 4 minutes longer above the horizon; it rises, in general, later by 13 minutes and sets 17 minutes later:

1st May,	rises:	9 h. 3 m. forenoon;	sets:	7 h. 11 m.	evening.
1st June	„	7 h. 3 m.	„	„ 5 h. 11 m.	„
1st July	„	5 h. 3 m.	„	„ 3 h. 11 m.	afternoon.
1st Aug.	„	3 h. 3 m.	„	„ 1 h. 11 m.	„
1st Sept.	„	1 h. 3 m. night;		„ 11 h. 11 m.	midday.
1st Dec.	„	7 h. 3 m. evening;		„ 5 h. 11 m.	morning.

In the calendar of the Avesta to Tishtrya is dedicated the fourth month, which falls between June and July, exactly during the time in which Sirius rises together with the sun. Under these circumstances the insertion of the Tishtrya-month cannot be regarded as a mere accident [1].

The veneration of Sirius, which, being the brightest star in the Northern sky, attracted at all times the attention of man, is apparently founded on the fact, that it shines in the firmament just at the time of the greatest solar heat, and that this heat diminishes in proportion as Sirius remains longer above the horizon, and as the time of his rising advances. This coincidence was in course of time looked upon as that of cause and effect. Sirius is reputed an adversary of the demons, who create the insupportable heat of the Irānian summer. From this star the enlivening rains are expected. Men and beasts await and yearn for its coming [2]:

'To Tishtrya, the bright sparkling star, we bring veneration:

'Whom the waters remember, stagnant and flowing waters, they that are in fountains and streams, the raining and pond-waters.

---

[1] Cf. Roth, *ZddmG.* vol. xxxiv, p. 713.
[2] Yt. VIII, 48; Cf. Yt. VIII, 5.

'When will arise for us Tishtrya, the shining, sparkling? When will the horse-strong fountains abound
with running waters?
'The beauteous; that over lands and fields and over
meadows are streaming. Then the sprouts of herbs
will rise with vigorous growth [1].'

The central point of the Tishtrya-myth is his combat against
the demon Apausha 'the burner.' Ten nights, so runs the
legend [2], Tishtrya makes his appearance in the shape of a
youth of fifteen, ten nights in the shape of a gold-horned
bull, and ten nights in that of a fallow-horse. Then his
adversary Apausha comes to meet him in the form of a
black horse, hairless on his tail, back and ears. Three
days and three nights they fight with each other. At first
Tishtrya is vanquished. But at last he succeeds, with the
help of Ahura Mazda, in conquering and driving away his
antagonist.

This legend, too, is explained by the real conditions of
Sirius. It is not immediately after the arrival of this star
that the heat diminishes; on the contrary, just at this time,
at the end of July and the beginning of August, it reaches
its highest degree. Vegetation grows dry and colourless,
the earth 'bare' and 'black,' moisture is more or less
evaporated. This is the time, during which Tishtrya is not
yet strong enough to vie with his adversary. Its duration is
30 days, at the termination of which begins the three days'
battle, that ends with Apausha's being routed. So the
diminution of heat falls, as it does in reality, in the last
days of August.

The Parikas are prominent adversaries of Tishtrya.
They, too, were represented as superhuman beings and
were specially connected with the shooting-stars. Tishtrya, therefore, is said to conquer the Parikas, that fly
about between heaven and earth as worm-stars [3].

---

[1] Yt. VIII, 41–42. Geldner, *Metrik*, § 96. I have accepted
Geldner's correction *aiwighzhārān* in the place of *aiwighzhārem*
(variant *aiwighzhārām*) in the second strophe.

[2] Yt. VIII, 13–34.   [3] Yt. VIII, 8.

The Evil Spirit has created the Parikas, that they may offer resistance to the rain-bestowing stars. One of them is peculiarly denominated the Parika of Scarcity[1]. When Tishtrya has routed wicked spirits,

'Then come forth the rainclouds bearing fertilizing water, clouds full of far-flying vapours, that are spreading far and wide, blessing the seven parts of the earth[2].'

This tradition, like the foregoing, finds its explanation in real phenomena. At the very time of the greatest heat, on the tenth of August, the earth traverses the meteoric swarm of the Perseides, and this night particularly abounds in shooting-stars. This phenomenon excited of course the liveliest interest, the more so as there existed at that time no second annual incident of the kind to claim attention. For the November swarm of the Leonides was, according to Leverrier's calculation, not before the year 126 after Christ compelled to enter into our solar system[3].

It was natural to think that the fall of meteors and the heat of the dog-days had some causal connection. But, since the appearance of Sirius falls in that period, the antagonism between this and the meteors, or as it is expressed in the dialect of mythology, between Tishtrya and the Parikas, was naturally suggested.

The companion of Tishtrya and his help-mate is the star Satavaisa. They work together principally in distributing moisture over the earth. The Fravashis let him wander between heaven and earth, that he may refresh, by the moisture of rain, men and beasts and plants[4]. Conformably to the opinion of the Parsees, he is lord and ruler of the Western sky, as Tishtrya is of the Eastern.

But here arises a difficulty. An explanation may easily be given of the popular opinion, which attributes the

---

[1] *Pairika · duzhyāirya.* Yt. VIII, 51.

[2] Yt. VIII, 40. *Urvāiti*sh should be read *uru-vāifi*sh as Geldner supposes (*Metrik*, § 57).

[3] Cf. Peschel, *Physische Erdkunde*, I, p. 114 seq.

[4] Yt. XIII, 43; see above, p. 118.

government of the South and the North each to a fixed star, according to its course. But how people happened to imagine that a star was reigning in the East or West is less easy to explain.

The idea cannot possibly have had its origin in observations of the general course of the star in question. It must rather start from a determined period of the year, during which this star is seen exactly in the East and correspondingly in the West. One thing must be granted : Satavaisa must be a star that, in its setting, is nearer the equator than either of the poles, consequently between North-West and South-East. Otherwise it could not be called ' Regent of the West.' It is, likewise, true that Sirius rises in the South-East.

Since Satavaisa is in every regard the counterpart of Tishtrya, I must return to it in order to define the latter. The time at which Tishtrya-Sirius develops its chief activity is Midsummer, or rather August. In this month it shines before sunrise in the Eastern sky.

We must, therefore, conclude that if Satavaisa is the counterpart of Tishtrya, it must stand at the same time, the beginning of August, *after sunset* in the West, in order to be reputed ruler of the West. So we arrive at the conclusion that Satavaisa must be identified with the star Antares in *Scorpio* [1]. Rising, in fact, on the first of August, between 1 and 2 in the afternoon, it is at 9 o'clock in the evening above the South-Western horizon and sets about an hour later.

But I think that Antares is no fit ruler of the West. At 38° North Latitude its course is too much in the South. Its culmination is only about 26 degrees above the horizon. We would rather give him a power similar to that of Fomalhaut which culminates at about 22 degrees.

The star Arcturus of *Bootes* seems to be more to our purpose. It is on the first of August at seven o'clock in the evening West-to-North in the sky and sets between 10 and 11. It culminates at 74 degrees more or less.

---

[1] So West, ' Pahlavi Texts,' part i, pp. 12–13 note.

In identifying Satavaisa with Antares or Arcturus, we always observe that at the time when it declines in the West, Fomalhaut is on the South-Eastern horizon, and Ursa Major low in the North-North-West.

But in determining Satavaisa I prefer by all means starting from another point of view. If Sirius is ruler of the East and Satavaisa of the West, both must stand at *the same time* in the sky, the former towards morning, the latter towards evening. So we must find for Satavaisa a star that shines in the Western sky *before sunrise in the beginning of August*. If this hypothesis is correct, Satavaisa and Wega in the constellation of Lyra must be one and the same star.

Wega rises on the 1st of August about noon and sets at four in the morning. So it is visible for a time together with Sirius. Hence results the surprising combination, that during this time Sirius is standing in the South-East, Fomalhaut in the South-West, Wega in the North-West near the horizon, and the stars Mizar and Alioth, ϵ and ζ of Ursa Major, almost exactly in the North. Thus we have four governors of the four points of the compass at the same time in the firmament, and the whole doctrine concerning them clears up in a most simple way from real circumstances, when we take as a starting-point the period in which Sirius, without doubt the most prominent of the four, shows its greatest activity and efficacy.

We can now understand that Tishtrya and Satavaisa are a closely connected couple. Sirius and Wega are two stars that may be said to relieve each other. When the former first appears in the morning sky, the latter is visible during the whole night. The more Sirius increases in brilliancy and the longer he remains in the sky, the more Wega decreases. Finally, on the first of December, when Sirius rises at seven in the evening and so remains visible all night, Wega disappears only an hour later below the North-Western horizon.

I shall not conclude without mentioning that in the names *Tishtryeni* and *Pauryeni* greater groups of stars are comprised [1]. Evidently they are in close correlation to *Tishtrya*

---

[1] Yt. VIII, 12.

or *Paurya*, by which denomination the same star is probably
meant; perhaps they are stars in his immediate neighbourhood.   We must further remark that the distribution of
water on the earth and the fostering of vegetation is not,
according to the view of the Avesta, the exclusive charge
and duty of Tishtrya and Satavaisa.   They are aided in
this by a whole body of stars, from which, as the Avesta
says, 'the water comes and the plants and the (fertile)
earth [1].'

---

§ 15. *Chronology and Calendar.*

IN describing the climatic conditions prevailing in the
dwelling-place of the Avesta people I remarked that, strictly
speaking, they divided their year into two parts only,
summer and winter [2].   Thus it is that we meet with a two-
fold calculation, by years and half-years [3].   Now I shall
demonstrate below that this fact is involved in the whole
arrangement of the calendar.

Though the dialect of the Avesta must be supposed
to have some distinct name for spring and originally one
also for the latter part of autumn [4], yet these periods of
transition are so short in Eastern Irān, that they were
entirely lost and merged in summer and winter.

The most prominent phenomenon was certainly the
winter with its intense and lasting cold.   Winter, therefore,
is used instead of 'year' in the dialect of the Avesta.   What

---

[1] *Stārō · āf*shch*ithra · urvarō-chithra · zemaschithra.*

[2] [Vide § 21 of *OKA*.]   *Yāre* or *saredha* 'year;' *zyāo* (*zim*)
or *aiwigāma* 'winter;' *hama* 'summer.'

[3] *Naęmem · yāre-drājō* and *yāre-drājō* are employed together in
Vd. III, 36 and 37; cf. Vd. VI, 1 and 43; V, 14.

[4] *Vaĝhra* 'spring' is indicated by Tomaschek (p. 20) as
employed in the Pamir dialects; *zaremaya* (Roth, *ZddmG*. vol.
xxxiv, pp. 702–703) means the same.   *Saredha* 'year'=Skr. *çarad*
'autumn' (in N. Pers. *sāl* 'year') seems to have also originally
denoted, in the dialect of the Avesta, 'the latter part of autumn' or
perhaps even 'winter,' because it appears (Vsp. II, 2) as an epithet
to *maidhyāirya*, ' the midwinter-day.'

observations may be drawn from this change of signification and analogous etymological facts in the Old-Indian dialect, I have already said before [1].

The Eastern Irānians looked upon the night as preceding the day. They reckoned, therefore, by nights, not by days. So the above-mentioned benediction of the fire, literally translated, runs in the following manner: 'In merry mind spend thy life, the nights which thou hast to live [2]!' This fact is of particular interest, since we find it also among the Indians, Germans, and Gauls [3]. From this similarity we might perhaps suppose that the custom of counting by nights existed in the very first ages of the Indo-Germanic race.

The month was employed to compute longer spaces of time, as, for instance, the pregnancy of women [4]. If the weather is bad, it is known that the body of dead people must not be brought to the *dakhma*. It must be kept for a time in a pit, *kata*, and is to remain here *two or three nights or a whole month together*, until the bad weather is gone [5].

If there is a dead body in any house, the fire must be directly removed from the hearth, that it may not be exposed to impurity. *Nine nights in winter and a month in summer* must pass by before it is permitted to bring it again into the house [6].

The Calendar of the Avesta has been often, in our time, the subject of accurate investigation [7]. Nevertheless I

---

[1] *Zim, zyāo* 'winter, year' (cf. also the foregoing note); see *OKA*. p. 144 seq.

[2] *Tāo · khshapanō*, Ys. LXII, 10; *vide supra*, p. 76. *Khshapan* 'night,' *ayare* 'day,' *ushaǧh* 'dawn, morning.'

[3] Zimmer, *AiL*. p. 360.

[4] Vd. V, 45 : *aęvō-māhīm, bimāhīm,* &c.

[5] *Bikhshaparem · vā · thrikhshaparem · vā · māzdrājahīm · vā,* Vd. V, 12 ; cf. also Vd. V, 54, 55, 56, &c.

[6] *Nava-khshaparem · upa-mānayen · aęlẹ̄ · yōi · Mazdayasna · aiwi-gāmẹ̄ · āat · hama · māzdrājahīm,* Vd. V, 42.

[7] Spiegel, *E.A.* vol. iii, p. 665 seq.; and again *ZddmG.* vol. xxxv, p. 642 seq.; Roth, *ZddmG.* vol. xxxiv, p. 698 seq. ; C. de Harlez,

hope to bring forward at least some new points and so to be allowed to enlarge in this place on its elucidation. The year was divided into 12 months of 30 days each, every month into two equal halves of fifteen days. The whole month is a period which elapses between two full or new moons (strictly 29½ days); half a month is the time between full-moon and new-moon. That the bipartition of the month must have been a very old custom will be proved below. Yet I think it very problematical to say that the people of the Avesta observed the week of seven days or that it was of any account in the business of civil life[1]. At any rate it was of course necessary to use a week of seven and of eight days alternately, since the month had 30 days.

The names of the months are, it is true, nowhere completely enumerated in the Avesta. But those that are mentioned in our texts[2] agree fully with the list of the calendar met with in the later Scriptures of the Parsees. So we are entitled to suppose that they were known as far back as the Avesta, and to insert them here without hesitation :

1st Month :	*Fravashinām*	. .	Farvardīn.
2nd „	*Ashahē-vahishtahē*		Ardabihisht.
3rd „	*Haurvatātō*	. . .	Khordād.
4th „	*Tishtryęhę*	. . .	Tīr.
5th „	*Ameretātō*	. . .	Amurdād.
6th „	*Khshathrahē-vāiryęhę*		Shahrēvar.
7th „	*Mithrahę*	. . .	Mihir.
8th „	*Apām*	. . . .	Ābān.
9th „	*Āthrō*	. . . .	Ādar.

Bulletin de l'Athénée Oriental, 1881, p. 79 seq., p. 159 seq.   I regret that I have not been able to read the Essay of Bezzenberger ; I know it only from quotations.

[1] This hypothesis is based only upon the use of the expression *vīshaptatha,* which is interpreted by Roth (l. c. 710, note 1) as 'between-seven' and translated by 'week.'

[2] These are the months *Asha-vahishta, Tishtrya, Khshathravarya, Mithra, Dathuō* i.e. 'of the Creator' (*Trad.* 'of the Law'), and *Spentā Ārmati.* Westergaard, 'Zend Texts,' p. 318 seq. Spiegel, *Av. üb.* vol. iii, p. 239 seq.

10th Month: *Dathushō* . . . . Dīn (better ' Creator ').
11th   „   *Vaɡhǫush Manaɡhō*   Bahman.
12th   „   *Spentayāo Ārmatōish* Spendārmad.

The order of the names is, as justly remarked by Roth, very striking. We should naturally think that Ahura Mazda, the Creator, would stand foremost, that after Him the other Amesha Spenta would follow in the usual order, and finally Mithra, Tishtrya, Āpō, Ātar, Fravashi. I must, however, confess that I have not found any satisfactory solution of the problem, and must, therefore, leave it to some more fortunate student.

Roth starts with the theory, that the tenth month must have formed originally the beginning of the year; thus the names of the other Amesha Spenta are, says he, in their due order, save that succeeding couples are separated by the insertion of the Fravashis and Tishtrya. The insertion of the former, he continues, must be accounted for by the fact that a sacred and solemn feast of the *manes* could not be removed from its fixed place in the year, while Tishtrya had a strong foothold in the time of the rising of Sirius.

There can be no doubt that much is explained by this hypothesis, yet many a difficulty still remains. As yet we know not why Spentā Ārmati follows immediately after Vohu-manō and Khshathra-varya stands last of all the Amesha Spenta, and certainly there must also be reasons for this fact. Finally, we should think it more natural that the feast of the manes, Hamaspatmaidhaya, fell in the month of the Fravashis, as the calculation of the calendar demands, rather than in the intercalary days inserted before it.

The day-names are also nowhere distinctly enumerated in the Avesta, yet there is in the Yasna a list. of genii completely agreeing with the day-list found in the traditional Scriptures of the Parsees[1]. This is no accident. The author of that passage evidently named the genii on

---

[1] Ys. XVI, 3 seq.; cf. Sir. I and II ; Spiegel, *E. A.* vol. iii, p. 667. Several names, viz. those of the 11th, 15th, 16th, 20th, 26th and 30th days, are also mentioned in the passage of the Avesta cited above (p. 144, note 2).

purpose after the order in which they rank in the calendar. The list runs as follows :

1. *Ahurahę̄ Mazdāo* . . .	Ormazd		
2. *Vağhēush Manağhō* .	. Bahman		
3. *Ashahę̄ vahishtahę̄* .	. Ardabihisht	The seven
4. *Khshathrahę̄ vairyęhę̄*	. Shahrēvar	Amsha-
5. *Spentayāo Ārmatōish*	. Spendārmad	spands.
6. *Haurvatātō*	Khordād	
7. *Ameretātō*	Amerdād	
8. *Dathushō*	Dīn[1], (probably) Creator.
9. *Āthrō*	Ādar . . . . Fire.
10. *Apãm*	Ābān. . . . Waters.
11. *Hvare-khshaętahę̄* . .	. Khorshēd . . Sun.
12. *Māoğhō*	Māh . . . . Moon.
13. *Tishtryęhę̄*	Tīr . . . . Sirius.
14. *Gēush*	Gōsh . . . . the Beasts.
15. *Dathushō*.	Dīn[1], (probably) Creator.
16. *Mithrahę̄*	Mihir. . . . Mithra.
17. *Sraoshahę̄*	Srōsh. . . . Srausha.
18. *Rashnaosh*	. Rashnu . . . Rashnu.
19. *Fravashinãm* . . .	. Farvardin . . the *Manes.*
20. *Verethraghnahę̄* . .	. Behrām . . . Vethraghna.
21. *Rāmanō*	. Rām . . . . Rāman.
22. *Vātahę̄*	. Vāt . . . . Wind.
23. *Dathushō*	. Dīn[1], (probably) Creator.
24. *Daęnayāo*	. Dīn . . . . the Law.
25. *Ashōish*	. Ard . . . . Ashi.
26. *Arshtātō*	. Ashtād . . . Arshtāt.
27. *Asmanō*	. Asmān . . . Heaven.
28. *Zemō*	. Zamyād. . . Earth.
29. *Māthrahę̄ Spentahę̄*	. . Māhrspand . . the Holy Word.
30. *Anaghranãm-raochağhãm* Anīrān . . . the 'Lights Without Beginning,' i. e. the Stars.

---

[1] [Rather *Dai-ja-Ādar*, *Dai-pa-Mihir*, *Dai-pa-Dīn*, Dai=Pers. دى, 'yesterday.' The eighth, fifteenth, and twenty-third days of the month are dedicated to Ahura Mazda, like the first day. They are, therefore, named from the day that follows. *Tr. note.*]

There must still be added the five intercalary days that are every year inserted in order to bring the solar and lunar years into harmony. They are dedicated to the five Gāthās or collections of holy hymns. The first and the last of them are mentioned in a recently quoted passage of the Avesta:

1. *Gāthayāo ahunavaithyāo*,
2. *Gāthayāo ushtavaithyāo*,
3. *Gāthayāo speñtāmainivāo*,
4. *Gāthayāo vohu-khshathrayāo*,
5. *Gāthayāo vahishtōishtōish.*

The list of names of days is in perfect order, yet it must occasion surprise that the day Dathush occurs three times. This might perhaps be explained by the fact, that the month of thirty fixed days of the solar year was preceded by a lunar month of varying length. If we divide the month into its natural halves of fifteen days each, we see that the first half begins with the day of Ahura Mazda, and terminates with that of the Creator; besides that in the very middle of each half-month an additional day, Dathushō, is inserted and proves superfluous by its very position. In my opinion there existed at first settled names only for twice fourteen days. As the synodical month had only twenty-nine days and a half, it was necessary that months of twenty-nine and thirty days should alternate. If needed, an intercalary day could be inserted in the middle of the first or the second half of the month, or in each of them, to keep pace with the lunar phases in the computation of time. Nor can it appear at all strange that these intercalated days were dedicated to the Creator.

During the transition from the lunar to the solar calendar, it was natural that the month of thirty days soon became the standard of calculation. The intercalary days had their settled fixed places as well as the other days. Now it led to no practical disadvantage that the month was not always conformable to the changes of the moon, for it had lost its original value and served only as a convenient subdivision of the year, which is too long for the wants of civil life.

The Irānian year had also its regularly recurring feasts [1]. In the first place, as stated by the Parsees, those days in every month were held sacred which had the same names as the months in which they fell. In the first month the nineteenth day (since it is dedicated to the *manes*); in the second month the third day; in the third month the sixteenth day; in the fourth month the thirteenth day; in the fifth month the seventh day; in the sixth month the fourth day; in the seventh month the sixteenth day; in the eighth month the tenth day; in the ninth month the ninth day; in the tenth month the first day, perhaps also the eighth, fifteenth and twenty-third; in the eleventh month the second day; in the twelfth month the fifth day.

To these days are to be added the six principal feasts, the so-called GĀHANBĀRS, which are annexed, as Roth justly remarks, to the different seasons, and their importance for civil life. But I cannot believe that their names were originally the names of the seasons. I should prefer to think that they became such in later times. The names of the annual feasts are:

1. MAIDHYŌ-ZAREMAYA, in the month of Asha-vahishta on the day of Dathushō before Mithra (the fifteenth day of the second month).
2. MAIDHYŌSHEMA, in the month of Tishtrya on the day of Dathushō before Mithra (the fifteenth day of the fourth month).
3. PAITSH-HAHYA, in the month of Khshathra-varya on the day of Anaghranãm (the thirtieth day of the sixth month).
4. AYĀTHREMA, in the month of Mithra on the day of Anaghranãm (the thirtieth day of the seventh month).
5. MAIDHYĀIRYA, in the month of Dathushō on the day of Verthraghna (the twentieth day of the tenth month).
6. HAMASPATMAEDHAYA, on the day of Vahishtōishti, and thus on the last of the five intercalary days [2].

---

[1] *Yāriya · ratavō*, literally 'yearly times.'
[2] Ys. I, 9; II, 9; Visp. I, 2; Āfr. Gāhanbār, 7 seq. The opinion

Each of these feasts comprises five days, so that the principal *dies solemnis* falls on the last of them. The feast Hamaspatmaidhaya extends, therefore, over all the intercalary days; the feast Madhyō-zarmaya lasted in the second month from the eleventh to the fifteenth day; the feast Madhyōshma, in the fourth month, likewise from the eleventh to the fifteenth day; the feast Maidhyārya, in the tenth month, from the sixteenth to the twentieth day. And so, too, the other feasts.

It is possible that the prolonged duration of these holidays, as well as their later relation to the six periods of creation, is nothing but an addition of more modern times. The first feast is designed to celebrate the creation of the heavens, the second that of water, the third of the earth, the fourth the creation of plants, the fifth that of animals, and the sixth the creation of man. It cannot be denied that this connection of the annual feasts with the history of creation cannot be regarded as an invention of the priests thus to render the Gāhanbārs more venerable. Originally they were certainly nothing but rural feasts, and, therefore, originated in rural life.

This is proved both by the meanings of the names given to the several feasts, and by the epithets which they receive in the Avesta.

Madhyō-zarmaya denotes ' midspring,' Madhyōshma 'midsummer,' Madhyārya 'midwinter' or, more accurately, 'midyear.' The first is called the time of blossoming, the second the time of the hay crop, the third the autumn or winter time [1]. Patish-hahya is generally understood as the

---

of Roth, that we have old names of the seasons in the *Gāhanbārs*, is contradicted, I think, by his own etymologies. If *maidhyō-shema* means ' midsummer,' *maidhyō-saremaya* 'midspring' and *maidhyāirya* ' midwinter,' then these names can only denote originally certain single days. That it may be implied from the epithet *saredha* added to *maidhyāirya*, that in later times these names came to signify seasons, is quite erroneously explained by Roth. It means ' year,' perhaps originally ' autumn,' ' late autumn,' about the last period before midwinter-day.

[1] Vsp. I, 2, *maidhyō-zaremaya payaŋha, maidhyōshema vāstrō-*

time of the corn crop, harvest time, and so is fitly called 'corn-bearing[1].' Ayāthrema is, according to Roth's ingenious exposition, the time in which the cattle return from the mountain-pastures into the valleys, and the rams are allowed to go to the ewes[2]. The explanation of the name Hamaspatmaidhaya offers the greatest difficulty. In the opinion of Roth this is the time in which the farmer makes his preparations for the sowing. I would rather adopt the opinion of C. de Harlez in referring this name to the great feast of the *manes* and the solemn preparations for it[3].

The Gāhanbārs have in Afrīn-e-Gāhanbār each its peculiar number. The first number signifies the anniversary on which the first feast falls, each additional number the interval between the feast in question and the one previous. All these numbers must, therefore, make up:

1.	Madhyō-zarmaya	.	.	.	45
2.	Madhyōshma	.	.	.	60
3.	Patish-hahya	.	.	.	75
4.	Ayāthrema	.	.	.	30
5.	Madhyārya	.	.	.	80
6.	Hamaspatmaidhaya	.	.	.	75
					───
	Total	.	.	.	365

Assuming that Madhyōshma must fall on midsummer-

---

dūlainya, maidhyāirya saredha (*vide* p. 146 of *OKA.*). Spiegel and Hübschmann have recently pointed out (*ZddmG.* vol. xxxv, pp. 643 and 665–666) that *maidhyōshema* can have no connection with *hama*, and that the *maidhyō-shad* quoted by Roth as analogous to it is merely a misreading for *maidhyōi-shad.*

[1] *Paitish-hahya* (cf. also the correct explanation in Spiegel, *Av. üb.* vol. ii, pp. 7–8, de Harlez, *Av. tr.* vol. ii, p. 34, and Bezzenberger in *ZddmG.* vol. xxxv, p. 643) from *hahya*=Skr. *sasya* + *paiti* (as *paiti-puthra, paitish-ayag̃h*).

[2] *Ayāthrema · fraourvaeshīra · varshni-harshīa* ; the former from *āyāthra*=Skr. *ājātra* from root *yā*+*ā* ; *fraourvaeshīra* from root *urvis* (certainly not identical with *vṛt* !) + *fra* ; *varshni-harshīa* from *varshni*=Skr. *vṛshan*+*harez* 'to let loose '=Skr. *sṛj.*

[3] *Hamaspatmaḍdhaya · aretō-kerethna* ; the former is not easily to be explained, the latter is certainly from *areta*=*asha*+*kerethna* from root *kar.*

day, the twenty-first of June, Roth has made out that the old Irānian year began on the ninth of March, since the one hundred and fifth day of the year was fixed for this feast. If this calculation cannot be said to be absolutely certain, since the assumption on which it is based can be considered only hypothetical, it appears at any rate most probable. Besides, it is quite in unison with the statements of the Parsees, who say that the first month corresponds to March, the second to April, &c.

Hence result the following dates for each month;

1. Farvardin . . 9th March — 7th April.
2. Ardabihisht . 8th April — 7th May.
3. Khordād . . 8th May — 6th June.
4. Tīr . . . . 7th June — 6th July.
5. Amerdād . . 7th July — 5th August.
6. Shahrēvar . . 6th August — 4th September.
7. Mihir . . . 5th September — 4th October.
8. Ābān . . . 5th October — 3rd November.
9. Ādar . . . 4th November — 3rd December.
10. Dīn . . . . 4th December — 2nd January.
11. Bahman . . 3rd January — 1st February.
12. Spendārmad . 2nd February — 3rd March.

The five intercalary days, 4th–8th March.

The annual feasts are celebrated as follows:

1. Madhyō-zarmaya . on the (18th —) 22nd April.
2. Madhyōshma. . . „ (17th —) 21st June.
3. Patish-haya . . . „ (31st Aug.—) 4th September.
4. Ayāthrema . . . „ (30th Sept.—) 4th October.
5. Madhyārya . . . „ (19th —) 23rd December.
6. Hamaspatmaidhaya „ (4th —) 8th March.

We have thus fixed the year as it originally stood in the Avesta Calendar. It is a moveable year; and, consisting only of 365 days, it must every fourth year fall one day in arrears when compared with the solar year. It is no part of my task to solve the question how this inconvenience was obviated, since I am only obliged to prove the original institution of the fixed year[1].

---

[1] Cf. Von Gutschmid *Über das Iranische Jahr* in the ' Transac-

The calendar of the Avesta has resulted, as one may observe at a glance, from a combination of solar and lunar chronology. I shall now attempt to describe the manner of this combination.

The month of thirty days, employed in the solar year, was evidently preceded by a quite primitive mode of calculation from one new-moon or full-moon to another, or more probably from new-moon to full-moon, and again from full-moon to new. This is indicated, as I have said already[1], by the arrangement of the days, particularly by the repeated use of the day Dathushō, which became necessary on account of the variability of the synodical month.

Additional proof of the originally lunar character of the Avesta calendar is afforded by the numbers which indicate the intervals between the several Gāhanbārs.

Spiegel has observed that all these numbers are divisible by five[2]. Hence he concludes that the Gāhanbārs belong to a calendar in which every week consists of five days. However I cannot agree with this conclusion, since a week of five days is rather uncommon.

I am convinced that the Gāhanbār numbers are based on the synodical half-month of fifteen days; this half-month must be regarded as the basis of the whole chronology in general. This I infer from the fact that all those numbers are multiples of fifteen.

The number of the Madhyārya-feast seems to form an exception. But even here the seeming difficulty is overcome in the simplest manner, by resolving 80 into $75 + 5$, i.e. into five half-months and five intercalary days.

The Gāhanbār numbers further show clearly that the year was divided into two half-years:

1. $45 + 60$ $\qquad + 75 = 180$
2. $30 + 75 (+ 5)$ $\quad + 75 = 180 (185)$.

Probably the half-year was more employed in civil life than the complete year. Being a shorter period it was

---

tions of the Scientific Society of Saxony,' 1862, 1 seq.; Spiegel, *E. A.* vol. iii, pp. 669—670.

[1] *Vide supra* p. 147.   [2] *ZddmG.* vol. xxxv, p. 645, note 2.

more convenient for calculations and agreed moreover with the generally known and popular division of the year into summer and winter. This may be seen from the very distribution of the Gāhanbārs over these half-years :

1. Madhyō-zarmaya,   2. Ayāthrema,
   Madhyōshma,   *Madhyārya*,
   Patish-haya,   Hamaspatmaidhaya.

It is evident that each of the two solstices forms the centre and turning point of a half year, so that, indeed, the first more or less corresponds with the warm, the second with the cold season.

But we can trace the calendar to a still more primitive form. Since the name Madhyārya means literally not ' midwinter,' but ' midyear,' the year must necessarily have once begun with the summer solstice, or still more correctly with the day next following. Only in this case the *Bruma* (or the winter solstice) forms also the middle of the year.

But since the Madhyārya itself is associated with the number 80, we might justly conclude that along with the combination of the lunar and solar calendars the five intercalary days of the winter solstice have been inserted. The oldest calendar may be, therefore, thus arranged :

1st Month : 22nd June — 21st July,
2nd   „   22nd July — 20th August,
3rd   „   21st August — 19th September,
4th   „   20th September — 19th October,
5th   „   20th October — 18th November,
6th   „   19th November — 18th December.
     Intercalary days 19th — 23rd December.
7th Month : 24th December — 22nd January,
8th   „   23rd January — 21st February,
9th   „   22nd February — 23rd March,
10th   „   24th March — 22nd April,
11th   „   23rd April — 22nd May,
12th   „   23rd May — 21st June.

Here the winter solstice forms, indeed, the centre of the whole year ; for the 21st of December falls exactly on the middle of the intercalary days.

The intercalary days and the additional days of the synodical month may both have been dedicated to Ahura Mazda, the 'Creator'; and now we have, I think, arrived at the point, proceeding from which we can explain why the month falling about the winter solstice was called DATHUSHŌ.

The whole calendar was, therefore, calculated from the winter solstice, the original centre of the year; it was afterwards put back by 105 days, and, indeed, in such a manner that the intercalary days also were no longer inserted at the time of the winter solstice but before the beginning of the new year. The reason lay evidently in the fact that the official, I should like to say the ecclesiastical, calendar was to be brought in harmony with the popular division of the year into a winter and a summer half-year. This could only be done by putting the winter and summer solstices, which had always before formed the division between the two half-years, almost in the middle of them.

What may have really occasioned this alteration of the calendar, I cannot say; however I am satisfied with having made an attempt at reducing the calendar of the Avesta to its primitive form as far as possible.

Finally, the divisions of the day are still to be treated of.

The Avesta recognizes five parts of the day[1]. They are called in due order: 1) HĀVANI, 2) RAPITHWINA, 3) UZAYERINA, 4) AWISRUTHREMA, 5) USHAHINA[2]. The second is, here at least, without doubt midday, for its name serves, just as in our languages, to denote the southern sky[3]. About, or till the time Rapithwina, Tishtrya and Apausha fight against each other[4]. This, it is true, is very strange, since Tishtrya is an astral *yazata*. But the recollection of this fact had apparently disappeared, before the idea was formed.

---

[1] *Asnya raiavō* or *ayara raiavō.*

[2] *Hāvani, Rapithwina, Uzayçirina, Aiwisruthrema* with the constant epithet *aibigaya,* and *Ushahina.* *Vide* Ys. I, 3 seq., II, 3 seq. (here are also the names of the genii to whom the single parts of the day are consecrated), Gāh. I–V.

[3] *Vide supra* p. 133. The name seems to be connected with *pitu* 'food.'

[4] Yt. VIII, 25.

And if the feud between Tishtrya and Apausha symbolizes only the opposition between the cool weather after summer and the heat of summer, the time of midday seems to be very appropriately selected.

At the same time takes place the combat between Kersāspa and the dragon :

> On him (the dragon) did Kersāspa cook in the iron kettle his meat *about the time of midday*, and the dragon grew hot and began to sweat; and he burst forth from beneath the kettle and poured out the boiling water, and affrighted started back the manly-hearted Kersāspa [1].

Moreover, there cannot be any doubt that *Ushahina* must be *the time about dawn* [2]. In the same way we learn from the signification of the name itself that *Uzayerina* is that hour of the day in which the stars rise, i.e. *the evening* [3].

Hāvani comes between Ushahina and Rapithwina and is, consequently, *the forenoon*. This period is so named probably from the circumstance [4] that in it the sacrificial ceremonies are performed and in particular the sacred *hauma* beverage is prepared. For this reason the Yazata Hauma visits Zaratushtra at the time Hāvani, just as he is going to purify the fireplace. Finally, the time *Awisruthrema* falls between Uzayerina and Ushahina, and is, therefore, *the midnight*, the time for being watchful and wakeful [5].

Now we shall see that the genii to whom the single parts of the day are consecrated, are by no means arbitrarily chosen, but stand in real, and for the most part clear, relation to the several periods which they preside over.

---

[1] Yt. IX, 11; Yt. XIX, 40.

[2] From *ushaĝh*=Skr. *ushas* 'dawn.'

[3] *Uzayçirina* is derived from *uzayara*; it is used (Vd. XXI, 5, 9, 13) for the rising of the sun, moon and stars (from root *ir + uz*).

[4] *Hāvani* from rt. *hu*=Skr. *su*.

[5] *Aiwisruthrema* evidently comes from *aiwisruthra*, 'watch, guard' (from root *sru + aiwi*=Skr. *abhi-çru*); comp. *ayāthrema* from *āyāthra*.

Ushahina belongs to Srausha.   He is reputed the genius of wakefulness, and it is his duty at early morning to awaken mankind from slumber and to chase away the demon of sleep.   He is aided in his task by his herald, Chanticleer (the domestic cock).

Hāvani, or the forenoon, is under the care of Mithra, because he is the yazata of the rising and heaven-ascending sun.   Sunrise seems to have been considered, at least in later times, the beginning of the day, and not midday; for *Hāvani* opens the dance or circular course of day.   At an earlier period the night was thought to precede the day, and hence people were accustomed to reckon time by nights.

Awisruthrema is ruled by the *manes,* who guard human kind at this time, and the genii, e. g. Valour, Victory, and Superiority, by whose aid nightly dangers are warded off. Noon, finally, is consecrated to the genius of fire, and evening to that of water.

§ 16.   *Religion and Superstition.*

WE cannot omit in this place one of the highest spiritual gifts of mankind—Religion.   The position in which a people place themselves with regard to their Deity is without doubt an important phenomenon in their intellectual life and is characteristic of their manner of viewing things.

And yet I must restrict my remarks to what is indispensable.   The religion of the Avesta and the ideas connected with the different genii have already been described by several authors.   A new and exhaustive description would afford sufficient matter for a special investigation and would at present lead us too far from our task.   I must, therefore, content myself with touching upon some peculiarities of the Avesta religion, illustrative of its spirit and intrinsic excellence.

In comparing the religion of the Avesta with that of the closely related Vedic Indians, a radical difference will force itself upon our observation [1].

---

[1] [Compare the following remarks of Mr. William D. Whitney (Professor of Sanskrit and Comparative Philology in Yale College)

In the Rig-veda it would be difficult to say who appears as the principal deity; Varuna and Indra are known to be represented as fighting for the ascendancy. And, besides, to every poet that god appears the most great, powerful

---

in his Chapter on 'The Avesta.' *Vide* 'Oriental and Linguistic Studies,' p. 191 :

'The Zoroastrian religion is one of the most prominent among the forms of belief which have prevailed upon the earth, by reason both of the influence which it has exerted and of its own intrinsic character. . . . The later Jewish faith is believed by many to exhibit evident traces of Zoroastrian doctrines, borrowed during the captivity in Babylonia; and the creeds of some Oriental Christian sects, as well as of a portion of the adherents of Islam, have derived essential features from the same source. But the influence which its position only gave it the opportunity of exercising, was assured to it by its own exalted character. Of all the religions of Indo-European origin, of all the religions of the ancient gentile world, it may fairly be claimed to have been the most noble and worthy of admiration, for the depth of its philosophy, the spirituality of .its views and doctrines, and the purity of its morality. Valuable notices respecting it had been given by the classical writers, yet they had been altogether insufficient to convey a clear view even of its then condition in the western provinces to which it had spread, much less to illustrate its origin, and the history of its development in the land of its birth. Had the Avesta no other merit than that of laying before us a full picture of the ancient Persian religion, it would be a document of incalculable value to the student of antiquity.'

Also compare Rev. Dr. Mitchell on the merits of Zoroastrianism, in his short tract on 'The Zend-Avesta,' pp. 49–50 :

'There are several characteristics which entitle the Zoroastrian faith to a high place among Gentile systems of religion. (1) It ascribes no immoral attributes to the object of worship. Ahura Mazda, the supreme divinity, stands ethically much higher than the popular gods of Pagan nations generally. The Avesta, as we have seen, retains much of nature-worship; but evil qualities are never ascribed either to the physical object or the being who presides over it. (2) The Avesta sanctions no immoral acts as a part of worship. (3) None of the prescribed forms of worship is marked by cruelty. (4) In the great contest between light and darkness, the Avesta exhorts the true worshipper not to remain

and venerable, to whom his songs are addressed. To him he ascribes all the qualities and powers which make up, in his opinion, the nature of the Deity. In the Avesta, on the contrary, rank and order are minutely and exactly established.

As the chief of the whole world, visible and invisible, ranks Ahura Mazda. He is the Creator and Lord of the Universe, no one equals him in honour and power. Next to Him rank, as the highest of the genii, the six Amesha Spenta : Vohu-manō, Asha-vahishta, Khshathra-varya, Spentā-Ārmati, Harvatāt, and Amertāt. To each of them a peculiar sphere of activity and dominion in this visible world is allotted. To Vohu manō is confided the protection of beasts, perhaps originally of mankind too, to Asha the care of fire, to Khshathra of metals, to Ārmati of the earth, and to the two last of water and of plants. The Amesha Spenta are followed by the *yasatas*, the great host of inferior genii, among whom Mithra, Anāhita, and others are prominent.

With the same systematic accuracy and uniformity is the empire of the evil spirits organized. The first of the demons, the counterpart of Ahura in everything, is Angra Manyu, who is all death. Round him are grouped, next in

---

passive, but to contend with all his might against the productions of the Evil Principle. (5) One remarkable characteristic of the system is the absence of image-worship. (6) The Avesta never despairs of the future of humanity ; it affirms the final victory of good over evil.

'In regard to all these points there is a striking difference between Zoroastrianism and Hinduism. It is not easy to explain how the former system struggled successfully against that fatal gravitation downwards, which made primitive Hinduism sink deeper and deeper in the mire ; but the fact, at all events, is undeniable.

'Assuredly, we have no wish to undervalue the importance of the great characteristics of Zoroastrianism that have now been mentioned ; and we might point to yet other merits, such as (7) its encouragement of agriculture, (8) its inculcation of truth in thought. word, and deed, (9) the position of respect it assigns to women. and (10) the kindness towards, at least, Zoroastrians which it inculcates.' *Tr.*]

order, the six Arch-daivas, who, sometimes in their very names, are opposed to the Amesha Spenta. The widest circle is formed by the great army of minor demons and infernal fiends.

Thus the whole spiritual world is divided into two great equally organized parties, the party of light and good, and that of darkness and evil. Nevertheless, we cannot speak of a proper dualism, since, though both spirits, the good and the evil, co-exist from the beginning [1], yet, according to the doctrine of the Avesta, the latter will succumb in the decisive battle at the end of the world [2].

Like the invisible world, the visible is also divided between two diametrically opposite parties. Every man is either good or bad, every animal a creature either of light or of darkness ; even more, in nearly every object there is a combination of both powers. Such a separation was suggested in Irān by external circumstances ; the extraordinarily great differences of the climate, the sudden transitions from cold to heat, the immediate proximity of fertile fields and deserts, and even the historical and social separation into nomad hordes and sedentary farmers. Yet the consistent manner in which this separation is everywhere followed out in the Avesta must be the work of a conscious speculation.

Whatever the religion of the Avesta has lost in poetical strength and life on the one side, it has gained, without doubt, on the other, in moral profundity. It approaches monotheism by far more nearly than the Vedic religion ; as it knows one Eternal Lord and God, of whom the other genii are servants and helpmates.

Personifications of natural powers are by no means the

---

[1] Ys. XXX, 4 :
    ' When both spirits came together from the beginning to create
    Life and death, and as the world should be at its end
    The evil one chose the impious, but to the pious there came
      the Best Mind.'
    In Ys. XXX, 3 Ahura and Angra Manyu are mentioned as twins, *yēma*.
[2] *Vide supra* pp. 110–111 ; Yt. XIX, *ad finem*.

ideal of the orthodox Zoroastrian; and though Mithra and Anāhita may have had partisans and worshippers enough among the common people, in the system itself they give place to deities that prove to be mere hypostases or personifications of ethical conceptions.   Vohu-manō is, literally translated, *the good mind*, Asha-vahishta, *the best piety*, Ārmati, *the devoted and devout resignation*; and these names are, in hundreds of passages in the Avesta, employed in their purely abstract signification.   These notions cannot be said to have been exalted into real personages.

Since every individual must necessarily decide either for the party of Ahura or that of Angra Manyu, indifferentism is impossible, and every one must exactly know and fulfil the duties which are imposed upon him by the Deity.   The less the forms of the divine beings of the Avesta may have satisfied the imagination, the more impression must have been made by its peculiarly moral energy on every heart and mind.

We must confess that a people contented with such a religion lacks fancy and poetical elevation, but it has a highly respectable moral soberness.   A nation of this description will produce no great poet, but will attain a high degree of ethical perception.

Before I discuss the Ethics of the Avesta I insert here, by way of an appendix, some words concerning witchcraft, enchantment and similar superstitions which, though existing among the old Irānian people, do not seem to have had any great importance or diffusion.   If the whole world be supposed to be full of evil spirits and demons, as in the Avesta, you may easily perceive that people thought themselves menaced and endangered by these dismal powers, and endeavoured to frustrate their baneful efforts. To heretics and misbelievers was ascribed some influence on the vegetation of the earth[1]; they were commonly thought to possess evidently supernatural or magical powers.   In this way only will it be intelligible that *Yātu* denotes a

---

[1] Vd. IX, 53–57 ; XVIII, 63.

heretic or an apostate as well as a sorcerer; *Parika* is a foreign, unbelieving woman, but at the same time also a sorceress with superhuman demoniacal faculties [1].

Not man alone, but beasts also were assaulted by these demons; the enchantment of cattle especially was generally believed in. If a bull started or a cow stumbled down a precipice, it was thought to have been caused by demons [2]. Everything bad in this world was believed to come from them. The best protection and shelter against them were prayers. Yet we may understand that peculiar words were thought peculiarly efficacious in certain cases, and regarded as a counter-charm able to repel the attacks of evil spirits. People especially believed that maladies could be driven away by health-giving sayings [3], nay, this manner of curing diseases was considered the very best and most appropriate.

But enchanting power was ascribed not only to sayings and prayers, but also to certain objects. The feathers and bones of the bird *Vārajan* or *Vārenjana*, denoting perhaps the owl, were believed to protect against wounds and to lay enemies under a spell so that they could by no means gain victory [4].

'Of the thick-feathered bird *Vārenjana* a feather seek to thee, O Zarathushtra! by it fortify thy body and bewitch thy enemies.

'For if a man wears bones of this fleet bird or feathers of this fleet bird:

'No powerful ruler can kill him or make him flee; rich honour is brought home, rich glory secured to him and shelter by the feather of the bird.'

---

[1] That *yātu* must have meant 'witchcraft' already in the Arian time, is proved by the Old-Indian *yātu* 'wizard,' and the New-Persian *jādu* with the same signification.

[2] Therefore an evil spirit *Snāvidhaka* has the names *Srvō-jan* (probably 'killing horned cattle,' from *sru, srva* 'horn') and *aseǧhō-gao* 'enchanting cattle' (Skr. *āças* and *aças*). Cf. also Ys. XXXII, 12.

[3] Vd. VII, 44; *vachāo · baęshazya*, Vd. IX, 27. See below.

[4] Yt. XIV, 35; Geldner, *Metrik*, § 142.

§ 17. *Morality.*

Piety in thoughts, words and works, was the chief precept of the Zoroastrian religion[1]. In it everything else is included; it is the sum of all precepts, the doctrine that is always repeated anew, that is, I dare say, met with on every page of the Avesta. He who thinks, speaks and acts well, or, as it is said, according to religion[2], is a perfect worshipper of Mazda (*Mazdayasna*) and a worthy follower of Zarathushtra. This triple injunction is a summary of the whole ethical life of the Zoroastrian.

It would be superfluous to attempt proving this from any passage of the later Avesta; I will put forward here only one strophe from the Gāthās to prove that this doctrine existed already in the oldest period of the Mazdayasnian community:

> ' The two spirits, that first existed,
> The twins, announced to me in a dream,
> *What good was and what evil*
> *In thoughts, and words, and works.*
> Of this the pious choose
> The right, but not the bad ones[3].'

It affords, indeed, proof of a great ethical tendency and of a very sober and profound way of thinking, that the Avesta people, or at least the priests of their religion, arrived at the truth that sins by thought must be ranked with sins

---

[1] *Humata, hūkhta, huvarsh*ta ' good thoughts, words and works'; united they form *asha*=Skr. *r̥ta* 'piety.' According to Darmesteter (*Ormuzd et Ahriman*, p. 8 seq.) these three notions had originally a liturgical signification, viz.=Skr. *sumati* 'devotion,' *sūkta* 'saying, prayer,' *sukr̥ta* 'sacrifice.' But I have no doubt that they developed already in the Avesta into really ethical notions.

[2] *Anumatēē · daēnayāo, anūkhtēē · daēnayāo, anuvarsh*tēē *daēnayāo*, Yt. V, 18. Cf. *Vsp.* II, 5.

[3] Ys. XXX, 3 ; similarly Ys. XLV, 8.

by deed, and that, therefore, the actual root and source of everything good or bad must be sought for in the mind. It would not be easy to find a people that attained, under equal or similar historical conditions, to such a height of ethical knowledge. In some Varuna-hymns there occasionally appear similar ideas of the guilt of sin, and the reconciliation of Conscience with the Deity; but they are only isolated flashes, whereas we have, in the Avesta, a settled and established doctrine that is, or should be, common to every one.

Externality and work-righteousness are by no means wanting in the religion of the Avesta. Offences can be expiated by punctiliously prescribed rites of expiation, and here it seems, indeed, that more stress was laid on the external performance of the expiatory ordinance than on the internal renewal and purification of the mind[1]. Even a kind of indulgence is not unheard of. To certain meritorious works is attributed the effect of removing all guilt and sin from him who performs them. Or it was possible to wipe out, by peculiarly severe atonements, not only the special sin on account of which the atonement was performed, but also other offences committed in former times or unconsciously[2]. Nor should we claim too much, nor

---

[1] [Comp. Mr. Cook's remarks on the opening chapter of the Gāthās in 'The Origin of Religion and Language,' p. 216: 'It is especially to be remarked that there is not in it (Ys. XXVIII), from first to last, a trace of so-called naturalism. No phenomena of nature are personified, invoked or noticed. The universe is conceived as the creation, not as the manifestation, of one Supreme Being, who is, however, not isolated, but surrounded by spiritual principles, which embody, so to speak, or vividly represent His highest attributes, perfect purity as Asha, perfect goodness as Vohumanō. Man approaches this Deity, and is favoured by Him so far as he reflects those attributes. No offering but that of a pure good spirit is suggested; prayer owes all its efficacy to their presence. The seer has one desire—to know the Supreme Being as He is, and knowing Him to communicate to others the blessings of that gift.' *Tr.*]

[2] *Vide* e. g. Vd. V, 26, with which you may compare Vd. III,

expect in the ancient world ideas not formed before the time of our modern and Christian culture.

As cardinal virtues of the old Irānian must be considered *truthfulness* and *fidelity, charity* and *benevolence*.

The love of truth is praised as a prominent characteristic of the Western Irānian by the Western writers. Herodotus expressly states that the Persians think nothing so shameful as a lie; after which, says he, ranks the contracting of debts, for this reason particularly, that such as contract debts are now and then compelled to take refuge in falsehood[1]. Covenants are sacred and inviolable to the Avesta, those which are pledged by a mere word not less than those which are pledged with hand or pawn[2]. The covenant is called *mithra,* doubtless after the *yazata* Mithra, the all-seeing genius of the sun, who, penetrating the whole world with his clear light, sees all things, even the most hidden, and so becomes the guardian and protector of truth, fidelity and covenants. He who betrays a covenant betrays the *yazata* himself, and becomes a betrayer of Mithra or a breaker of covenants[3]. This expression is used almost in the same meaning as *daēva* or *drvañtō,* 'the demons,' 'the evil ones.' The strict observance of a plighted word is regarded as characteristic of the Irānian and the adherent

---

21 and IX, 50. Conformably to Vd. XIII, 7 the killing of a *zarimyaḡura* seems to have effected a remission of sins.

[1] Herodotus, i, 138; Spiegel, *E. A.* vol. iii, p. 684 seq. Darius too expresses, in an inscription (H. 14 seq.), his detestation of 'lying,' if the word *drauga,* which is here used, means nothing less than 'revolt, uproar,' cf. *Bh.* I, 38 : 'The army revolted and the lie (uproar) increased in the provinces.'

[2] Vd. IV, 2 ; cf. also Yt. X *passim.*

[3] *Mithrō-druj.* A pernicious betrayer of Mithra destroys the whole land (Yt. X, 2), probably because he draws down the vengeance of the *yazata.* Mithra takes away in his rage, strength and courage from the Mithra-deceivers (Yt. X, 23) ; their dwellings shall be deserted and desolate (Yt. X, 38). The *mithrō-druj* and the *mithrō-zya* are named along with thieves, robbers, &c. (Ys. LXI, 3). *Verthraghna,* likewise, deprives the Mithra-deceivers of their strength (Yt. XIV, 63).

of Zarathushtra, and he who is wanting in fidelity and veracity cuts himself off from the national and religious community.

Lying is a creation of the evil spirits, and in by-gone days it was exceedingly powerful on earth. No sooner than after the birth of Zarathushtra were bounds set to it. For he revealed to man the holy religion, the most efficacious weapon against lying and deceit. It is therefore that the demons break forth into the wild complaint: 'Born, alas! is the pious Zarathushtra in the house of Porushaspa! How can we contrive destruction against him? He is a blow (thunderbolt) to the demons, he is an adversary of the demons, he is the demons' enemy! Down tumble the worshippers of the demons, down the *druj-nasush* produced by the demons, down the falsely-spoken lie[1]!'

Charity of course was restricted to followers of the same creed. This cannot seem strange considering the great gulf which Zoroastrians maintained between themselves and the adherents of other doctrines. To succour an unbeliever would be like a strengthening of the dominion of Evil. But charity to poor and distressed brethren is prescribed in the Avesta. Their prayers should be heard; he who grants them not is committing sin. In the Gāthās it is said:

'What is your power, and what your riches,
That I may join you, O Mazda, with my deeds,
In sanctity and pious mind
To nourish the poor man, devoted to you?
We have renounced all
The demons and *Khrafstra-men*[2]!'

In the Vendidād the precept of mercy is proclaimed no less explicitly in the following passage: 'He who does not grant the prayer of a begging man will become a thief of

---

[1] Vd. XIX, 46: *draogha · mithaokhta.*

[2] Ys. XXXIV, 5. In the first verse we should read *hakhmi*, which is strengthened by the manuscript K 5, Bartholomä, *Gāthās*, p. 39; in the last line *parē* must be expunged.

prayer by depriving him that made it [1].' From these words it becomes evident that the Mazdayasna must regard a request made to him as a deposit. If he does not grant it he keeps back, in a certain measure, the deposit, and commits in this way a theft to the damage of the asker.

*   *   *   *   *   *   *

---

[1] Vd. IV, 1.   My opinion agrees with that of Harlez (*Av. tr.* I, p. 114); another opinion, but too ingenious, is that of Spiegel, *Comm.* vol. i, p. 116.

CHAPTER IV.

ECONOMICAL LIFE.

§ 18. *Cattle-Breeding.*

THE beasts fed and tended by the Avesta people are divided into large groups, herds and flocks[1]. In the first group are numbered cattle, horses, camels and asses; in the second, goats and sheep. The rearing of poultry was, likewise, known to the old Irānians. It is certain that they knew of the cock, perhaps also of pigeons[2]. The dog must also be mentioned as a domestic animal of the Avesta people. He was their faithful companion on their wanderings and a careful guardian of their herds. He was, therefore, highly esteemed and treated with kindness, nay, even with veneration, by the worshippers of Mazda.

CATTLE.

The cattle, which are now reared in Central Asia and in the North-Eastern parts of Irān, by no means excel in beauty or other good qualities. In the plains there grows only a short and salty kind of grass[3]. The valleys in the high mountains of the Hindukush are, on account of the exceedingly rugged and barren quality of the soil, less adapted to the breeding of cattle than of sheep and goats. It is true that even the inhabitants of Wakhān and the Eastern

---

[1] Beasts, as opposed to men, are generally called *pasu*. At the same time this word when used with *anumaya* means 'flock,' as opposed to *staora* 'herd.'

[2] Tame poultry are meant by *vaya* in the *Yima*-legend, if this word (Vd. II, 8) is equivalent to *pasu*, *staora* and *svan*, that is, to animals which are all domestic. Pigeons may be understood by *vayaȶibya · paterȶaȶibya*, which are offered to Mithra together with *pasu* and *staora* (Yt. X, 119), i. e. with other domestic animals.

[3] Vámbéry, *Skizzen*, 198; Polak, *Persien*, II, 98; Spiegel, *E. A.* vol. i, p. 261; Khanikoff, *Bokhārā*, p. 302: 'The horned cattle of Bokhārā are in a very miserable state.'

parts of the Pāmir possess herds of cattle[1]; but, from an agricultural point of view, they are in every respect of inferior importance to sheep and goats.

With the old Irānian people things were quite different, according to what we learn in the Avesta. Hence we must conclude that in those times the rearing of cattle[2] was by far more popular and general than the breeding of flocks. Sheep and goats are mentioned only occasionally without any further remarks. But the cow plays, in all parts of the Avesta, the most ancient as well as the most modern, a very prominent part and her excellence was generally valued and acknowledged.

There is a double reason for this fact.

Cattle excel, indeed, all other domestic animals in usefulness for a farming population. They afforded to the old Irānian nearly everything he wanted in his frugal life. They must have been used in farming, for drawing carriages[3], and also, in all likelihood, for bearing heavy loads[4]. The milk of the cow was a favourite and universal article of food ; butter and cheese were made of it. The flesh seems also to have been dressed for eating[5]. Bows were strung with the sinews of the ox, and the manner of working the hides of slaughtered beasts seems to have been known.

Besides, it must not be forgotten that the Avesta was

---

[1] Gordon, ' Pāmir,' pp. 113, 136. Cows and sheep are, according to Wood (' Journey,' p. 249), the domestic animals of the inhabitants of Shignān, Roshān, and Darwāz.

[2] *Gao* 'cattle,' *ukhshan* ' ox, bull,' also *gao-arshan* (Yt. XIV, 7) ' male cattle,' *gāo-daęnu* ' female cattle, cow.' *Gaodāyu* or *gaodaya* ' cattle-breeder,' *gaodhana* (=Skr. *godhana*) ' possession of cattle,' *vāstra* or *gaoyaoiti* (=Skr. *gavyūti*) ' pasture.' The star-yazata Tishtrya and the genius Verthraghna appear in the Avesta as gold-horned bulls (like Indra, the Vritra-killer, Parjanya and others, in the Rig-veda). Yt. VIII, 16; XIV, 7.

[3] Yt. X, 38.

[4] Perhaps the expressions *gao-azi* and *gao-vazi* (derived from root *az*=Skr. *aj*, and from root *vaz*=Skr. *vah*) must denote the double use of cattle as beasts of draught and beasts of burden. The inhabitants of the Pāmir in our days employ yaks for bearing loads.

[5] *Vide* p. 228 of *OKA.*

written especially according to the ideas and in the interest of a settled population of farmers and herdsmen. But cattle-breeding really demands a life by far more sedentary than the breeding of restless, migratory sheep and goats. The latter are, therefore, the peculiar beasts of nomadic tribes of herdsmen, whereas horned cattle form the property of settled farmers.

The descriptions of the Avesta must, therefore, refer to a certain portion only of the population, but the real conditions do not completely correspond to the picture as we see it. Although we have no grounds for supposing that cattle-breeding was in the old ages in as low a state as it is at present in Central Asia, yet it was probably restricted to certain regions and to a small portion of the people. Sheep and goats were certainly not less cared for than now, since the country is naturally well adapted to the rearing of them. They were certainly more liked and valued than might appear from the texts of the Avesta.

Natural pastures are not wanting in the country of the Avesta people. They are found in the valleys of the high mountains, nay, even on the Pāmir. Many of them could not be brought under tillage on account of their situation. The desire to profit by them for cattle-breeding was enhanced by the fact that there was no abundance of soil easy to till, and, therefore, even the smallest possible portions had to be employed for growing fodder.

So it was natural that pastoral habits were also developed among the sedentary and farming population who kept cattle as well. As the inhabitants now living in Wakhān drive their herds in summer to the neighbouring steppes of the Pāmir[1], just as the nearest mountain regions serve in summer as a pasture-ground to the inhabitants of the Yāghnōb; so it was certainly even in olden times. A sojourn in the brisk mountain air and the wholesome nutritious pasture could not but cause the herds to thrive.

This system of pasturing has of course no resemblance

---

[1] Gordon, 'Pāmir,' p. 136; Schuyler, 'Turkistān,' p. 278. Cf. particularly, Wood, 'Journey,' p. 210: 'In the summer, the women, like the pastoral inhabitants of the Alps, encamp in the higher

with the continual and regular change of feeding-grounds, as it was, and is, customary among nomadic and semi-nomadic tribes. Permanence of abode was by no means prejudiced by it. The owner of the farm remained with the greatest part of his servants in the valley and followed agricultural pursuits. Only the *shepherds* or the *herdsmen*[1] accompanied the animals.

On the mountains the cattle remained during the night in the open air, and were only penned in by fences or hurdles[2]. The dogs took care that no thieves or wolves attacked the herd or dispersed it. 'If anybody,' it is therefore ordered, 'wounds a dog that watches cattle, or cuts off his ear or foot, and if then a thief or a wolf comes unperceived upon the herds and carries off ten head of cattle, he [i.e. the man who injured the dog] must give compensation according to the amount (of the damage)[3].'

The wolf being certainly the most terrible enemy of

---

valleys interspersed among the snowy mountains, and devote their whole time to the dairy. The men remain on the plains, and attend to the agricultural parts of the establishments, but occasionally visit the upper stations; and all speak in rapture of these summer wanderings.'

[1] *Zaotare* 'driver,' Ys. XI, 1; *vāstare* 'herdsman,' Ys. XXIX, 1, according to the very probable conjecture of Westergaard.

[2] *Ashīa* 'hurdle' = Skr. *asta*. Hence Vd. XIV, 17: 'On twice ninety hurdles, whose fencings (*harethra* 'fencing,' from rt. *har*) are no longer useful, solid enclosures shall be raised.'

[3] Vd. XIII, 10, *dasa* 'ten,' is apparently a signification of an unsettled plurality. 'Herd' is expressed in this passage by the word *gaętha*, the meanings of which have developed, as I think, in the following way:—

Original meaning:
'Possession, homestead, household.'

Livestock, herds, flocks.	Estate, premises, fields.
Animals, world generally.	People living on the premises, colonists.

Below I shall demonstrate the different meanings of this word by quotations.

grazing cattle[1] on pasture-grounds, is very justly called the 'herd-killer[2].' For greater security the herdsmen not unfrequently remained with the herds even during the night, and the fires that were then lit[3] served as well to warm their bodies as to scare away these unwelcome visitors. In winter the pastures are inaccessible on account of the deep snow. Already at the beginning of October the cattle were invariably brought back into the valleys, and now the feast of 'driving in'[4] could be celebrated. It commenced at the same time as the winter half of the year.

It was necessary that the cattle should be sheltered in safe and substantial stables during the cold months and that the necessary fodder should be provided.

As the Avesta enjoins the expiation of different faults by constructing roads, bridges, canals and divers useful works, so likewise does it order it by the erection of *stables*. Several precepts, therefore, are given respecting the size and fashion of the building, which, it is to be regretted, we cannot fully understand[5]. Besides the stables for cattle, stables for horses and camels are also mentioned, and, moreover, pens for sheep and goats[6].

In order to feed the cattle during the winter in their stables it was necessary to cultivate grass with a view to

---

[1] *Yatha · vā · vehrkām · azrō-daidhīm · gaęthām · avi · frapataiti* 'as a wolf (*vehrkō*!) that dashes into the feeding herd on the pasture-ground.' I refer *azrō-daidhīm* to *gaęthām* and trace *azra* to Skr. *ajra* 'fields' (Grassman's *Wtb. sub voce*).

[2] *Gaęthō-jan* 'beating the herds.' [3] Vd. VIII, 94.

[4] *Ayāthrema*, see above, p. 150, and also p. 146 of *OKA*.

[5] *Nmānem ·gavayanem* (a house for cows) .... *chithīm · nisirinuyāt*, Vd. XIV, 14. The stable shall be: *dvadasa · vītāra upema, nava · vītāra · madhema, khshvash · vītāra · nitema*; according to Darmesteter: 'twelve *Vītāras* in the largest part of the house, nine *Vītāras* in the middle part, six *Vītāras* in the smallest part. Cf. Spiegel, *Comm.* vol. i, p. 342; de Harlez, *Av. tr.* vol. i, p. 224, n. 4.

[6] *Gavō-stāna, aspō-stāna, ushtrō-stāna* (Skr. *gosthāna, açva-sthāna, ushtra-sthāna*), *pasush-hasta* (*hasta* from the root *had* 'to settle'). It must not be overlooked that the stables for flocks have a different denomination from those for herds! Cf. Yt. X, 86. In Yt. V, 59 the hurdle is called *pasu-vastra*; see p. 48, n. 1 of *OKA*.

providing a store of hay. But there can be no doubt that
stall-feeding was limited to the utmost possible degree.
Grass is considered an object of farming as well as corn
and fruit-trees [1]. Wherever the natural fertility was not
sufficient, the productiveness of the meadows was increased
by artificial irrigation [2]. The harvesting of hay took place
in the month of June, just as in all countries of a moderate
temperature. Midsummer-day is, therefore, the time of
grass-mowing [3].

Several species of horned cattle were distinguished.
There seem to have been five [4]; however, more specific statements cannot be made from our texts. It would be very
interesting to learn whether the *yak* was known to the
Avesta. I cannot think it probable from the names by
which it is now denominated in the Pāmir-dialects [5]. The
yak, besides, is found more frequently in the territories of
Eastern Turkestān, particularly in Tibet. It is very doubtful whether it ever was a native of the Pāmir [6]. But since it
is at present on the Pāmir a domesticated animal of
exceeding value, it will not seem to be superfluous to say
something about it here according to Wood's description [7].

---

[1] Vd. III, 4–5.

[2] The produce of the meadows is called *vāstrem-beretem* or
vāstrō-beretem or *beretō-vāstrem* (Vsp. I, 9; II, 11; Vd. II, 24).
The artificial laying out of a meadow seems to be denoted (Vd.
XV, 42) by *uz-dā*.

[3] *Maidhyōshema vāstro dātainya.* See above, p. 150, and also
p. 146 of *OKA*.

[4]˙Hence, I think, the epithet *pañchōhaya* (Yt. XIII, 10). Another
appellative is *pouru-saredha* ' consisting of many species.'

[5] It is called (Tomaschek, *Pamirdialekte*, p. 32) either *staur* (Av.
staora) or *daugh* (from the root *yuj* ' yoke-beast'). In the Avesta
staora is a collective appellation for all kinds of animals which are
driven in herds. In Vd. VII, 41 it denotes a single beast. But
here also we must not suppose that the yak is denoted. The passage treats of an *upema, madhema* and *nitema staora*, by which
names probably are meant a camel, a horse, and an ox.

[6] Faiz-Bakhsh relates that the wild yak is met with on the
Pāmir (in Yule, ' Essay' LXIV); by Gordon, on the contrary, this
is expressly denied (' Pāmir,' p. 159).

[7] ' Journey,' pp. 208–211. Wood remarks that in Badakhshān

The yak is about double the size of an ox. Shaw, indeed, killed in Tibet an old yak which measured 10 ft. from the nose to the root of the tail, and was 5½ ft. high at the shoulder[1]. Its colour is generally black; white ones are rare. Its hair is exceedingly thick and long, hanging down to the ground on its sides. The tail is tufted and its hair extremely fine; white tails, as is known, are greatly valued in India.

The home of the yak is in the mountains. Wherever the thermometer does not rise above freezing-point, the climate is suited to it; in warmer districts it will degenerate and die off[2]. In summer, therefore, the yak-herds are driven from the low-lying regions into the valleys surrounded by snow-capped mountains. The women follow these herds, while the men remain in the valley to work in the fields. Now and then they go to their herds and speak with rapture of their wanderings on the mountains.

The yak is chiefly used for riding and carrying loads. Wherever a man can walk, the yak may be ridden. It is to the inhabitants of the Pāmir countries what the reindeer is to the Lapps of Northern Europe. Like the elephant, it possesses a wonderful knowledge of what will bear its weight. After a fresh fall of snow, travellers make the yaks walk at the head of the caravan. They are then sure that these beasts will avoid, with admirable sagacity, the hidden clefts and crevices. At the same time they are the pioneers of the caravan, for which they make an excellent road by leading the way.

The milk of the female is excellent, though its quantity

and Wakhān the yak is called *kāsh-gau* ' ox of kash.' Here, therefore, it is reputed a bovine animal.

[1] *Reise*, p. 75.

[2] Wood relates that he bought a yak in Ishkāshim for Dr. Lord, and sent it to Kunduz under the care of two trustworthy men. Though it was still winter, the yak died on the way. Several years before a nobleman of Afghānistān succeeded in bringing two yaks as far as Cabul. But here also the climate was not cold enough. They died in the beginning of spring. At present, it is true, domesticated yaks of Chinese origin are to be met with in our Zoological Gardens.

is not so great as that of the common cow. The flesh of
the yak is also eaten. Its hair is worked into carpets or
cloth.

THE HORSE.

As cattle are the principal domestic animals of the
farmer and herdsman, the horse might well be said to be
of an aristocratic character [1]. He is chiefly esteemed by
the warrior whom he serves on his campaigns as a friend
and companion in his battles and victories.

Hence the word *aspa* 'horse' is in the Avesta dialect of
frequent use in the formation of proper names. These
names mostly denote personifications of the legendary
heroes of Eastern Irān. I mention *Erzrāspa* 'having
ruddy horses,' *Kersāspa* 'having lean horses,' *Arvataspa*
'master of warlike horses,' *Hitāspa* 'driving harnessed
horses,' *Huaspa* 'having good horses,' and so on. There
might be added a number of similarly formed names from
Western Irān, transmitted in Oriental writings, as Prex-
aspes, Sataspes, Hystaspes.

The horses serve not only men but also [*figuratively*]
the celestial *yazatas*. Apām-napāt, the genius of the clouds,
and the *sun-yazata* drive warlike horses. The car of Ashi,
likewise, of Srausha, and of Usha 'the Dawn,' is thought to
be drawn by [*heavenly*] horses [2]. In the shape of light-red
horses appear the genii Tishtrya and Verthraghna [3], sometimes also represented as clear-coloured bulls. The car of
Mithra is drawn by horses of the same colour :—

---

[1] The 'horse' is plainly *aspa*. The stallion is called *aspō-arsha*
=Skr. *açvah · vṛshā*, the mare *aspi* or *aspō-daęnu*. A special or, as
it seems, more poetical expression is *erenava* (Ys. IX, 22). It is
translated into Pahlavi by *asp*, and certainly signifies 'runner.'
Geldner (*Metrik*, pp. 130–131) believes *erenava* to be the prize
given in chariot-races.

[2] Cf the epithets *aurvat-aspa*, Yt. II, 9; VI, 1 and 4; Ys. XXII,
24; and *reñjat-aspa* 'driving nimble, fleet horses,' Gāh. V, 5. According to Weinhold (*Altnord. Leben*, pp. 48–49), horses are also
considered to be gods by the old Germans of the North.

[3] Yt. VIII, 18; XIV, 9. The opponent of Tishtrya, Apausha,
appears, however, in the shape of a black horse; *Vide supra*, p. 138.

'Whom draw heavenly coursers, red, light, seen far and wide, blessed, active, fleet, obeying the heavenly will[1].

The Avesta people distinguished horses especially by their colour. First in order stand the white; besides, fallow and reddish-brown, dark-brown and black horses are specified [2]. Evidently white horses are reputed sacred, white being the colour of light. Hence they are chiefly used by the *yazatas* [3], such as Ardvi-sūra. Of Mithra also it is said :

'His chariot is drawn by four horses, white, uncoloured, eating heavenly food, immortal [4].'

The Persians are expressly stated by Herodotus to consider white horses as sacred [5]. And this custom can be traced also to people of other than Irānian race.

In the Vedic hymns the fire-god Agni is compared to a white horse. White is the colour of the horse which is given to Pedu by the Açvins, the Indian *Dioscurides*. In a poetical way the sun himself is called a white horse that carries the goddess of dawn up the sky :

'Bringing the eye of the gods, conducting the white beautiful steed, the happy Ushas appeared, decorated with rays, bestowing gifts, presiding over the uni verse [6].'

The Hellenes, likewise, regarded white horses as sacred. They are chiefly used by light and sun-gods. The Dioscurides ride light-white steeds, and horses of the same colour are harnessed to the car of *Eos* or Dawn[7].

By the Germans white horses were valued above all others; generally they were even forbidden to be used for worldly purposes. They were consecrated to the gods

---

[1] Yt. X, 68 and 136. Mithra is, therefore, called *aurushāspa*.

[2] *Spaęta* or *spaętila*=Skr. *çveta* ' white ;' *zairi*=*hari* ' fallow ;' *erezra*=*rjra* ' light-red ;' *aurusha*=*arusha* ' chesnut ;' *syāva*=*çyāva* ' bay ;' *sāma* ' black.'

[3] Yt. V, 13.   [4] Yt. X, 125.   [5] Herod. I, 189.

[6] Rv. VII, 77. 3; cf. Grassmann's *Wtb.* under the word *çveta*, Zimmer, *AiL.* p. 231.

[7] Preller, *Griech. Mythologie*, I², 335 ; II², 191.

and reared in sacred groves. Kings only were allowed the special privilege of riding white horses [1].

Not less care was necessary in breeding horses than in breeding cattle. The slightest neglect was regarded as a great offence, and followed by punishment. In the Avesta the horse itself is made to pronounce a curse against the neglectful master :

> 'Never more shalt thou harness horses, nor ride on horseback, nor yoke horses to the carriage, thou who askest not strength for me in numerous assembly, in populous companionship [2].'

The old Irānian, especially the warrior, frequently repeats his desire to possess horses. The warlike hero implores the *yazatas* to give strength and endurance to his team. And the divine beings bestow 'herds of horses and wealth in horses' on those that offer sacrifice and veneration [3]. Horses are the pride of the heroes and their dearest and most cherished possession :

> 'Thee, O Anāhita ! valiant heroes implore to grant them fleet horses.'

> 'To her, Anāhita, offered the Hvovides, to her the Nautarides; those asked for riches, these for the possession of fleet horses. Soon were the Hvovides blessed with riches; but the Nautaride Vishtāspa was in our country owner of the swiftest horses [4].'

Among the qualities of the horse his swiftness is the most prominent. In a poetical manner he is, therefore, classed with the wind, clouds, fog, and winged birds [5]. Next in estimation is his endurance, and, justly, also his keen sight. The stallion is able to see a horse-hair lying

---

[1] Tacitus, *Germ.* IX, 10; Grimm. *Deutsche Mythologie*, II⁴, 552–553; Weinhold, *Altnord. Leben*, p. 47.

[2] Ys. XI, 2. *Ebenda* 1, *vide* the curse of the cattle. Compare to this Geldner, *Metrik*, § 116.

[3] *Aspyām · ishtīm, aspyām · vāthwām*—Yt. VIII, 19; cf. Yt. X, 3 and 11.

[4] Yt. V, 86 (*āsu-aspya*) and 98. Cf. Yt. XIII, 52.

[5] Ys. LVII, 28.

on the ground in the most dark, tempestuous, and rainy night, when the sky is covered with clouds [1]. He is chiefly employed, as already mentioned, in warfare. Joyfully snorting [2] he draws the chariot of his master into the thick of the fight. He is no less esteemed in the chariot-race; for here also he bears the hero to honour and glory. Chariot-races were without doubt customary among the Avesta people. Husrava applies to Anāhita, praying : 'Grant to me that I may drive, among all the teams, the foremost on the long race-course [3].' Wherever a hero asks strength and endurance for his team, we may consider that he thinks of chariot-races as well as of battles. But the remarks of the Avesta are so few that it would be superfluous to treat of the sports of the people of Eastern Irān in a special section.

Among the old Indians chariot-races were far more in favour than among the Avesta people. In the Vedic period they were carried on with peculiar spirit. Numerous passages of the Rig-veda, nay, whole songs treat of this chivalrous sport. In later times they fell into complete disuse because the people degenerated under the influence of sacerdotal dominion and grew still more unwarlike [4].

The use of chariots, particularly in battle, was a general custom among the Eastern Irānians as well as the Indians of the Vedic, and the Achaians of the Homeric, periods. But it was also usual to ride on horseback. It is of course evident that the nomad hordes of the desert never used any vehicle, but always went on horseback. Mithra, therefore, is said to batter down with his club, men and horses of

---

[1] Yt. XIV, 31 and XVI, 10. Compare with this what is asserted as a characteristic of the horse by Scheitlin (in Brehm, *Thierleben*, II, 354 seq.).

[2] *Ravō-fraothman*, Yt. XVII, 12. As a charger he is called *aspa-aurvat* or simply *aurvat*=Phlv. *asp-i-kārīzār*—Ys. XI, 2.

[3] Yt. V, 50; XIX, 77. The length of the race-course *charetu* or *chareta* (Phlv. *asp-rās*) seems to have been employed, like the Greek σтάδιον, for measuring distances. See Vd. II, 25 and 33.

[4] Zimmer, *AiL.* 291.

the enemies and to chase away men and horses[1]. These enemies are apparently nomads, hardy riders who, as it were, grow up together with their horses and conquer or perish together with them.

Here I again call attention to the curse of the horse against the neglectful owner : 'Nor longer shalt thou ride henceforward on horseback.' In the Avesta the warriors are also said to pray to the *yazatas* 'on the backs of their horses'[2] to grant strength and endurance to them and their coursers. This evinces that riding (on horseback) was known to all classes of the people. Riding was probably resorted to when great distances were to be traversed in the shortest possible time. The journey which a well-mounted rider was able to perform in a day was, therefore, made use of for a certainly primitive standard of measure[3].

The predilection of the Vedic Indians for the horse and their passion for chariot-races can hardly be explained from the conditions of Indian life[4]. In India the horse does not thrive, as even Herodotus expressly states[5]. . In later time horses were brought from the country of the Bālhika, i.e. from Bactria[6].

Here again we surely find in the Vedic culture a relic of former times. This custom originates in the period in which the Arians still encamped on the northern slope of the Paropamisus. Here, in the regions bordering on the desert, the land is, more than elsewhere, adapted to the breeding and training of horses. Here we find the requisite fat pastures and free open plains which serve for exercise. In these regions horse-breeding was at all times cultivated in great perfection.

I will not speak at length of the breeding of the Turco-

---

[1] *Hō · paoiryō · gadhām · nijaiñti* * *aspaęcha · paiti · viraęcha* * *hathra · tar*sh*ta · thrāoğhayęiti* * *uvaya · aspa-vīracha.*   Yt. X, 101.

[2] *Baręshaęshu · paiti · aspanām.*   Ys. X, 11.

[3] So it is asserted (Yt. V, 4) of the canals and branches of Ardvi-sūra or the Oxus: *kaschitcha · apaghzhāranām* * *chathware-satem ayare-barām* * *hu-aspāi · nairę · baremnāi,* 'and each of the water-courses is a journey of forty days for a good rider.'

[4] *Vide* also Roth, *ZddmG.* xxxv, p. 686.   [5] Herod. iii, 106.

[6] Cf. *B. R.* under the words *bālhi* and *bālhika.*

man horses, whose admirable swiftness and incomparable endurance are praised by every traveller without exception[1]. It is certain and it is affirmed by national tradition that the Turcoman horses, though on the whole indigenous, have a considerable admixture of Arabian blood. What is certainly of greater importance is that the high value which the Median horses had, in ancient times, in the eyes of a part of the Avesta people, was established, without doubt, on Median ground. Special praise is given to the horses of *Nisäa*, which must not be confounded with the *Nisaya* of the Vendidad. They are already mentioned by Herodotus, and Arrian and Strabo agree with his assertion[2].

The Eastern parts of Irān also are excellently adapted to horse-breeding. Curtius relates that Bactria abounded in good horses. One tribe of the Bactrians seems to have had the name *Zariaspi* 'with fallow horses,' and this name was given afterwards to the capital. The chief forces of the Bactrians consisted of their dreaded horsemen[3].

Horse-breeding is still successfully carried on in Balkh[4]. The horses of Herāt are likewise greatly valued. They are small, indeed, but strong and hardy. A great number of them are exported every year[5]. In short, we may justly say that all Irān is adapted to horse-breeding, and that the ground and soil are so conditioned that the inhabitants must have been attracted to it at all times.

---

[1] Ferrier, *Voyages*, I, pp. 183–185; Vámbéry, *Reise*, p. 368; the same, *Skizzen*, p. 198; McGregor, 'Journey,' I, pp. 267–268; Grodekoff, 'Ride,' 128. So too Fraser, Conolly, Abbott in the compilation of divers notices by Marvin, *Merv*, pp. 162–176.

[2] Herod. iii, 106, vii, 40; Arr. vii, 17; Strabo, pp. 529–530. Cf. the excursion in Ritter, *Asien*, IX, p. 363 seq. Darius, too, in an inscription at Persepolis (H. 8–9) praises the abundance of horses in his country.

[3] Curtius, IV, 12, 6; V, 8, 4; VII, 4, 26 and 30; cf. Forbiger, *H. a. G.* II, 555 seq.; Kiepert, *A. G.* § 54 and 59, note.

[4] Elphinstone, 'Kabul,' vol. I, p. 466. Horses in Kunduz according to Wood, 'Journey,' p. 143.

[5] Elphinstone, 'Kabul,' vol. I, p. 266; Malleson, 'Herāt,' p. 92. According to Wood ('Journey,' p. 249) horses are rather rare on the upper Oxus. In the upper Zerafshān they are, according to Schuyler (*Turkistān*, I, 278), replaced by asses.

We may assert even more. It is very probable that Central Asia is the original home of the horse, that here man began to compel to his service this noblest of all domestic animals. From the broad expanse of this continent, whose gravelly and sandy steppes afforded a free space to wander in, the horse went down, on all sides, through the high mountains of Northern India, into the valleys of Turkistān, into the tracts and plains near the Oxus and the Jaxartes. Even in our days numerous herds of horses, called Tarpans, rove freely about in Central Asia. It cannot be stated with certainty whether they have returned to the wild state or whether they are to be regarded as the wild sires of our domesticated animals [1].

THE CAMEL.

The camel is found all over Central Asia. In our own days it is extensively reared in the territories which must have been the home of the Avesta people. For the inhabitants of many countries it is even more useful than the horse itself; in desert districts it is almost indispensably necessary [2].

The camels of Bokhārā are highly renowned. Here, as well as in Khiva and in the other Khanates of Central Asia, both the single and the double-humped species are bred. The latter is especially the domestic and royal animal of the wandering Kirghiz. On account of its great fleetness and hardihood it is employed in the Turcoman deserts for the special purpose of carrying express messengers [3].

---

[1] Brehm, *Thierleben*, II, p. 335; Hehn, *Culturpflanzen*, p. 20 seq. Compare besides Middendorff, *Einblicke in das Ferghanah-Thal*, p. 264 seq. Mém. de l'Ac. de St. Pétersbourg VII. sér. t. xxix. No. 1.

[2] An account of the camel and its distribution is given by Ritter, *Asien*, XIII, p. 609 seq. Compare besides Brehm, *Thierleben*, II, p. 399 seq.; and especially Polak, *Persien*, II, p. 98; Spiegel, *E. A.* I, p. 260.

[3] Burnes, 'Bokhārā,' II, p. 210; III, p. 153; Khanikoff, 'Bokhārā,' p. 202; Vámbéry, *Reise*, pp. 368–369; and also *Skizzen*, p. 198. Schuyler, *Turkistān*, I, p. 130: 'Of course one sees everywhere in the streets numbers of camels.' Middendorff, *Ferghanah*, pp. 293 seq.

In Afghānistān the two-humped camel is oftenest seen. It is also called the Bactrian camel, because it seems to be a native of the districts in the North of the Hindukush and is chiefly found there [1]. The breed in particular request is that of Andkhui, a variety called *Ner*. The Ner-camels are conspicuous by the thick hair which grows down from their necks and breasts, by their slender form and uncommon strength [2].

The inhabitants of the Pāmir also and of the valleys and tracts on the Upper Oxus cultivate the camel as a domestic animal [3]. The two-humped camel of the Pāmir-Kirghiz is described by Wood. It is not so ugly as the Arabian camel, but combines with the good qualities of the latter a noble carriage in which it is surpassed only by the horse. A Kirghiz horde consisting of a hundred families, whose encampment was passed by Wood between Ishkāshim and Kalai-Panja, had, besides 2000 yaks and 4000 sheep, no less than a thousand camels of this description.

The nomads of Central Asia in particular esteem the camel above all other domestic animals, almost to the point of adoration. We cannot wonder at this when we consider its great strength, patience, and the trifling cost of maintaining it. Fed by a few thistles which are despised by other beasts, it wanders for weeks, nay for months, across the desert without being fatigued. Moreover, it is so docile and obedient, that a child is able to govern a whole troop of these beasts by a single word [4].

In the breeding season the character of the male camel is entirely changed. It grows wild, stubborn, vicious and intractable. It becomes dangerous even to its human masters, and there are instances in which men have been bitten to death by such mad camels [5].

The Eastern Irānians of antiquity kept the camel [6] as a

---

[1] Elphinstone, 'Kabul,' vol. I, p. 227; Stein, *Petermanns Mittheilungen*, 1879. 24.   [2] Vámbéry, *Reise*, p. 213.

[3] Gordon, 'Pamir,' p. 113; Wood, 'Journey,' pp. 212–213, 246.

[4] Vámbéry, *Skizzen*, p. 54.   [5] Schuyler, *Turkistān*, I, p. 20.

[6] *Ush*tra 'camel' = N.P. *shutur*. The corresponding expressions in the Pāmir dialects are found in *Tomaschek*, p. 31.

domesticated animal as well as the tribes now dwelling in the plains on the Sīr and Amu.   It is already mentioned even in the Gāthās:

> 'That I ask of Thee; give me truly answer, O
>   Ahura!
> When shall I get justly and rightly my reward,
> Ten mares with their stallions and a camel[1]?'

As far back as we can in general trace the culture of the Avesta people in past times, they must have attended to the breeding of camels.   Yet the contexts lead us to suppose that in the earliest times the camel was more valued than the horse, or at least was less common.

In the later Avesta the camel ranks, wherever the domestic animals are regularly enumerated according to their value and importance, between the horse and the cow, standing before the latter and after the former[2].   Yet there are also exceptions.   For curing the wife of the master of a village a cow must be given as fee to the physician ; for curing the wife of the chief of a district a mare, and for the wife of the governor of a province a she-camel. The latter is here, indeed, more highly priced than a horse or cow[3].

Camels were no less desired by the old Irānians than herds of cattle and horses.   A Tūrānian seems to have been praised for possessing 700 camels[4].   If this passage is urged, it will perhaps prove that the less sedentary Tūrānian tribes, the nomads, devoted special attention to the training of this useful animal.

How much the camel was esteemed in old Irān may be seen from the fact that a great deal of personal names are formed by combination with *ushtra*.   I mention *Arava-ushtra* 'having wild camels,' *Vōhu-ushtra* 'having good camels,' and *Avāraushtra*, but more than all the name of the prophet *Zarathushtra* himself, and that of his friend and follower *Frashaushtra*.

---

[1] Ys. XLIV, 18.
[2] Vd. XXII, 3–4, 20 : *aspa, ushtra, gao, anumaya.*
[3] Vd. VII, 42.   Cf. also Vd. XIV, 11.   [4] Yt. IX, 30.

A full and particular description of the camel, less poetical indeed, but rather circumstantial, is given in the following passage of the Avesta :

'A fourth time came driving Verthraghna, whom Ahura had created, in the form of a load-bearing camel, a biting, swift-footed, a submissive, rambling, a hair-covered, dwelling with man ; that of all productive males has the greatest power and the greatest courage; that roves among the females; for those (females) are best protected, whom a burden-carrying camel protects ; a slender, bony, strong-humped, a . . . gay-looking, courageous, a stately, tall, mighty ; that casts up whitish foam towards its head in its courage and its strength [1].'

Before I finish this section I must allude to a remarkable matter. To the old Irānian word for 'camel' corresponds, in the Indian language, *ushtra*, which is found both in Vedic and in later literature. Here it has, agreeably to the dialect of the Avesta, the signification of 'camel [2];' in the Rig-veda, however, it seems to mean rather a buffalo (or humped ox), as we should, indeed, conclude from the context of certain passages.

---

[1] Yt. XIV, 12–13. The epithets are the following : (1) *Vadh-airi.* We might at first recall to mind the Skr. *vadhri* ' castrated,' and regard the *a* between *dh* and *r* as a Svarabhakti vowel. But this suggestion is expressly excluded by the third strophe. I therefore adhere to the explanation of Geldner (*Metrik*, p. 8 n.)· (2) *Dadāsu* ' biting.' (3) *Aiwi-tachina*, literally, 'running to and fro,' hence ' swift.' (4) *Urvat* ' friendly, submissive.' (5) *Frasparena*, from *spar* ‒ N.P. *sapardan* ' pede calcare, viam terere' ('to beat the road by the foot or spur'). (6) *Gaethu* ' hairy' (?) ‒ *gaçsu* (see my Manual under this word). (7) *Mashyō-vaĝha*, from *m.* + *vāĝha* from root *vaĝh* = Skr. *vas* ' to dwell.' (8) *Ash-bāzu* ' with strong fore-feet.' (9) *Stui-kaofa* ' with high, strong hump.' (10) *Smarshna* (?). (11) *Daęma-jira.* (12) *Sāra* ' valiant,' from root *sā* = Skr. *çā* ' to sharpen'; cf. German *Schneidig* (sharp). (13) *Raęva.* (14) *Be-reza.* (15) *Amavat.* To these are to be added from Yt. XVII, 13 *Uzyamana · zemat* ' starting from the ground,' *ash-manaĝh* ' coura-geous,' and *peretamana* ' warlike.'

[2] *Vide B.R. sub voce.*

Sometimes one may hesitate between these two meanings in the Vedic songs[1]. Thus it is in the Dānastutis, in which the poets praise the gifts with which they have been honoured by princes. Here the *ushtras* are enumerated among the gifts along with horses and cows[2]. But there can scarcely be any doubt that buffaloes are meant, when the *ushtras* are said to walk by fours under a yolk[3]. And the same meaning I think correct whenever Pushan, chasing his enemies before him, is compared to an *ushtra*[4]. For elsewhere in the Rig-veda the bull is the symbol of untamed strength and force[5].

From the change of signification in this single word we may again derive a portion of the history of civilization. The Indo-Irānian tribe certainly denoted by *ushtra* only the camel. On the northern slope of the Hindukush or still further to the North he may have learned to breed and train this domestic animal. With the Irānian people who remained in the original seats, it preserved at all times its high importance and its old name. But the Indians took the camel with them when wandering into the low plains of the Indus and its five tributaries. Here it must have become more and more rare, because it was not found in a wild state in this neighbourhood. The number of the camels which they had brought with them decreased more and more, for in India the camel thrives only in a few tracts which are specially favourable to its increase, as in Mārwār[6]. The losses could not well be replaced by beasts tamed anew.

---

[1] Ludwig, indeed, in his translation of the Rig-veda, renders *ushtra* at one time by 'camel,' at another by 'buffalo.'

[2] Rv. VIII, 5, 37; XLVI, 22.

[3] 'Up to the heavens reached *Kakuha*, who gave me four-yoked *ushtras*; by glory the people of Yadu.' Rv. VIII, 6, 48.

[4] Rv. I, 138, 2. Here Ludwig (Rv. I, 154) translates *ushtra* by 'camel.'

[5] In Rv. VIII, 46, 31 the *ushtra* is said to bellow. The word *krad*, employed in this passage, generally designates the bellowing of bulls and the neighing of horses.

[6] Lassen, *Indische Alterthumskunde*, I², 349. In the upper part

In the Zebu or hump-backed bull which is a native of India the Vedic Arians found a substitute for the camel which continued to die out. Like the camel it became the favourite beast of burden, and was finally known by the same name *ushtra*.

But the remembrance of the camel and its useful services was not lost. Perhaps the species had never become entirely extinct, though surviving only in a few individuals. In a later time it became again more common because camels began to be introduced from the bordering districts of the West. In this way the old name, which had in the Vedic period an unsettled meaning, but the original signification of which had never been wholly forgotten, acquired new importance, and the camel was again de-nominated by the name *ushtra* as before.

THE ASS.

Among the domestic animals of the Avesta people the ass is also mentioned, though only in a single passage of our texts. In usefulness it stands next to the horse and camel. A female ass is the fee which must be paid to a physician who has succeeded in healing the wife of the chief of a family[1]. For curing ladies of higher rank a cow, a mare, or a female camel must be given.

* * * * * * *

Among the Indians of the Vedic time also, the ass was greatly valued as a domestic animal. It was mainly employed for carrying heavy burdens; but the male ass was also yoked to carriages[2].

---

of India the camel must have existed in pre-historic times. In 1834 the bones of this animal were found in a fossil state on the spurs of the Himālaya ('Journal of the Asiatic Society of Bengal,' 1835, vol. iv, pp. 517, 694, in Ritter, *Asien*, XIII, p. 634).

[1] Vd. VII, 42 : *kathwa-daęnu*. With *kathwa* compare, from the Pāmir dialects (*Tomaschek*, p. 31), the word *kuāt*, which means 'the colt of an ass' in Wakhī.

[2] Zimmer, *AiL.* pp. 232–233.

At present great attention and care are paid to the breeding of asses in Persia and Turkistān. This animal is, in our northern countries, not seldom headstrong, lazy and wilful, though there is no reason at all for making him the type of dulness and stupidity. In southern countries he makes a more favourable impression. There he is a fine and sturdy beast, and is besides no less active than enduring [1].

Particularly numerous and renowned are the asses of Bokhārā and Khīva [2]. Every year many are brought to Persia, Bagdād, Damascus and Egypt by the Hājis. In Tāshkend they are nearly as common as horses. Here they are of small stature and of white or gray colour; they are able to carry heavy loads. In Khokand, it is true, they are very seldom met with, but on the upper Zerafshān, where horses are rare, they are used as beasts of burden [3].

It is not at all improbable that it was in Central Asia that the ass, like the horse, was first brought under the power of man. At least the sandy and gravelly steppes of Central Asia are the original home of the *onager* or wild ass. He is a most handsome and swift animal, very shy, and, therefore, very difficult to hunt [4]. Great herds of wild asses roam about near the Aral and Caspian and in the deserts in the North of the Garmsil, according to the reports of travellers [5].

SHEEP AND GOATS.

We know already that greater value and importance are attributed by the Avesta to the breeding of cattle than to

[1] Brehm, *Thierleben*, vol. II, p. 365 seq.

[2] Khanikoff, *Bokhārā*, p. 202; cf. Vámbéry, *Skizzen*, p. 199; *idem*, *Reise*, p. 369. Regarding the Persian ass, see Spiegel, *E. A.* vol. I, p. 260. Cf. Middendorff, *Ferghanah*, p. 281.

[3] Schuyler, *Turkistān*, I, pp. 130, 278.

[4] Brehm. *Thierleben*, vol. II, p. 361 seq.

[5] Vámbéry, *Reise*, pp. 96, 98; Ferrier, *Voyages*, vol. II, p. 294, and other passages. Cf. p. 98 of *OKA*.

that of sheep and goats [1]. Probably, whilst cattle were the chief property of the settled portion of the people, nomadic or semi-nomadic tribes devoted their time to breeding small cattle, viz. goats and sheep.

The usefulness of goats and sheep was certainly not unknown to the Avesta. Their milk was occasionally drunk, their flesh was doubtless eaten, and their hair and wool were made into cloth [2].

It is easy to explain why the sheep is the symbol of shy timidity. The wolf is its most dangerous enemy. As a sheep is afraid of the wolf, the demons are afraid of the soul of a pious dead person [3].

The old Irānian farmers kept, not only their herds of cattle, but also their flocks on the pastures of the neighbouring mountains during summer. In autumn they returned into the valleys and were here sheltered against the severity of frost and snow in warm penfolds during the whole winter time [4]. After their return at the end of September the rams were allowed to go to the ewes [5]. The lambs, then, were born in the beginning of March, and were able, when they had passed a summer on the pastures and grown vigorous, to endure the hard Irānian winter with less risk than lambs born in July or August.

The breeding of flocks flourishes in full vigour in the districts of the Sīr and the Amu and in Afghānistān even in our days [6]. To a great extent it is favoured by the climate and the natural conditions of the soil. On account of their being so prolific and so easily driven, sheep and

---

[1] Sheep *maęsha*, ewe *maęshi · daęnu*, or *maeshi* alone, ram *maęsha · varshni*, goat *buza* or *iza*.

[2] Vd. V, 52; VII, 15; for cloth made of goat-hair we have *vastra · izaęna*, vide p. 224 of *OKA*.

[3] Vd. XIX, 33. Cf. *Aogemadaechā*, p. 19; Yt. XXIV, 27.

[4] Cf. *supra*, p. 171.

[5] Cf. *supra*, p. 150; Roth. *ZddmG*. vol. xxxiv, pp. 704-705.

[6] In Persia also mutton is in favour and cloth is made from the wool of sheep and the hair of goats. Spiegel, *E. A.* vol. I, pp. 260-261; Polak, *Persien*, vol. II, pp. 96-98.

goats are much affected by wandering herdsmen [1]. Their
transport causes no difficulty, even marches of considerable
length are by no means hurtful to them. They easily
mount the highest valleys and defiles of the mountains, and
even poor pastures, difficult of access, where cattle would
starve, are sufficient for their sustenance.

Besides, they more easily resist the cold of winter than
cattle, and by no means require such careful and regular
tending. The inhabitants, therefore, of rugged and barren
mountainous tracts in which the winters are severe and
long, always rear them in preference to any other domestic
animal.

So sheep and goats are the most valued animals in the
mountainous regions of Eastern Irān. They are found on
the Pāmir and in the valleys on the Upper Oxus, in Siri-
kul, Wakhān, Shignān and Roshan [2]. They are likewise
the chief property of the nomad Aimaks and Hezāres and
of the wandering herdsmen on the borders of the Khāsh
desert [3].

No less valuable are sheep and goats to the Afghāns and
Kāfirs [4]. On the way to Kabul, Burnes met with thousands
of sheep which belonged to the tribe of the Ghilzāis [5].
They were being marched, as the snows had disappeared,
into the high valleys of the Hindukush, there to spend the
summer.

The fat-tailed sheep of Bokhārā are everywhere known [6].
Their flesh is, as Vámbéry asserts [7], the best he ever
tasted in Asia. But it is of course an idle fable to say that
the tails of these sheep are sometimes of such weight as to

---

[1] Roscher, *Nationaloekonomik des Ackerbaus*, § 12, note 3.

[2] Gordon, ' Pamir,' pp. 113, 136 ; Wood, ' Journey,' pp. 212–
213, 249. Compare also Middendorff, *Ferghanah*, pp. 289
seq.

[3] Ferrier, *Voyages*, vol. i, p. 364 ; vol. ii, p. 294, &c.

[4] Masson, ' Narrative,' vol. i, p. 212 ; vol. ii, pp. 206, 325.

[5] *Bokhārā*, vol. ii, p. 109.

[6] Burnes, *Bokhārā*, vol. iii, p. 151 ; Vámbéry, *Skizzen*, p. 196.

[7] *Reise*, p. 368.

necessitate the animals dragging them along behind them
on little wheels [1].

*   *   *   *   *   *   *

THE DOMESTIC COCK.

To what extent poultry were bred by the old Irānian
people cannot be determined, since our sources of information are very scanty. They were certainly not unknown,
for fowls are spoken of in the Avesta along with other
domestic animals [2]. Mention is made of the domestic cock [3]
particularly, which was highly regarded among the Avesta
people. He seems to be indigenous to Irān. At a comparatively late period he was brought from Western Asia to
Europe; for as late as in the Greek comedians he is called
the ' Persian bird [4].'

Watchfulness and early rising are reputed a great virtue
by the Mazda-worshippers. In it they were aided by the
cock which, at early dawn, awakens sleepers by his crowing.
For this reason he is so highly praised and even held
sacred in the Avesta.

The cock is the herald of the *yazata* Srausha, who is
active at the early sun-rise [5]. With a loud voice he utters
his cry at break of day and chases away the evil spirits of

---

[1] Schuyler, *Turkistān*, I, 326.

[2] Cf. above, p. 167.

[3] *Parodarsh*, literally ' the foreseer.' He was so called, I think,
because he announced and heralded the approach of day by his
crowing. The partridge, I suppose, is meant by *kahrka*, for which
expressions corresponding with the former meaning are also to be
found in the Pāmir dialects (*Tomaschek*, p. 38).

[4] Hehn, *Culturpflanzen*, p. 277 seq.

[5] Vd. XVIII, 15 seq. For ' herald' we have in the original
text *sraoshā-vareza* ' maker of obedience.' Commonly ' priest ' is
understood by this word (Spiegel, *Comm.* vol. i, p. 173). The
meaning seems to be that the cock announces to man the time .
prescribed for the performance of the matutinal ceremonies, as a
priest enjoins upon the people the due observance of religious
precepts.

night and darkness. The Avesta ascribes to his crowing the following meaning: 'Rise, ye men! praise the genius of piety, curse the demons! If not, Būshyāsta, the evil spirit of sleep, might assault you, who endeavours to pour sleep on all living creatures that are awake at day-break (saying): "Sleep long, O man!"—But this does not become you [1].'

It is said in another place that the cry of the cock is heard even before it dawns in the East [2]. He calls people to light the fire of the hearth. But then his mightiest adversary, the demon of sleep, breaks in and craftily whispers to the awaking: 'Do sleep, ye men! sleep ye, who live in sin, sleep ye who spend your life in sinning!'

With such as did not zealously follow the precepts of the religion of Mazda and especially disliked the commandment of early rising, the cock was certainly no favourite. To the sluggard his rousing cry was not seldom very unwelcome. Therefore, they resorted to mockery and contempt in order to discredit, as far as possible, the cock, whose voice sounded sweet and agreeable only to the active and industrious. The Avesta actually mentions two appellations of the cock, one of them expressly stated to be used by evil-speaking men. Of course such defamation of a most useful and honest animal could not but provoke the indignation of the religious and orthodox Irānian and cause him to denounce such infamy.

One of these names is *Kartō-dansu* [3]. Literally, it means 'cutting with knives,' and evidently alludes to the shrill, insupportable cry of the cock. The second name, *Kahrkatās*, cannot easily be explained; perhaps it must be translated

---

[1] The conclusion offers some perplexities and the text is mutilated. That *hvafsa-dareghō · mashyāka* must be the words of Būshyāsta, appears from the passage to be presently brought forward. *Hvafsa* I think to be the imperative of the inchoatine or inceptive *hvafs* from *hvap*; but in this case we might expect the adv. *dareghem*.

[2] Yt. XXII, 41–42.

[3] *Karelō-dāsu* from *karela*, 'knife,' and *dāsu* from the root *dās* = Skr. *damç*.

by 'fowl-biter[1].' It is not impossible that the meaning is obscene. The latter name, for certain, was already popular in the Arian time. It is also found in the Rig-veda in the form *Krika-dāsu*, and is used here also in a contemptuous way to denote the cock. A poet who is fond of sleep gives him this name in a short song in which he curses in a coarse way everything that might trouble his repose: the braying of the ass, the sighing of the wind or the rustling of the forest, and the cry of the cock:

> 'Put to death, O Indra! the ass that brays so piteously!
> Chase away with the bird *Kundrināchī* the wind far over the forest!
> Kill every one that makes a noise, curse the *Krika-dāsu!*'[2]

THE DOG.

Between the manner in which the dog was treated by the Avesta people, and that in which he is now treated by the inhabitants of Persia, there is a great difference. It is well known that he is regarded as an impure animal by Moslems. With the introduction of Muhammedanism into Central and Anterior Asia he has indeed lost all his former dignity and value.

It is narrated by Schuyler that every family of the Sarts has at least *one* dog[3]; but he is by no means treated as a

---

[1] *Kahrkatās*, Vd. XVIII, 15. Darmesteter, *Notes sur l'Avesta*, 20. It will scarcely be possible to separate this word from *kahrka*, N.P. *kark* 'fowl' (cf. *kahrkāsa*). Indeed we are tempted to see in *kareta* and *kahrka* nothing but collateral forms of Skr. *karṇa* (formed with suffix *ta* and *ka* instead of *na*), and in *tās* a mutilation of *dās*. In this case the two names might be rendered by 'ear-mangler.'

[2] Rv. I, 29, 5–7. The *dāçu* in Skr. *kṛkadāçu* corresponds, it cannot be denied, more with the *dāsu* of *karetō-dāsu*. But it proves at the same time, that *tās* may be regarded only as a mutilation.

[3] *Turkistān*, I, 130.

favourite, but rather maltreated. He is seldom fed, being
generally left to provide for himself. Their dogs are
accordingly lean, weakly and half-starved. They are employed for no other purpose than for watching the houses.
By day and night they ramble about in the vicinity of the
house, giving the alarm whenever a stranger approaches.

With the modern Persians the word 'dog' is a by-word
of the most insulting kind. As such it is employed in
divers contumelious expressions, as for instance: 'Whose
dog was your father?' or 'You son of a dog!' It may be
remarked that a similar usage is found in the Rig-veda,
whereas, on the contrary, such forms of abuse are quite
impossible in the Avesta :

> 'He, the god, may choose like a man the song of the
> pressed Soma; chase away *the avaricious dog*, as
> the Bhrigus the enemy!'
> 'Crush round about *the yelping dogs*, kill the enemies,
> for you are able to do it, ye Açvins!
> Reward every song of the bard with riches, bless ye
> both, ye truthful, my hymn!'[1]

There are excellent dogs in Wakhān. It seems also that
they are here better treated, because the minds of the
people are not yet fully imbued with the spirit of Islāmism.
According to Wood, they differ essentially from the Indian
dogs[2]. They have long ears and a tufted tail, are commonly
of a black or reddish-brown colour, in the latter case sometimes spotted. Their shape is lean and more adapted for
speed than strength. They are very wild and most watchful, and will attack dogs of double their strength.

In the Avesta the dog is esteemed a faithful companion
and friend of man[3]. He is particularly useful in taking
care of his master's property, especially by protecting herds
and flocks from all damage.

---

[1] Rv. IX, 101. 13 (otherwise explained by Ludwig, Rv. II, 512);
I, 182, 4.

[2] Wood, 'Journey,' p. 246.

[3] *Span* 'dog' = Skr. *çvan*; a monograph of the dog is the Essay
of Hovelacque, *Le chien dans l'Avesta, les soins qui lui sont dus*,
son éloge in the *Revue de Linguistique*, VIII, p. 187 seq.

The Vendidād represents Ahura Mazda as uttering the following words:

'I created the dog in his own clothes and shoes, with keen scent and sharp teeth as the property of man to protect his folds; I created the dog as a guard against enemies. If he is attentive and cares for the flocks, and if he, O Zarathushtra, is watchful with his voice, no thief nor wolf will come unperceived into the villages to carry away booty'[1].

The dog is, therefore, less the servant of man than his friend and house-companion. Along with wives and children he forms the ornament of the house and a guarantee of its permanence. Numerous dogs are no less desired by the Mazda-worshipper than great herds and a rich harvest[2].

Everywhere the dog appears immediately after man. Of all beasts he stands next to him, almost on a footing of equality. The *yazata* of earth is offended, whenever dead dogs or dead men are deposited in her lap, and the exhumation of such bodies is a work of the greatest merit[3].

The dog is sacred and inviolable. It is a great crime to beat, to wound, or to kill him. Whoever caused the death of a dog by his neglect had to undergo a very severe punishment. Every damage suffered by herds or other property, in consequence of injury to the watch-dog, was expiated in the same way as a sin consciously committed[4].

These views of the Avesta completely agree with the narration of Herodotus respecting the Magi, who, he says, kill everything living except man and the dog[5].

The duties of dogs are various. Hence they are divided into several varieties.

---

[1] Vd. XIII, 39 seq. This passage offers considerable difficulties. *Draonaǧh* must be compared with Skr. *draviṇas*. I translate *masu* by 'watchful,' on the basis of tradition, which interprets *māshak* as *zīnāvand*. Beginning from the words *yęzi · asti · ash-khrathwa* the original metrical form of the passage may easily be recognized.

[2] Vd. III, 3.

[3] Vd. III, 8, 12; cf. also Vd. III, 36 seq.

[4] Vd. XIII, 10 seq.   [5] Herod., I, 140.

First in rank stands the dog 'that watches the herds [1].'
It is his duty to run round the herd on the pasture in order
to scare away wolves and thieves. From the fact that he
was ranked highest of all we may conclude how much
pastoral life was still affected by the Avesta people, and
how they regarded herds and flocks as their most valuable
property. The sheep-dog of the herdsmen now living in
the Pâmir is described as being large, of a pale-yellow colour,
with small erect black ears, black muzzle and thin straight
tail [2].

Second to him stands the farm-house dog 'that watches
the village [3].' He remains near the settlements and has to
protect them from the same enemies. For personal safety
served the dog 'that goes to the blood [4],' that is to say,
who had been taught to keep hold of a man. Finally, we
must mention the dog that had learnt to play tricks and,
therefore, was less useful, kept only for sport and pastime [5].

All kinds are named together in the passage which treats
of the killing of a dog and its consequences :

> 'Whoever kills a dog that watches the herds, or one that
> watches the village, or one that goes to the blood, or
> one that has learnt tricks; more dreadfully for us
> and more hideously will his soul wander into the
> world to come, than a wolf which roves about in the
> horrible vast forest [6].'

In a strange panegyric, the tenour of which has little

---

[1] *Spā · yō · pasu*sh-*haurvō*. Compare for this and the following
statement, Vd. XIII, 17 seq.

[2] *Vide* Tomaschek, *Pāmirdialekte*, p. 29.

[3] *Spā · yō · vish-haurvō*.

[4] *Spā · yō · vōhunazgō*. Cf. Spiegel, *Comm.* vol. i, p. 176.

[5] *Spā · yō · drakhtō-hunarō*.

[6] Vd. XIII, 8. Towards the end the passage is metrical and
may be restored in the following manner : *Khraosyōtaracha · nō ·
ahmā*t * *vayōtaracha · hvō · urva* * *parāiti (parō-) asnā*t · *aghvṛ* *
yatha · vehrkō · vayō-tūitē * *dramnō · barezi*sh*tē · razūirē*. The
translation is difficult; that of Spiegel and de Harlez must be rejected. *Vayōtara* and *vayōtūta* (?) are certainly connected with

interest for us, his qualities are compared to those of a priest, a warrior, a farmer, a slave, a ferocious beast, a bawd and a babe! The first he equals in poverty and contentment, the second in watchfulness, the third in activity and restlessness. He flatters like a slave or a bawd, roves about in the darkness like a thief or wild beast, and his tongue protrudes from his mouth like that of an infant[1]. In short, he has something of the nature of each of them; he combines the characteristics of nearly all beings.

The dog is recommended with earnestness to the care of man by the writers of the Avesta. He who gives him bad or insufficient food must expect the severest punishment. It is not allowed to cast before him bones which have not been bruised, nor any hot food to burn his mouth with[2].

Female dogs big with young must be particularly taken care of. For the lives of many were threatened, if they were hurt by any accident. If such an animal was frightened away, and fell, in consequence, into a cistern or a ditch or a canal, such an offence could by no means be expiated[3].

Skr. *bhī, bhaya.* Instead of *dramnę* I conjecture *dramnō* (from root *drā* 'to run'). The former originated from its connection with *vayō-tūitę.*—A division of dogs still more detailed will be found in Vd. V, 29. In this passage *spā·jaxhush, aiwizhush* and *vīzhush* are obscure. With *sukuruna* compare *skön* 'whelp' in Wakhi (Tomaschek, *Pamirdialekte*, p. 29); *spā-taurunō* is perhaps the greyhound, an excellent breed of which is found in Persia.

[1] Hence the strange epithet of *hizu-drājağh.* In just the same way the dog is called *dīrgha-jihvya* (Rv. VI, 101, 1). Perhaps the word may have, in the Avesta, at least a metaphoric signification, I suppose, 'talkative,' to which N.P. *sabĭn-dirās* might be compared.

[2] Vd. XIII, 20 seq.; XV, 3.

[3] Vd. XV, 5. The word used here for bitch is *gadhwa.* It certainly cannot mean 'cat.' In the preceding context dogs only are spoken of; nor is it probable that the cat was so early known. See Hehn, *Culturpflanzen,* p. 531. Now indeed cats are very frequent in Turkistān and fine specimens are seen there. Schuyler, *Turkistān,* vol. i, p. 130.

What a contrast between these precepts and the way in which dogs are now treated in Central Asia! A peculiar purifying power was attributed to the dog. Among other evidences this appears from the ceremony of the *Sagdid*, although the latter has also an idealistic background. Ways by which dead bodies had been carried, were purified by leading over them a dog with certain marks. At sight of him fled away the *Druj Nasush* [1] which had taken possession of the way [2].

. . . .

It is known that dogs which have lapsed into a kind of savage state are a plague to several countries of the Orient. It seems to have been so already in Old Irān. At least there occurred, according to the Avesta, instances of men being killed by dogs [3]. It was, we may suppose, particularly half-savage dogs which trailed forth carcasses and, like foxes and wolves, devoured the corpses exposed on the Dakhmas [4].

§ 19. *Agriculture.*

THE combination of the terms 'cattle-breeder' and 'husbandman' is in the Avesta the constant and official denomination of the peasantry [5]. Thus by the very idiom itself the double nature of husbandry is indicated.

In a like manner the words 'fields' and 'herds' are

---

[1] *Vide* Introduction, p. xxxix.   [2] Cf. *supra*, pp. 76, 81.
[3] Vd. VII, 4.   [4] Vd. V, 3; VI, 46.
[5] *Vāstrya · fshuyās.* The former word is derived from *vāstra* 'pasture,' and represents the farmer as the owner of herds and flocks. But *fshuyās* is, in my opinion, a derivative of the root *fshu*, which must be connected with Skr. *psā* 'food' (cf. also *psur*). By food we must understand corn. It is also called *hvaretha* in the Avesta. Cf. Spiegel, *E. A.* vol. iii, p. 654 seq. In Ys. XXIX, 6 the words *fshuyañtaçcha · vāstryāicha* 'husbandman and owner of cattle' are even used separately.

frequently employed together[1]. Yima, the herdsman of
the people, prays to Druvāspa: 'Grant me that I may
bestow *fields* and *herds* on the creatures of Mazda, that
I may bestow immortality on the creatures of Mazda!'
Then he asks of Anāhita the boon, that he may wrest from
the demons riches and bliss, fields and herds, abundance
and power[2].

The nature of the soil in the country of the Avesta
people is on the whole more favourable to cattle-breeding
than to agriculture. There is abundance of pasture, but
the soil adapted to tillage is rather scanty.

By glancing at present conditions we shall be better able
to judge of the husbandry of this people in antiquity.

The cultivable and cultivated land in Central Asia is of
two kinds. It lies either on the slopes of the mountains or
immediately on the banks of rivers. In the former it
derives the necessary moisture from springs and atmo-
spherical deposits, in the latter from artificial irrigation.

Thus the rude and barren tracks of the higher mountains
are, on the whole, excluded from agriculture. It is only
in the wider and more open valleys, as in those of the
Panja, the Kokcha, the Herīrūd and other rivers that corn
can be produced in considerable quantities, as far as climate
and temperature will allow. In the glen-like transverse
valleys only isolated parcels of the soil can be brought
under tillage. The pastures alone are as a rule of real
value for the husbandry of the people in Central Asia.

Low-lying plains and plateaus are for the most part no
less unfit for the cultivation of corn. Even along the banks
of rivers it is only possible when the construction of water-
channels is not rendered impracticable by the configuration
of the land. Wherever the surface of the river lies beneath
the bottom of the valley, wherever the bank rises steeply,
its waters are often quite useless.

Schuyler says with respect to the Russian dominions[3]:

---

[1] *Fshaoni · vāthwa*. The former is, indeed, connected with
fshuyat and means '.corn, cornfield.'

[2] Yt. IX, 9; V, 26. Cf. Yt. XIX, 32.

[3] *Turkislān*, vol. i, p. 284.

'A map of Central Asia, on which all the arable lands were carefully marked, would be at once instructive and curious, so narrow would be the green strips along the rivers and at the foot of the mountains.' According to his calculations, in the district of Zerafshān only about one-sixth part of the soil is cultivable. In adding the districts of Khōjend and Kurama this proportion will be still less favourable, since in those provinces there are vast deserts. In the latter case there remain only about two twenty-fifth parts of useful ground, in Central Asia altogether no more than one-sixtieth part.

As to the districts in the South of the Amu I have no statistical computation like that of Schuyler for Turkistān. But in reading the accounts of the journeys of Wood, Ferrier, Grodekoff and others, we may probably conjecture that the nature of the soil must be very similar there.

The northern slopes of the Hindūkush apparently contain in their valleys a rather considerable extent of cultivable land. Even far from the banks of rivers good pasture-land is found ; but, for want of moisture, the ground is not fit for raising large crops of corn. This is expressly stated by Wood with respect to the district lying between Kurum and Abi-Kunduz[1]. The plateau between Kurum and Siripūl, which has been traversed by Ferrier, appears to be of a similar nature[2].

If soil of natural productiveness were found in abundance, the water of the rivers would not be utilized as was actually the case.

In the upper and middle course of a river the ground does not always allow the turning-off of the waters into channels. And yet a great number of such channels were passed by Ferrier, as he approached the Dehās on his way from Kurum[3]. The river Sīripūl, also, has such low flat

---

[1] Wood, 'Journey,' pp. 135-136. The plain between the streams that water Kunduz and Kurum has an undulating surface, and, though unfit for agriculture, affords excellent pasturage.

[2] Ferrier, *Voyages*, I, pp. 417-418.

[3] Ibid. p. 419.

banks near this town, though it is situated in the mountains, that its water can be made use of for irrigation in spring [1]. Naturally, artificial irrigation is not employed to any great degree before the rivers enter level land. Consequently, some of the most considerable settlements are situated on the very verge of the desert. The flat districts in the neighbourhood of Balkh are traversed by numerous channels, which distribute the water over the whole plain on which lie the ruins of ancient Bactria. This, in old times, caused its great fertility, and is at present the cause of the marshy state of its soil, where cultivation does not flourish [2].

But the water of the river is absorbed by this manner of irrigation to such a degree that it disappears in the sands of the steppes without reaching the Oxus. Yet, even in the North-East of Balkh, there are ruins of considerable extent in the midst of the desert. They are called Siyāh-gird [3]. They certainly afford proof that in earlier times the quantity of water flowing from the mountains was by far greater, or at least that cultivation was far more efficient than now-a-days.

What has been said of Balkh is no less true with regard to Kunduz and Khulm, Shibārjān and Andkhūi, and particularly with regard to the oasis of Merv [4].

The situation of the Herīrūd is apparently more favourable. Its valley is broad and open, and arable land is found in greater extent even near the middle course of the stream. The district of Haraiva, therefore, was doubtless, in early times, already an important centre of cultivation. The same may be said with respect to the tracts situated to the West on the Keshef, the Atrek and Gurgān, which led the people up into the more fertile fields of Media.

A large tract of fertile ground is also found about the lake of Hāmūn, but the soil is not seldom marshy. It was

---

[1] Cf. p. 70 of *Osīrānische Kultur*.

[2] Grodekoff, 'Ride,' p. 80; Ferrier, 'Voyages,' vol. i, pp. 389–391; Burnes, 'Bokhārā,' vol. ii, p. 207; Elphinstone, 'Kabul,' vol. ii, p. 213.

[3] Grodekoff, 'Ride,' pp. 13–14.

[4] Comp. pp. 60, 62, 69, 70, 71 of *OKA*.

without doubt necessary to drain it in many places, before tilling and sowing were possible. East of the lake of Hāmūn waterless deserts extend as far as the mountains, only a few strips affording suitable pastures to nomad tribes, at least in winter. Arable land is found only in narrow strips along the rivers Farārūd, Khāshrūd, and especially the Hilmend. But cultivation is here rendered possible only by artificial irrigation.

In the mountainous regions of the Aimāks and Hezāres there is abundance of natural pasture. It may be regarded as certain that agriculture is possible in some places, but in comparison with cattle-breeding it will doubtless remain unimportant.

I shall now pass over to the province South-West of Cābul, between the inner Suleimān range and the Hilmend. It has the general character of a rather sterile plateau traversed by ranges of mountains. There are sufficient pastures ; but fields and gardens are confined, for the most part, to the banks of rivers, namely the Arghandāb, the Tarnak, and the Arghesān. Here also the ground everywhere requires an artificial supply of water in order to repay cultivation.

The mountains of Pishīn are rocky, cold, devoid of vegetation. Even the plateau of Tōba, praised for its beauty, consists almost exclusively of pastures. Corn is grown in small tracts, where the ground can be watered. The Shōrawak too owes its productiveness exclusively to artificial irrigation [1].

We know little about the nature of the soil of the upper Kurum and Gōmal, where pasture-land is certainly abundant; however, arable land cannot be wanting since there is no lack of irrigation. The valley of the Cābulrūd is no less adapted for extensive cultivation. But in the mountains of Kōhistān, Kāfiristān and Chitrāl, the land available for tillage is, for the most part, restricted to the wider valleys and the more gentle slopes. Pasture-land is here also very common. The rugged and rocky parts of the highest mountains are absolutely useless for cultivation.

---

[1] Comp. pp. 110, 112 of *OKA.*

With such conditions of soil, husbandry must naturally increase and flourish. It is a matter of course that every spot of land, even the smallest, is profited by, if it can be cultivated. As the sterility of the soil is caused by the deficiency of moisture, artificial irrigation is especially employed in a most rational way, and advantage is taken of the water of rivers, lakes and springs as far as possible. Indeed the irrigation of the soil is carried out with admirable care throughout Turkistān, Afghānistān and Persia.

The Persians evince great ability and skill in their system of irrigation. And yet it is followed by people who have no technical knowledge at all, and whose appliances must be called to some extent defective. We cannot but admire whatever the Persians accomplish in finding out springs, in digging subterranean channels, in dividing and diverting rivers. Hundreds of villages have been created by turning the course of rivers or by separating *one* river into several branches[1].

The beauty of the aqueducts in the environs of Herāt is praised by many a traveller[2]. The system of irrigation practised in Afghān Turkistān, especially in the neighbourhood of Balkh, Andkhūi and Shibargān, has been referred to by me on several occasions. Nor is it less certain that the oasis of Khiva owes its fertility solely to the channels cut from the Oxus.

Nowhere, I think, is the art of watering fields more perfect, nowhere is every drop of water turned to better account than in the valley of the Zerafshān. We are perfectly right in stating that here population can only increase if the supply of water increases.

According to Radloff[3], it might be difficult, even for scientifically trained engineers, to make anything more skilfully than has been done by the people that dwell on the banks of the Zerafshān. The picturesqueness of the

---

[1] Polak, *Persien*, vol. ii, pp. 116, 119; cf. Ritter, *Asien*, VIII, p. 448; Roscher, *Nationalökonomik*, § 36, note 6.

[2] *Vide* pp. 73–74 of *OKA*.

[3] *Zeitschrift der Gesellschaft für Erdkunde*, vol. vi, p. 407 seq. Comp. Khanikoff, *Bokhārā*, p. 46.

neighbourhood of Samarkand depends entirely on artificial irrigation. Without such a supply of water the valley would be sterile and barren. But now the banks of the river are crowned by blossoming gardens and groves of fruit-bearing trees, by waving fields and smiling meadows, wherein feed numerous herds. And not far from here lies the most dreary desert of the globe!

The system of irrigation adopted by the inhabitants of the district of Zerafshān is described at length by Schuyler [1].

Between Penjkend and the lake of Dengiz into which the Zerafshān flows, 85 principal channels are numbered. Their whole length amounts to 2500 kilometres. The numerous branches and ditches, which divide from the channels and distribute the water over fields and gardens, are not included in this reckoning.

The first great channel, called Bulungur, branches off near Penjkend from the right bank. It waters the tracts to the North of the river and is one of the oldest in the valley of the Zerafshān.

Further down, on the left side, begins the channel Dargam [2]. This supplies Samarkand and the territory on the left side of the Zerafshān with the necessary moisture.

At the foot of the hill Chupān-ata, not far from Samarkand, the river divides into two different streams. The Northern is called Ak-daryā, 'white stream;' and the Southern, Karā-daryā, 'black stream.' They enclose an island of considerable fertility. Its length is 113 kilometres, its greatest breadth 14 kilometres. Above Katta-kurgān the Karā-daryā sends off the channel Nari-pāi, which returns after a course of 80 kilometres into the Zerafshān near Kermin. The whole Eastern part of Bokhārā depends on the Karā-daryā and Nari-pāi for its water-supply.

The town of Bokhārā and the province in the North of it are watered by the Sheheri-rūd and other channels, which branch off from the Zerafshān below Kermin. Almost all

---

[1] Schuyler, *Turkistān*, vol. i, p. 286 seq.
[2] *Vide* p. 33 of *OKA*.

the rest of the water of this river is distributed over the country by ditches and channels; only a very small portion reaches the lake of Dengiz.

At the first colonization of the country the Arians, indeed, commenced with cultivating tracts that were naturally productive. But very soon misfortunes, attended with great danger, began to be felt. The rainfall in Turkistān and Eastern Irān is extremely unequal, the success of the harvest is, therefore, very uncertain [1]. Bad harvests and times of pressing want and distress must have been experienced.

In the early times, therefore, the project was planned of employing the water of rivers for the irrigation of the fields. The colonists settled on the banks of a river and extended their fields as far as artificial irrigation was possible.

The Avesta people had already no inconsiderable technical skill for irrigation. In the Gāthās, it is true, this subject is not spoken of. We shall see that this is to be accounted for not only by the scantiness of the texts, but

---

[1] Schuyler, *Turkistān*, vol. i, p. 292 : 'Experience shows, too, that the harvests on these (rain) lands are exceedingly variable. Thus, for example, in 1862, the extensive rain-lands to the south of Katta-kurgān, called Chul, produced 1,106,000 bushels of wheat ; in 1868 : 155,620; in 1870 : 486 ; and in 1871 : 12,430. . . . The great famine of 1870 is still remembered. From 1810 to 1811 there was no winter, and no rain fell in the spring, wherefore the harvest in the rain-lands failed entirely, and there was such a famine that men sold their children, their sisters and mothers, and either killed the old people or left them to starve. In 1835 there was another famine from the same causes, but less disastrous in its consequences, as there had been a remarkably good harvest in the preceding year. In the winter of 1869–70 there was no snow and very little rain in the following spring, so that the wheat on the rain-lands had no sooner sprouted than it dried up.' These facts are taken from an essay written by Grebenkin on the 'Causes of the Bad Harvests in Bokhārā,' published in the *Turkistān Gazette*, 1872, Nos. 17 and 18.

that it is also founded on the economical state of the first
period of Zoroastrian civilization.

In the later Avesta we see that agriculture was highly
developed. All the means are already known and employed by which nature is assisted and its deficiencies
relieved in Central Asia even in our days [1].

Both the draining of morasses and the irrigation of arid
soil are praised as highly meritorious [2]. Such draining
was indispensable in some regions, as for instance on the
Hāmūn; while irrigation was almost necessary in all parts
of the country. The religion of Mazda invites its adherents
to ceaseless activity in agriculture no less than in other pursuits. It bids them fight against sterility and barrenness,
and create instead of them affluence and culture.

Only the cultivated ground is the property of Mazda.
Regions devoid of cultivation are haunted by evil spirits.
Wherever, therefore, a follower of the Avesta religion
settles, it will be his first duty to render the soil productive.
It is a triumph of the good cause whenever a portion of
arable ground is wrung from the death-like desert. In the
Vendidād the genius of the earth is said to rejoice at the
soil being tilled and corn produced, and to mourn at its
remaining barren and sterile. The earth is like a woman,
who misses her vocation when she grows old childless, but
who is proud in happiness and beauty when healthy sons
owe their lives to her [3].

This view will explain why in the Avesta belief and
unbelief are so often brought in immediate connection with
the vegetable life of nature.

At the birth of Zarathushtra the waters and plants
increase. On the contrary, a sinner who has defiled

---

[1] Terms of agriculture are : *aiwi-varez* 'to work the soil' (N.P.
barzīdan, barzīgār, barzīgārī) ; *kāraj* ' to beget, to produce (fruit)' ;
yaokarshti (from *yava + karshti*, from root *karesh* = Skr. *kṛsh*, cf.
kṛshti, charshaṇi ' cultivation of corn ').

[2] Vd. III, 4–5.

[3] This idea is chiefly made use of in the third chapter of the
Vendidād, and forms the key-note of the whole passage. Cf.
ZddmG. vol. xxxiv, p. 421 note.

himself by touching a dead body, will cause the pastures to be parched by heat or herds and flocks to be endangered by enormous masses of snow in winter[1].

A misbeliever, an *Ashemaugha*, takes away all fertility from the country he dwells in. Only after he has suffered merited death is it that prosperity and affluence, bliss and plenty, will return to it[2].

The prostitute, who mingles the seed of the pious and impious, is said to dry up by her looks a third part of the running waters, and to stunt a third part of the beautiful gold-coloured plants. The attacks of evil spirits are directed peculiarly against the fertility of the earth. The good spirits endeavour to keep off these assaults :

> 'When the Evil Spirit sought to overwhelm the creations of the Good and Holy Spirit, there intervened, hostile to him, Vohu-manō and the Fire. They both overthrew the enmity of the evil, wicked Spirit, that he might never check the course of waters, nor prevent the growth of plants. At once the blissful waters of the high Creator, of the powerful Ahura Mazda, began to flow and His plants began to sprout[3].'

The practical side of the Zoroastrian religion was, of course, of the greatest importance for civilization. What happy influence it exercised in Persia has been shown in an excellent manner by Ritter[4]. By the cultivation of the ground, the construction of fountains and the planting of trees the rigour of the Irānian soil and climate were gradually and imperceptibly mitigated.

It is certainly not unknown that the last followers of the Zoroastrian religion on Persian ground, the Guebers in Yezd and Kirmān, chiefly attended to horticulture. It was not by the severity of external circumstances alone that they were compelled to do so[5]. They were in no less

---

[1] Yt. XIII, 93; Vd. VII, 26–27.   [2] Vd. IX, 53–57.
[3] Yt. XIII, 77–78. Cf. Geldner, *Metrik*, § 81.
[4] *Asien*, vol. viii, p. 275.
[5] Khanikoff, *Mémoire*, p. 203 : 'Empêchés par la concurrance

degree influenced by their religious precepts and their habitual esteem for agricultural pursuits. Artificial irrigation is, according to the Avesta, an indispensable requisite in agriculture [1]. In the district of Zerafshān there is a custom of dividing the field into squares in growing lucern and grain which demand an equal distribution of water. They are separated by small ridges a few inches high. When they are filled with water, the opening from the canal is closed and the water is left to soak into the soil [2].

Probably, in old times as at present, the main channel was first dug. From it there branched off, if wanted, secondary channels and ditches which distributed the water over the fields. It is characteristic of the regard for public utility in the Avesta people, that in the Vendidād the construction of water-channels is enjoined as compensation for trespasses [3].

On fields too distant from the river wells were dug in search of springs [4]. The water was then drawn up, we must suppose, by means of suitable appliances.

In the construction of wells the modern Persians show

des musulmans de prendre une part active dans le commerce et dans l'industrie manufacturière, les Guèbres se livrent presque exclusivement au jardinage.'

[1] *Nātat · āpem · hiñchaiti · avi · yavō-charānem*, Vd. V, 5 ; *mācha · paschaçla · Mazdayasna · tām · zām · kārayen, mā · āpō · harezayen*, Vd. VI, 2.

[2] Schuyler, *Turkistān*, vol. i, p. 289.

[3] Vd. XIV, 12 ; V, 5. The ditches made for irrigation are called *vaidhi* or *vāidhi*. In the Pāmir dialects (*Tomaschek*, p. 24) is found *wādh, widdh* with the same signification. A greater channel is called *urudh*, Vd. XIII, 38. The order of the expressions, *maçgha, chāiti, vaçma, urudh, āp-nāvya*, is to be observed. The enumeration is made apparently from the smallest to the larger. Justi translates ' river,' but this is probably denoted by the last expression. I would refer also to Vsp. XVI, 3 : *shōithrya · apascha · zemascha · urvarāoscha*, ' the waters, fields and herbs appertaining to a settlement.'

[4] *Chāiti* or *chāt*=N.P. *chāh* '*puteus, fovea.*' Vd. XIII, 38 ; VI, 33.

special ability. They combine them by horizontal stream-works, so as to form a whole net-work of subterranean channels. The water is drawn up in the following manner : the bucket, fastened to a rope, is sunk into the well ; the rope runs round a beam; oxen yoked to its opposite end draw up the bucket when filled. In order to lighten the work the team is commonly driven down an inclined plane [1].

In regions where water was particularly scarce, cisterns seem to have been constructed [2]. The rain-water gathered there appears to have served for men and herds. It was scarcely sufficient for irrigating the fields.

The Avesta distinguishes three stages in agricultural pursuits : *watering, ploughing up*, and *ploughing down* [3]. The ploughing up was immediately followed by the sowing of corn. Then the seed was covered with earth. Of the form of the plough and of the harrow nothing certain can be stated. At present agricultural implements are very simple and primitive in Turkistan. Hence we may suppose that they were no less so in ancient days.

According to the statements of the Avesta, the irrigation of the soil must have preceded the work of the plough. It was considered a preliminary condition of tilling and sowing. But it was not thought sufficient to water the fields only once. It was repeated two or three times [4]. In agreement with this is the actual custom of the peasantry in the environs of Samarkand in growing wheat.

'Winter-wheat and barley are sown about the middle of September, and worked in with a rude harrow. Winter-

---

[1] Polak, *Persien*, vol. i, p. 120.

[2] Such cisterns are probably meant (Vd. XV, 39) by *avakana* (from root *kan* ' to dig ').

[3] Vd. VI, 6 : *hikhti, karshti* (from root *karesh* 'to draw furrows'), *parakañti*.

[4] Vd. XIV, 13 : ' Arable and productive land (*sãm · karshyãm · raodhyãm*) shall be given to pious men in good piety for the expiation of the soul. Creator! of what kind must the land be? Such (a land) *as is twice watered.*' Vd. V, 5 ; *ana · tã · vaidhīm ayão, ana-bilīm, ana · thritīm ; pascha · tūirīm.*

wheat is irrigated two or three times, barley only once, and the harvest ripens about the end of May[1].'

We do not learn anything further of the tasks and labours of the farmer until the harvest-time. Nor can it be stated, as I have already remarked[2], what kind of grain was cultivated. At present, wheat is general in Turkistān. In the district of Zerafshān one-fourth part of the watered land is sown with wheat, about one-fifteenth only with barley[3]. The agricultural system followed by the Avesta people especially resembles that which is at present employed with respect to wheat. Yet I dare not hence draw any natural conclusion with regard to the ancient practice.

The time for gathering the harvest was, of course, very different according to climate and temperature, and even according to the season of sowing in different provinces. By the beginning of September the crop was everywhere brought home, even in the coldest districts. At this time, therefore, the harvest-feast was celebrated[4].

When the corn was cut, it was probably trodden out by horses and oxen driven over the sheaves spread on the ground. This method is still generally practised. Whatever was not immediately consumed was preserved in *barns*. The separation of the grain from the chaff was performed by *winnowing* or *fanning*. In the *mill*, the construction of which was certainly most primitive, the corn was ground and so meal was made[5].

---

[1] Schuyler, *Turkistān*, vol. i, p. 290.
[2] Comp. pp. 151–152 of *OKA*.
[3] Schuyler, *Turkistān*, vol. i, p. 291.
[4] *Paiti*sh-*hahya*. Vide p. 146 of *OKA*. Hence, therefore, we must not conclude that the climate was exceptionally rigorous. How is it possible to lay down a universally valid law for territories of such diametrically opposite character, as Balkh and Kabul, Seïstān and Ghazna, the districts of Panja and Zerafschān? The harvest certainly took place one or two months later in the mountain valleys than in the hot plains.
[5] *Yavan* ' barn ' (Vd. XVII, 3); *sudhu*sh ' winnowing-fan ' (from rt. *sudh*=Skr. *çudh* ' to cleanse '), Vd. III, 32 ; *pish*t*ra* ' mill ' (from rt. *pish* ' to grind '); *guñda* ' meal.' Schuyler, *Turkistān*, vol. i,

Not only corn, but also grass and fruit-trees were objects of cultivation with the Avesta people:

'Creator of this material world, Thou Holy One! Where, thirdly, is the Earth most gladdened? Ahura Mazda answered: Wherever grain is mostly produced, O son of Spitama, Zarathushtra, and grass and fruit-bearing trees; wherever arid land is changed into watered, and marshy into dry land[1].'

We know that in Old-Irān stall-feeding was necessary during winter. This required the storing of hay in spite of abundant pastures. According to the passage cited above it will scarcely be contested that *grass was grown*[2]. But it was certainly restricted as far as possible on account of the small extent of productive land. But a portion of the winter fodder might have been also obtained from pastures.

It is a matter of importance that *the Avesta people also cultivated trees*. This circumstance proves that they were a fully-settled people. He who cultivates grain, takes care of his immediate wants, but he who rears trees, thinks less of his own advantage than of that of his children and grandchildren who shall one day enjoy the fruits of his labour. He supposes that his progeny will dwell on the same land, will plough the same field. Confiding in their love and reverence for himself he will leave them his land in the best possible condition.

I have already spoken about the abundance of fruit in Turkistān and Eastern Irān[3]. Persia and Afghanistān, which are more favourably situated, are famous for their splendid gardens.

In his description of the inhabitants of Zerafshān in connection with the subject of horticulture, Schuyler says:

---

p. 290: 'The grain, instead of being thrashed, is trodden out by oxen and horses, and then cleaned by being tossed in the air.'

[1] Vd. III, 4.

[2] Also in Vd. XV, 41–42 the question seems to refer to artificially laid-out meadows (*yō · aᵉtem · vāstrem · uᵭdasta · vāstri*sh). It is true that Geldner translates 'hurdle.'

[3] *Vide* p. 151 of *OKA*.

'The gardens are the glory of all this land. The long rows of poplars and elm-trees, the vineyards, the dark foliage of the pomegranate over the walls, transport one at once to the plains of Lombardy or of Southern France. In the early spring the outskirts of the city and indeed the whole valley are one mass of white and pink with the bloom of almond and peach, of cherry and apple, of apricot and plum trees, which perfume the air for miles around. Nowhere are fruits more abundant, and of some varieties it can be said that nowhere are they better[1].'

Little can be stated with certainty as to the system of managing farms followed by the Avesta people. It may have varied in different provinces.

A system of fields having permanent pasturage is best adapted to the conditions of the soil. It is characteristic of this system that the ground is divided into two principal portions, of which one is employed for growing corn, the other as permanent pasture[2]. The former lies nearer to the centre, or the settlement, in order to lessen the work in the fields. In Irān it was limited to the banks of rivers, or slopes naturally irrigated.

Manuring was unknown. Had it ever been practised, it would have been mentioned among the preparatory stages of agriculture not less than irrigation. Nor do we know whether several species of grain were cultivated or whether the rotation of crops was understood. It was necessary, therefore, to let the soil lie fallow at certain periods. It was also not impossible to turn it into grass-land, since the cultivation of meadows was at least not quite unknown.

Finally, I again refer here to the state of husbandry in the district of Zerafshān, as known to us and as described by Schuyler[3]:

'Farmers possessing only four or five acres endeavour by careful cultivation to get as much out of their land as

---

[1] *Turkistān*, vol. i, p. 296.
[2] Roscher, *Nationalökonomik*, § 25.
[3] *Turkistān*, vol. i, pp. 289-290.

possible, without allowing it to lie fallow too long. In general the larger farmers pursue a modification of the three-field system. The field, after lying fallow for a year, is sown with winter-wheat or barley. The next year, after this crop is reaped, the land is again ploughed up and sown for the second harvest with millet, sesame, lentils, carrots or poppies.'

§ 20. *Manufactures.*

EVERY manufacture begins in the family. Originally, it is exclusively a domestic industry. Wherever it has already begun to become a profession, it is not the exclusive occupation. Farming is carried on at the same time as a subsidiary employment, as is not seldom the case in our villages.

Not before considerable numbers crowd together in one place, or before a lively commercial intercourse allowing the constant exchange of manufactured articles in return for natural productions, arises, will industry make any great progress. This progress, therefore, coincides with the gradual development of villages into towns. Then, by reason of the increasing demand, the manufacturer is able to support himself and his family by his industry. He finds it no longer profitable to work in the fields. All his energy is devoted to his craft; increasing custom sharpens his ingenuity, and thus industry thrives not merely in extent but also in excellence.

With the Avesta people it is true that manufactures did not develope in such a normal way. And yet the following sketch may serve as a standard whereby to judge the state of industry in Old-Irān at the period described in the Avesta.

The articles of manufacture in use among the Avesta people were many and various, in fact, too varied to allow us to think of them as merely the productions of domestic industry in the full sense of the word. Thus we are compelled to assume that there was a distinct class of handicraftsmen.

With these brief observations I proceed to enter more closely into this question.

Special skill seems to have been shewn in the working of metals. The manufacture of instruments of gold and brass or bronze was the most important branch of this industry; but silver, copper and lead too seem to have been worked [1]. We must not forget that the Avesta texts are too scanty to furnish an idea of the instruments which they made use of, or of their mode of working and technical knowledge.

Gold was the best known and most precious metal. No less on account of its brilliancy and splendour, than on account of the little difficulty which it offers to the workman, it was employed first of all metals in different parts of the world.

In Old-Irān jewellery was chiefly made of gold. The Avesta [2] speaks of golden fillets, ear-rings and necklaces. Gold cups or bowls seem to have been used on the occasions of the Hauma consecration [3]. Gold was also employed for the embellishment of arms, particularly the hilts of daggers and swords. The dagger, which the legendary king Yima wore as a badge of his sovereign power, is styled 'decorated with gold [4].' Finally, it must be mentioned that gold embroidery on garments, coverings and carpets was not quite unknown [5].

---

[1] *Vide* pp. 147–148 of *OKA*. The workshop (?) of a worker in metals is called *pisra*. The particular class is denoted by the compounds: *zaranyō-saēpa, erezatō-saēpa,* &c. *Pisra* may be connected with Skr. *piç* 'to adorn, to decorate, to work skilfully'; *saēpa* must be derived from rt. *sip*, which has been preserved in N.P. *siflan* 'to harden.' For the whole statement compare Vd. VIII, 87 seq., where you will find a list of manufactures in which fire is used.

[2] *Zaranyō-pusa* 'with golden fillets' (Yt. XV, 57; XIX, 41); *zaranyō-mina* 'with a golden necklace' (Yt. XV, 57). Cf. Yt. V, 127 and p. 227 of *OKA*.

[3] *Tashti · zaranaēn*. Ys. X, 17.

[4] *Ashtra · zaranyō-paēsa.* Vd. II, 7. Cf. Skr. *hiranya-peças.*

[5] See pp. 223, 225, 227 of *OKA*.

Gold is principally mentioned wherever divine beings or things belonging to them are spoken of.

The chariot and the chariot-wheels of the *wind-yazata* Vayu and of Mithra are made of gold. The former wears a girdle, a helmet, and arms of gold; the latter is clad in a gold coat-of-mail [1]. The very hoofs of the horses of Mithra and Srausha are shod with gold or silver [2].

It is hardly necessary to say that these words are merely metaphorical. Certainly no one will conclude from such descriptions that helmets or mail-coats, nay, even chariots and wheels and horse-shoes, were made of gold! Yet by these figures of speech it is proved beyond doubt that these precious metals were worked to no little extent. We see also that gold was considered a symbol of affluence and splendour and therefore reckoned among the possessions of divine beings.

Besides vessels of gold there were others of silver, brass and copper, and likewise of stone, clay and wood [3]. Those of brass or lead were of least value. The most common things only, used in every-day life, were made of these materials. It must be remarked that vessels of lead were apt to become very dangerous to health [4].

Silver was considered inferior only to gold. But the former was worked far less than the latter. The cup in which the Hauma is purified is made either of gold or silver. Mithra wears on his head a helmet of silver [5].

Arms and weapons are chiefly made of brass or bronze, e.g., helmets and coats-of-mail, arrow-heads and metal-heads of clubs, as well as the blades of swords and daggers [6].

---

[1] Yt. XV, 57; X, 112, 124, 136.

[2] Yt. X, 125; Ys. LVII, 27.

[3] Vd. VII, 74 seq. treats of the cleansing of such vessels. Cf. *hāvana · ayağhaęna* (Ys. XXII, 2).

[4] *Ayağhaęnem · vā · srum · vā · nilema · khshathra · vairya.* Vd. XVI, 6.

[5] Ys. X, 17; Yt. X, 112.

[6] An iron-foundry is called *fra-hich* (Yt. X, 96). Compare Skr. *sam-sich*, Athrawa-veda, XI, 8, 13 (B.R. *sub voce*).

In the Avesta, therefore, the word 'brass' is metaphorically employed for arms. Clubs were also covered with plates and knobs of *copper* to increase their size and weight [1]. I come now to pottery. Earthen vessels have already been mentioned above. They were usually baked in kilns [2] specially constructed for the purpose. The art of making and burning tiles was also well known. But glass, as I think, was not yet made. The belief that the old Irānians manufactured glass would lead to important conclusions in the history of civilization. But it rests only on an incorrect interpretation of the text [3].

I would, likewise, ascribe the use of coal as fuel to the age of the Avesta [4]. The melting of metals required a fire of intense heat. This want may first have led to the use of coal. The material was less deficient in old times, we may suppose, than now-a-days.

The art of *weaving*, though very old and known already in the Indo-Germanic period, is mentioned quite casually in the Avesta [5]. With it is mentioned the art of working the skins of beasts into garments. Since Anāhita especially is represented as clad in skins, I conjecture that the robes of the nobility in particular were trimmed with fur. The

---

[1] Hence *chakushanām-haosafnaęnanām*, Yt. X, 130.

[2] *Tanūra*, N.P. *tanūr*, seems to denote the potter's kiln.

[3] Vd. VIII, 84–85 says *khumba*t · *hacha* · *zemaini-pachikā*t and *khumba*t · *hacha* · *yāmō-pachikā*t. The first I translate 'from a potter's kiln, where clay is burned,' the latter 'from a potter's kiln, where vessels are burned.' The former term refers to the making of tiles, the latter to pottery in its proper sense. It cannot be thought strange that the making of the two articles was regarded as a *single* manufacture, and both are therefore called *khumba*. Of course *yāma* is connected with N.P. *jām* '*poculum*.'

[4] I infer this from Vd. VIII, 95, where I identify the word *skairya* with N.P. *sakār*, *sagār* 'coal.' Thus also Geldner.

[5] *Vap* 'to weave.' Cf. *vastra-ubdaęna* 'woven garments.' More difficult of interpretation is *izaęna* · *vastra*, which can scarcely be separated from * *iza*, Skr. *aja*, *ajā* 'goat.' It does not, therefore, signify garments of skins, but those made from the hair of goats. Cf. p. 224, note 5 of *OKA*.

passage referred to proves at the same time that they knew well the seasons in which it was either profitable or the reverse to hunt beasts for their fur.

The building of carriages and the making of harness attained a high degree of perfection among the old Irānians and the old Indians. But it is to be regretted that many of the terms in question are obscure in the Avesta.

A distinction was made, I think, between war-chariots and baggage-wagons[1]. The former bore a driver and a combatant; the latter served for the carriage of goods during peace.

As a rule there were two horses to each chariot. They stood on the right and left sides of the pole, and their halters were fastened to it by means of iron hooks[2]. Sometimes a carriage-and-four was used[3]. Rich and noble gentlemen chiefly indulged in this luxury. The chariots of the *yazatas*, therefore, are especially described as drawn by four horses.

---

§ 21. *Medicine and Commerce.*

THE art of healing appears in the Avesta as a profession of a higher order. It plays no unimportant part in our texts. It had apparently already attained a certain degree of perfection; and, as I am inclined to believe, the priests all devoted themselves to this profession[4].

---

[1] Av. *ratha* and *vāsha*. A horse completely harnessed is called *aspa-yukhta.*

[2] *Ākhna* and *aiwi-dāna* (= Skr. *abhidhānī*; cf. also Tomaschek, *Pāmirdialekte*, p. 73). Also in Yt. X, 125 some parts of the harness are enumerated, e. g. *hām-isa, Sima*; but I cannot make out their meaning.

[3] *Vāsha · chathru-yukhta*, Vd. VII, 41.

[4] *Baęshaza*, 'art of healing,' 'medicine,' and 'physician.' The last is also called *thamanaǧhvat.* Again medicine is *baęshaəya*. Cf. Skr. *bhishaj* and *bheshaja*. The expression *vimādhāǧh* for 'curing' (Vd. VII, 38) deserves attention, because it is akin to Latin *medeor, medicus, medicina*. Compare, for the whole, Spiegel, *E.A.* vol. iii, pp. 581–582.

Diseases were of course considered by the old Irānians to be the creations of Evil. They make their appearance in numberless forms. There are ten thousand, as the Bundehish asserts [1]. Angra Manyu created them on earth to damage the pious people. But Ahura Mazda set bounds no less to this plague than to all other works of the demons. He made the healing plants to grow, by the juice of which patients are healed [2].

Fevers chiefly are endemic in ancient as well as in modern Irān. They appear in different forms, and are, therefore, denoted in the Avesta by different names. Some of those names, for reasons which are apparent, originally mean 'flame' or 'heat [3].'

The puerperal fever in particular is also mentioned in the Avesta as occurring to women in child-bed, and often endangering their lives. Like all other fevers, it is accompanied by a tormenting thirst [4].

Women, moreover, are exposed to divers diseases. Among them the Avesta mentions the disorder of the *menstruum*, consisting in an abnormal duration of hemorrhage [5].

Head-aches also afflicted the Irānian [6]. *Caries*, or consumption [7]—the term in question is obscure—destroyed the

---

[1] *Bdh.* IX, 4; West, 'Pahlavi Texts,' part i, p. 31.

[2] Vd. XX, 3–4; XXII, 2.

[3] *Dazhu* (Vd. XX, 3), from rt. *daz* = Skr. *dah* 'to burn.' Next comp. *tafnu* = Phlv. *tapashn* (N.P. *tabish* 'febris'); *sārasti* or *sārastya* (Phlv. *garm* 'heat, flame'; according to Darmesteter, Vd. p. 221, n. 1, it must mean the ague); *naęza* and *naezaǧh* (Phlv. *tanput* = N.P. *tanbad* 'rigor febris*, feverish chill;' yet in Yt. XIV, 33 it is used metaphorically for 'fire').

[4] *Yezicha · hę̄ · hām · tafnō · jasā*t · *avi · tanuyę̄ · zōishnuyę̄, yę̄zicha · hę̄ · dva · yaska · avi · achishtō · ājasā*t, *yascha · sudhō · yascha · tarshnō*, Vd. VII, 70. The word *zōishnu* may be connected with the root *zan* 'to bear (children).'

[5] Vd. XVI, 8 seq. I will no longer assert with confidence that *pishtra* and *skeñda* in Vd. V, 59, denote sexual diseases.

[6] *Sārana*, from *sāra* 'head.'

[7] *Vazemnō-asti*. Consumption, as a consequence of unnatural practices, is probably meant in Vd. XVIII, 54 by 'we dry away from him his tongue and his fat.'

strength of his body. An excess of sexual desire [1] might likewise become a sort of disease.

A grave national evil existed in divers cutaneous disorders, among which I shall only specify the itch. Most terrible was leprosy, which covers and destroys the body of the patient. It rages now-a-days too all over Central Asia and certain tracts of Persia [2].

The bite of snakes caused death by poisoning. This may be understood by 'the calamity caused by serpents,' spoken of in the Avesta. Some plants, too, contained deadly venom, which might be fatal to the incautious [3].

Furthermore, there are enumerated in the Avesta a series, for the most part of bodily defects and infirmities, which were regarded as emblems of the evil spirit. There were people with a hump on their breasts or backs, stammerers, dwarfs or hunch-backed people and such as had overgrown teeth [4]. To these must be added the blind and the deaf, the halt and the lame, the dumb and the idiotic. They are all marked by the devil [*disease*] and therefore excluded from the sacrifices of the pure *yazata* Anāhita [5].

---

[1] *Vāvereshi* (Yt. XIII, 131) is certainly connected with Skr. *vṛsh*, *vṛshan*. In Vd. VII, 58, which may be regarded more or less as a parallel passage, we read *aghōsḥish · pourushu · asti · varesō*, but the text is corrupt. I should like to change the first word into *aghaoshtish* (cf. *maidhyoshema*, perhaps for *maidhyaoshma* according to *ZddmG*. vol. xxxv, p. 666), 'evil desire,' from *agha ushti*.

[2] *Garenu* = N.P. *gar*, and *pāman* = Skr. *pāman* 'itch'; *paęsō · vilaretō-tanu*sh = N.P. *pēs* 'leprosy.' Cf. Polak, *Persien*, vol. ii, p. 305 ; Schuyler, *Turkistān*, vol. i, pp. 147–148.

[3] *Azhi-karsh*tem *tbaęshō.*—*Kapasti* = N.P. *kabast* 'poison.' I must pass over other names of diseases, as *azhana, azhahva, kurugha, duruka*, since they are not intelligible.

[4] Vd. II, 29 : *frakava, apakava, apāvaya, kasvi, vīmitō-dañtan*. The translation of the different terms is based upon tradition.

[5] Ys. V, 93. *Añda* = Skr. *andha* 'blind.' *Karena* 'deaf,' comp. Tomaschek, *Pamirdialekte*, p. 83 (Skr. *karṇa* 'ear '). *Drva* perhaps = *dhruva* 'fixed, not being able to move,' hence 'lame.' *Mūra* = Skr. *mūra* 'silly, idiotic.' *Ara* may perhaps be derived from the root *rā* = Skr. *rā* 'to utter a sound,' with the primitive *a*, hence

'Healing by means of sayings (mâthra)' was considered the chief and most efficacious kind of medical treatment [1]. But nobody could utter religious sayings and prayers more efficaciously than priests. The physicians, therefore, belonged to the priestly order.

If prayers had not the wished-for effect and if the demons of disease would not depart from the patient, the physician was called in to help by his skill. According to the kind of disorder, therapeutics or surgery, 'the cure by means of plants' or 'the cure by means of apparatus' was employed [2].

The best healing powers have been given by Ahura Mazda to plants. especially the poisonous ones. In them deadly and healing qualities are combined [3]. To water also healing power was attributed both by the Irānians and the Indians [4]. Hence it is that Amertāt and Harvatāt, the genii of a long and healthy life, preside over water and plants.

The art of curing was thought very ancient. Its origin is traced back to the divine beings by tradition. This art was greatly valued by the Avesta people. The last three chapters of the Vendidād are almost exclusively devoted to it, and it is here that its origin is described.

Thrita [5], we are told, was the first 'of the helping, prudent, powerful, intelligent and rich men belonging to the

'dumb.' Finally, *ragha* comes from the root *ragh*=Skr. *las* ' to hobble.'

[1] *Mâthrō-baeshaza* (Vd. VII, 44). The *mâthra* and *vachāo* are expressly called *baeshaza* or *baeshazya* ' healing, curing.' Vd. IX, 27; X, 5; Yt. III, 5.

[2] *Urvarō-baeshaza* and *karetō-baeshaza*. Vd. VII, 44.

[3] Comp. *vish-chithrem* ' a remedy coming from poisonous plants.'

[4] Comp. Rv. I, 23. 19–21 ; Zimmer, *AiL.* p. 272.

[5] Av. *Thrita* corresponds to the Indian *Trita*, to which, as is known, the Greek Τρίτων, Τριτωνίς, Τριτογένεια are correlative. Evidently *Trita* was, originally, the deity of the water, either celestial or terrestrial. Since water was considered to possess sanative qualities, he might fitly be made the inventor and protector of medical science.

family of the *Paradhāta*,' who fought against sickness and death [1]. At his request Mazda causes the numberless multitude of healing plants to grow [2]. It is also he, according to tradition, who first contrived the double mode of treatment, either by plants having medicinal qualities or by surgical operations. With native simplicity he is said to have requested from Ahura Mazda as a boon a medicine coming from poisonous plants, and a metallic knife [3].

Medical treatment did not extend to men only, but also to beasts [4]. There are special precepts regarding the efforts which must be made in order to cure dogs that have run mad. . Medicine should be administered to them entirely in the same way as to man. If this is done in vain it is permitted to use violence [5].

He who intended to practise medicine was obliged to undergo a kind of preliminary examination, in connection with which the most characteristic feature was that surgical experiments were made on unbelievers. If they died under awkward hands, the loss was not considered a great one.

If he who underwent the examination failed in three operations, he was incapable for ever of becoming a physician. If, nevertheless, he practised medicine, and if one of his patients died in consequence of injudicious treatment, it was imputed to him as intentional murder. But if, on the contrary, he succeeded in three operations and the patients recovered, he was allowed to practise without any restriction [6].

If the physician was called to a sick person, he was obliged to answer the summons as soon as possible. But the Vendidād deprecates hastiness in the treatment of the sick. Great importance was evidently attached to a correct diagnosis. The physician must observe each symptom of

---

[1] Vd. XX, 1–2.

[2] *Urvarāo · baçshazyāo.* Vd. XX, 4.

[3] *Vish-chithrem · dim · ayasata · āyapta · khshathra · vairya,* Vd. XX, 3. The last term denotes firstly 'metal,' then 'a metallic tool,' 'a knife,' as in Vd. IX, 9.

[4] Vd. VII, 43.
[5] Vd. XIII, 35 seq.

[6] These regulations are found in Vd. VII, 36–40.

the disease and learn its nature before he decides on this or that remedy. If a disease has begun in the morning, the treatment is to commence in the day-time; if during the day, it shall be commenced in the night; if in the night, the physician has to commence by day-break [1]. This is a precept that was certainly dispensed with in cases of emergency.

The fee—which, it seems, was to be paid only after a successful cure—is laid down already in the Vendidād [2]. In speaking of the fee of a physician I enter upon the investigation of a very important matter in the civilization of the Avesta people, viz. the question of money.

The fee differs for men according to rank and calling, for beasts according to their utility. A priest is to be cured for a blessing. Therefore, he pays no taxes.

For curing the master of a house, the head of a village, the president of a community, and the sovereign of a country respectively, there should be paid an ass, an ox, a horse or camel, and a carriage with four horses. For ladies, payment must be made, according to their rank, of the corresponding female beasts, a she-ass, a cow, a mare or a she-camel. The cure of a child of a family, particularly of a son, seems to have cost a horse. For curing a domestic animal the one next in value was always given; for a horse a cow, for an ox an ass, for an ass a sheep, while, last of all, bread and milk were given for a sheep.

We see that natural products, especially domestic animals, were the regular medium of payment. Thus the circumstances of the Avesta people were quite similar to those of the old northern nations and of the first epochs of Rome. In the one, cattle were regarded as the standard of value and

---

[1] *Yęzi · uzirōhva · mereñchailę̄, arezahva · baęshazyā̆t ; yęzi · arezahva · mereñchailę̄, khshapōhva · baęshazyā̆t ; yęzi · khshapōhva · mereñchailę̄, ushahva · baęshazyā̆t,* Vd. XXI, 3. ' The sickness ' is here the grammatical subject. *Mereñch* cannot mean, of course, ' to kill,' but only ' to hurt, to prove hurtful.' Comp. Skr. *mṛch.*

[2] Vd. VII, 41–43.

money[1]; in the other, all bargains were originally effected by bartering domestic animals, and coined money was not substituted before the legislation of the decemvirs.

Even in the making of contracts cattle or sheep were given in pledge, according to the precepts of the Avesta. He who violated or revoked such a contract had to give, according to the agreement, one or more head from his herd or flock.

The fee payable to a priest for performing the purificatory ceremonies was settled in domestic animals just like the fees of physicians. And here it is expressly laid down that the beasts themselves shall be given as far as practicable. Only in exceptional cases it was allowed to expiatea fault or transgression by giving other movable goods [2].

No proof can be adduced that we ought to understand by movable goods also coined money. On the contrary, this is contradicted by all other conditions of commerce. Wherever coined money is once known and in general use, it is impossible to think that payment in animals can be customary or desirable, even in the case of priests, to whom such property in animals could not but be inconvenient, considering that the nature of their duties constantly called them away from their own homes.

At most, it might be conceded that the nobility amassed, here and there, in their houses, trinkets, jewels and other precious things which might perhaps serve as means of payment in some cases [3].

---

[1] Weinhold, *Altnordisches Leben*, p. 202.

[2] Vd. IX, 37–39: '. . . If they can afford it, the Mazdayasna shall deliver to that man these animals from out their herds or flocks. But if they cannot, they shall replace them by *some other goods* (*anyām · avaretanām*).' This translation of the passage, according to which the animals are evidently considered as being themselves *avareta*, proves that movable goods in general are only meant by it. The same is apparently signified by *shaęta* or *khshaęta* (= Phlv. *khvāstak*). If this is given as *weregild* ' compensation for a murder' (Vd. IV, 44), we cannot doubt that horses, cattle or sheep are meant more than anything else.

[3] This might be inferred from Yt. XIII, 67 : ' Just as a man,

Similar circumstances are found at least among cognate nations in a similar stage of civilization. So it is with the ancient Germans and the Indians of the Rig-veda. ' The chiefs of the Germans pay by means of horses and jewels; excellent horses and rings are given as gifts of honour ; horses and jewels are very often granted as rewards in " Beowulf." The same is the case with the Vedic tribes : *Nishka*, a golden ornament for the neck or breast, serves as a present together with horses : "A hundred *Nishka* were given me (says the poet of *Kakshivant*) by the king who stood in need ; with a hundred horses I was presented in one day." ' [1]

Of course we cannot speak properly of commercial intercourse, where a system of currency was entirely wanting. It was, I suppose, limited to the exchange of natural products between neighbouring communities.

But the desire to enter into commercial relations with other provinces cannot be said not to have existed in the time of the Avesta. The attempt was made to construct the first bridges and ways. The building of bridges in particular is highly meritorious, since streams and rivers are among the greatest obstacles to commerce [2]. In the garden *Vara*, laid out by Yima (who during the great deluge finds here an asylum with his family), there are bridges and roads, as signs of good order and management.

In conclusion, I shall mention some of the standards of measure used in the Avesta.

A dry measure used for grain and even for liquids was the *Danare* [3]. I cannot say how much it contained.

---

a valiant warrior, armed and watchful, drives (the enemies) away from his collected treasures (*hush-hām-beretat* . *hacha* . *shaetāt*).'
    [1] Zimmer, *AiL*. p. 259.
    [2] Comp. Vd. XIV, 16 ; XVIII, 74. 'Way' is *maregha* = Skr. *mārga*, (Vd. II, 26). ' Bridge' is *peshu* (= *peretu*, from the root *par* ' to pass over'), originally only a natural food. The bridge supported on piles or pillars is called more specifically *fraschinbana* (cf. *skemba*, Skr. *skambha*). Also *haętu* = Skr. *setu* means, I think, both ' ford ' and ' bridge.'
    [3] According to Vd. XVI, 7, a menstruating woman is to receive for (daily) food one Danar *tāyūra* (?) and two Danar *khshāudra*. De

The smaller linear measures are taken from parts of the human body, and especially the *finger*. Sometimes, too, the uppermost joint of the middle finger is employed as a still smaller unit. Then follows the *span*, next the *ell* (the fore-arm from the top of the finger to the elbow), and, finally, the whole *arm* [1]. The *foot* served for a further unit of measure; three feet make a *pace* [2]. A greater length was determined by the *Hāthra*. Three or four made a *Parasang* (*Farsang*) [3]. A very interesting measure of length is the *Chartu*. Like the stadion of old Greece it seems to have been the length of the race-ground settled by use. But it might perhaps have been the distance made by a horse and his rider in *one* run [4]. In this case the length of the *Chartu* would be entirely vague and unsettled.

§ 22. *The Settlements of the Avesta People.*

THE Avesta contains a whole series of expressions, having the general signification of 'colony' or 'settlement.'

Harlez (*Av. tr.* vol. i, p. 235, note 5) observes regarding the *dā-nare*: 'Mesure de capacité ou de poids dont la base est une certaine quantité de grain. Elle paraît peser environ 700 grains.'

[1] 'Finger'=*erezu* (the Skr. *dishthi* also is a linear measure, see B.R. *sub voce*); 'finger-point'= *tbishi*, Vd. XVII, 5, and 7; 'span'= *vītasti*, N.P. *bīdast*; 'ell'=*vībāzu*, *frabāzu* (Skr. *prabāhu*) or *frā-rathni* (Skr. *aratni*); 'arm'=*bāzu*=Skr. *bāhu*.

[2] 'Foot' = *padha*, as in *thripadha* and *navapadha*; also = *gāya* as in *aęvō-gāya* and *thri-gāya*. Vd. IX, 8, and 10.

[3] Justi (in his *Hdb.*) says that the word *hāthra* denotes 'A measure of distance 1000 feet longer than a *parasang.*' But compare the different meaning of it given by West, *Pahlavi Texts*, part i, p. 46, note 5, and p. 98, note 2; *Bdh.* XIV, 4; XVI, 7, 29.

[4] *Charetu* is, indeed, connected with the root *char* 'to run,' and *chareta* 'race-ground.' The 'Vara' of Yima is said to be a *chartu* long in every direction (Vd. II, 25). The tradition translates the word by *asp-rās* 'horse-way.'

Sometimes they designate merely the relations in which
the individual lives with his family and his domestics,
sometimes the hamlet or the village, sometimes even the
entire district attached to it, sometimes the country, so far
as it is in general cultivated and inhabited, in opposition to
the surrounding unoccupied regions [1].

---

[1] The most important expressions may be traced partly from the
root *khshi*, *shi*=Skr. *kshi*, partly from *had*=Skr. *sad* 'to sit down,'
partly also from *karesh*=Skr. *krsh* 'to make furrows, to cultivate
the field.' To *khshi* belong :—1. *Shiti* (such as *hu-shiti*=Skr. *sukshiti*, next *rāmō-shiti* 'quiet, secure settlement,' and *dareghō-shiti*
'lasting settlement' ; *yāirya hushiti* 'yearly, good dwelling' is to
be particularly noticed, because in this expression an allusion is contained to a changing of the field).—2. *Shōitheman* in *hushoitheman*
and *shayana*. The last one means the land generally inhabited,
hence *airyō-shayana*. Gava is a *shayana*, i.e. the habitable part in
Sughdha, Khnenta in Vehrkāna, Vaikerta in the land of the
Duzhaka.—3. *Shōithra* is the 'field.' Hence this word stands
together with conceptions such as *gaoyaoiti* 'pasture-ground,'
maethana 'dwelling,' *asagh* 'district.' Cf. also *shōithrya · apascha ·
zemascha · urvarāoscha* p. 207, note 3. In Ys. 31. 16 *shoithrya*
stands as elsewhere *zantu*.

To the root *had* belong *hademan*, 'settlement,' and *hadish*,
meaning the same. The latter word occurs thrice in the Vispered
with the characteristic epithet 'rich in fields.' The former one
belongs to the Gāthā dialect. To *karesh* belongs *karsha* in
karshō-rāza 'founding, disposing and ruling settlements.' With
this compare Ys. 11. 2 : 'The horse curses his rider : In future
shalt thou not trap, mount, or rein a courser, as thou implorest not
for strength for me in the numerous community, in the settlement
abounding in heroes.' From the Old-Indian *krshti* and *charshani*
may be taken for comparison, particularly *pancha-krshtayah* or
charshanayah 'the five tribes.' With such names the Arians
characterize themselves with pride as a nation pursuing agriculture. (Comp. also Joh. Schmidt, *K. Z.* XXV. p. 89). In the
Avesta *karshivat* still denotes the rustic or peasant.

Further expressions are : *maethana*, *maethanya*, and *maetha*
'lodging, dwelling, premises of a farm.' According to Yt. XIII.
57, *maethana* must concur with *shōithra*. Worthy of notice are
also such formations as *asagh*, *shōithra*, *gaoyaoiti*, *maethana*,
Ys. I. 16, II. 16, III. 18, where *maethana*, I believe, denotes

This of itself proves what importance fixed settlements had in developing the civilization of the Avesta nation.   It may be said with perfect justice that they generally formed the central point of their entire economical, religious and political life.   The settled agriculturists and breeders of cattle are on the one side, and the homeless, restless, wandering herdsmen are on the other : these are the two great bodies, sharply opposed to each other, into which the inhabitants of ancient Irān were divided.

'house and farm' as opposed to field (*shōithra*) and meadow (*gaoyaoiti*).   Herewith corresponds Ys. X. 7, *ahḗ · vīsḗ · uta · maēthanem* 'village and farm.'   These words belong, according to Geldner (*Metrik*, pp. 147 and 156, note 16), to the commentary.   Also *gaētha* denotes frequently 'settlement, premises of a farm.'   Thus in the word *hadha-gaētha* 'inmate.'   It originally means 'possession, property' (*vide* p. 170, note 3), from root *gi=ji* 'to conquer, to obtain by victory, to acquire.'   Comp. Skr. *jaya*, which has quite the same meaning.   Then *gaētha* often means 'people,' particularly, I think, in such expressions as *ashahḗ · gaēthāo* 'people of the pious,' Ys. XXXI. 1; Yt. V. 34; XIX. 41 and 93.   The transition of meaning from 'settlement' to 'people living in settlements, settlers,' is found also in Skr. *kshiti* and Av. *hademan*.   To the Av. *gaētha* corresponds Old-Persian *gaithā*.   The word stands near *mānya*, and denotes evidently the whole farm together with the farm-buildings as opposed to the dwelling-house in particular.   There is no doubt that *gaētha* often means 'the herds.'   I include here chiefly *drvō-gaētha* 'possessing healthy herds,' which stands near *haurva-fshu*, further Yt. VIII. 29, where *vāstra* and *gaētha*, 'fields and herds,' are combined.

It would be very interesting if we could ascertain whether *khshathra* (certainly = N. P. *shahar* 'town'); should that word come from *shōithra*, it must sound *shēhar*) may mean 'fortified settlement.'   It is striking that all the passages which may be adduced as proof, belong to the Gāthās.   Comp. Ys. 45. 9 and 46. 16, but chiefly 34. 3, where it is said that the farms lie in the fortified settlement (*vīspāo · gaēthāo · ā · khshathrōi*).   If the translation be correct, we might ascertain in the case of Irān, the normal development of the town from the village surrounded with wall and trenches.

Finally, I mention *vīs* 'village,' and *nmāna* 'single farm,' of which I shall speak further on.

Though my present subject is, therefore, the system of settlement adopted by the Avesta people, still I must again discuss all its social features. In the section on 'Cattle-Breeding and Agriculture,' I have only dwelt upon the extent to which the economical life of the Avesta people had developed itself; in order to avoid repetitions I have not in the first place considered the course of that development. This historical part of the question must here necessarily appear in the foreground as far as possible. The chief point now is to trace the natural beginnings of the division mentioned above, and to show how the separation became wider and wider in course of time. It had become gradually more and more hostile and incompensable, since one portion of the nation began to advance vigorously on the path of civilization, while the other remained stationary in its earlier stage of culture.

Fixed habitations are to the old Irānian the *beau-ideal* of good fortune, of rest, and of peace. They are a gift of the heavenly ones. Tishtrya is called 'the dispenser of the field.' He and Mithra bestow good and peaceful settlements and long-lasting habitations [1].

In quite a similar manner the Vedic Indian in his hymns prays for 'good settlements' from the Gods. Indra, Agni, Soma, grant them to the pious man [2]. To him before all they belong, who stands under heavenly protection. Or they are possessed by the powerful ruler who protects his people with a strong hand and keeps away the enemy from his borders [3].

Settlements can be naturally founded only in such places where there are rich pastures for cattle and sufficient arable land. Hence they are called 'the rich in fields.'

　　'When will, O Mazda! at the same time with piety,
　　　　devoted sense

---

[1] *Shōïthrahẹ̄ · bakhtare, hushayana, rāmō-shiti, dareghō-shiti* are in Yt. VIII. 2 and X. 4, appellatives of the two genii.

[2] *Sukshiti* (=*hushiti*), Rv. II. 10. 8; X. 20. 10; V. 6. 8; VI. 2. 11.; I. 91. 21; IX. 108. 13.

[3] Rv. I. 40. 8; VII. 74. 6.

Fall to our lot, and together with power a good settlement rich in fields[1]?'

The loyal attachment to it is closely connected with the high regard entertained for the settlement. The nomad roves from one pasture-ground to another; whenever he finds fodder for his herds, he halts; when there is none left he carelessly advances further. The settlers on the other hand display their native feeling. They foster a noble love and reverence for the land already cultivated by their ancestors and inherited from them. It is an injustice and a shame to abandon them. This is doubtless implied in the words:

'May we be such as preserve their settlements, Not such as forsake them[2].'

Let us transfer ourselves to that period of time in which the Arian or Indo-Iranian tribes advanced gradually from their original home towards the south.

It is well known that even thus early agriculture was no longer foreign to the Indo-Germans. The breeding of cattle was, however, paramount. When, in their wanderings and migrations, the Arians took possession of the districts on the northern slope of Paropamisus, they naturally led a life at least half-nomadic. Though they were not continually in motion, still we may assume a constant change of pasture-lands in winter and summer.

The breeding of cattle amongst the nomads, however, is everywhere on a large scale, while the mode of agriculture

---

[1] Ys. XLVIII. 11 *hushiti*sh · *vastravaiti.* Cf. Vsp. IX. 5, the epithets *ashavat · vāstravat· marezhdikavat· hvāthravat* with *hadhi*sh. As here, again, *asha* stands near *vāstra*, it may be taken for 'corn, bread,' as in Vd. III. 3 (*vide OIK.* p. 235, note 2, and p. 408, note 1). *Hvāthra* is naturally to be separated into *hu-āthra*, and opposed to *duzhāthra.*

[2] Yt. X, 75 : *buyama · tē · shōithrō-pānō** *mā · buyama · shōithrō-irichō.* The glossographers add here the current ideas *mā · nmānō-irichō mā visō-irichō,* &c., which appear to be a gloss, even because *shōithra* stands first, what is certainly not conformable to the system.

Q 2

which they pursue is characteristic as wasting to the soil Wherever they repose with their herds a suitable piece of land is brought under the plough to produce the necessary supply of corn. The pasturage having been consumed and the single harvest got in, and the colder season returning the exhausted soil is abandoned and another district is visited.

The nomadic way of living presupposes in consequence a very extensive territory with a thin population. With the increase in the number of inhabitants, people are obliged to remain content with a more confined space. The change of pasture-lands according to the seasons is discontinued. In colder districts on mountains a kind of husbandry peculiar to them takes its place; cattle are fed in stables during winter, and driven over the mountain-pastures during summer.

The abode becomes a permanent one, and houses of a more solid kind are naturally constructed. They are built to last longer and are more adapted to the requirements of the climate. The soil occupied is worked with the utmost regard to its capabilities; a ruthless and exhausting mode of cultivation would merely harm him who pursued it. More attention is paid to agriculture because relatively it pays better than the breeding of cattle. At the same time agriculture becomes more imperative, since a change of the fields no longer takes place, and the management of the farm becomes also more rational and systematic. Slowly and gradually, and not by violent fits and starts, takes place the development by which the nomadic tribes are changed into a settled nation devoted to agriculture.

To this transitional stage the Arians had evidently arrived even before their separation. But arable soil is not to be found in abundance even in the Hindukush districts. I might therefore believe that it was actually the want of such a soil which induced the Indian tribes to emigrate through the Suleiman passes.

Of the Irānian tribes, several persisted in their nomadic way of living. But those whom we designate as the

Avesta people are, in the earliest epoch when we hear of them, already in that stage of transition.

Here we have in my opinion reached a point where a very important difference prevails between the Gāthā period and that of the later Avesta.

In the Gāthās the 'cow' is the peculiar centre of the economical life. Agriculture is by no means unknown, but it is far from occupying the same place as the breeding of horned cattle. The perfection of the latter indeed is probably also a characteristic mark of the transition from nomadic life to fixed settlements. The more easily moveable small cattle, such as sheep and goats, form the principal property of wandering herdsmen.

Ahura Mazda is in the Gāthās emphatically called the 'Fashioner of the Cow.' It is He who created her for the benefit of mankind. The divine spirits themselves take care that she may find sufficient pasture. Several epithets of honour are conceded to her[1]. Nay more, an entire hymn treats exclusively of the wrongs and oppressions which she endures at the hands of her enemies the nomads. The heavenly powers themselves consult how that evil may be checked, and promise to send Zarathushtra as a saviour and helper upon the earth[2].

It is erroneous to assume that the growth of agriculture led the nation to settle down in permanent dwellings. The development of agriculture on the contrary is frequently the result of a more fixed establishment, both of which, however, are in turn perfected by a more studied and rational cultivation of cattle-breeding, especially the breeding of neat-cattle.

This the poets of the Gāthās knew very well:

'She, the cow, gave us good settlements and prosperity
And estates, she that was longed for by the good;

---

[1] *Gēush · tashā*, epithet of Ahura, Ys. XXIX, 2; XXXI, 9; *yē · ahmāi · gām · rānyō-skeretīm · hēm-tasha*t 'who created for us the delight-bestowing cow,' Ys. XLVII, 2. Besides *rānyō-skereti*, chiefly *hudhāo* ' bestowing good things' occurs as an epithet of the cow, which epithet is also usual in the later Avesta.

[2] Ys. XXIX.

For her caused the plants to germinate according to
the holy order
Ahura Mazda from the beginning of the first world[1].'

And how at this time agriculture and the breeding of
neat-cattle mutually influenced each other is expressed in
the following stanza :

'But she, the cow, selected of those two the active
countryman for herself
As her pious lord, the guardian of the good mind.
But he who did not follow agriculture did not participate
in the good religion, though he attempted to deceive[2].'

So also the Gāthās. But on the other hand quite
a different picture is presented in the younger Avesta.
But here also the possession of herds is highly esteemed.
Mithra is called 'the bestower of herds[3].' The yazatas are
entreated for bullocks and horses, and their possession is
looked upon as a gift of grace from the heavenly powers[4].
But the 'cow' does not in the least figure so prominently
as in the epoch described by the Gāthās.

The economical development has continually and regularly advanced. Agriculture has undergone important
technical improvement. At this time it is no longer of
secondary consideration, but stands on the same level with
cattle breeding; in fact it even appears to surpass the latter
in value and importance[5]. That transition which began in

---

[1] Ys. XLVIII, 6. *Hā* at the beginning of the stanza refers
doubtlessly to *gavōi* of the precedent stanza ; *vaghēu*sh *managhō* -
berekhdhē refers to *hā*, and is probably nom. sing.

[2] Ys. XXXI, 10. In line 2, on account of the metre, it is required to read *fshcñghim* (Spiegel, Comm. II, 243), which has no
difficulties at all, because of the following *m*, and admits also of an
orderly construction. Cf. Roth, *Yaçna*, XXXI, pp. 8–9, 24–25.
One feels induced to translate *vaghēu*sh *managhō* here and in other
passages in the Gāthās directly by 'cattle.'

[3] *Vāthvō-dāo*. Yt. X, 65.

[4] Yt. X, 28. Cf. above, p. 176.

[5] This is clearly to be seen from Vd. III. 4–5, where agriculture
and cattle-breeding are mentioned together, and even agriculture
before cattle-breeding.

the Arian period and continued in the Gāthās, is now complete. The Avesta people have become a firmly-settled nation of agriculturists.

I must here again lay stress on the fact that in the Gāthās the opposition is really not between herdsmen and husbandmen, but frequently between the nomads and the settled population. To the latter did the proclaimer of the new religion address himself. Amongst them did the new religion first find acceptance.

'For that I ask Thee, give me the right answer,
    O Ahura:
How shall I maintain pure the doctrine
Which shall be proclaimed before the liberal prince
As the true supreme power and as the best doctrine
    by thy follower, O Mazda,
Who lives *amongst the settlers* with piety and good
    mind [1]?'

'O Zarathushtra, who is thy pious friend
    In thy great work? Who is it that wishes to an-
    nounce it?
It is he himself, Kavi Vishtāspa, the one armed for
    battle,
And those whom besides, O Mazda, Thou selectest
    from the settlers,
Those will I praise with the prayers (*māthras*) of the
    pious mind [2].'

With the spread of the new doctrine therefore the increase of settlements goes hand in hand. When a hitherto nomadic tribe becomes converted to the Zoroastrian religion, it abandons its former unsettled mode of living, builds permanent dwellings, and cultivates the fields:

'For that do I ask Thee, give me the correct answer,
    O Ahura!
That is, for the doctrine which is the best of all that
    exists,

---

[1] Ys. XLIV, 9.
[2] Ys. XLVI, 14. *Hadēma* is, of course, not to be separated into *ha* + *dēma*, but stands for *hadema* = Skr. *sadman*.

Which, when it is followed, multiplies for me piously
the settlements.
Together with the words and works of devotion may
He grant it to me rightly!
My soul's wishes crave for Thee, O Mazda[1].'
'For this end do I approach Thee, Blissful Spirit,
Ahura Mazda, Thou Commander through the good
mind.
Through Whose deeds the settlements are piously
increased;
To them does their devoted sense teach the precepts
Of Thy Spirit, Whom nobody can deceive[2]!'

The divine beings support man in his work of civilization.
Hence they bear the name 'increasing and furthering the
settlements[3].' Ahura Mazda takes care of the farm-houses[4]
and Srausha is called 'the protector of the settlements of
the pious[5].'

The conversion of a Tūrānian tribe to Zoroastrianism is
already noticed in the Gāthās. Through it the settled
dwellings of those who are of 'devoted sense' are increased[6].
The Fryānas thus relinquished their nomadic life and joined
the number of the settlers.

The adversaries of the Mazda religion are nomads. How
these maintained their position near the settled population
of Irān is explained by the condition of the soil.

Even at the present day in Afghānistān permanently
settled tribes that pursue agriculture dwell near and amongst
nomadic people. The Ghilzai, to whom the territory on
the Tarnak river belongs, are partly wandering herdsmen
and partly peasants[7].

---

[1] Ys. XLIV, 10 : *yā · mōi · gaęthāo · ashā · frādhōit · hachēmnā.*
[2] Ys. XLIII, 16 : *yēhyā · shkyaothanāish · gaęthāo · ashā · frā-dhentę.* The same formula see Ys. XIX, 17. Cf. Vsp. II, 5; III, 4, &c.
[3] *Frādhat-gaętha, varedhat-gaętha.*   [4] Ys. LV, 4.
[5] *Hishārō · ashahę · gaęthāo.* Ys. LVII, 17.
[6] Ys. XLVI, 12 ; cf. p. 31.
[7] Masson, *Narrative,* II, 205 ; Elphinstone, *Kabul,* II, 172–175 ; Spiegel, *E. A.* I, 321 seqq.

The Sturiānī were originally nomads. Only a little before Elphinstone's sojourn in Afghānistān had they adopted agriculture and fixed settlements. A strife with a neighbouring tribe had narrowed their territory, and this necessitated a more careful cultivation of the soil. The Shīrānī pursue agriculture ; their neighbours the Vazīrī wander round about with their herds. So too the Nassers. These pass every autumn in constant warfare through the dominion of their bitterest enemies, the Vazīrī, in order to search for pasture-grounds in warmer districts during winter. In spring they return by the same way and amid the same perils to the cooler mountain-heights[1].

That nomadic tribes also embraced Zoroastrianism is not quite impossible, but it is also by no means certain.

We know for a fact that the Mazdayasnān dwelt sometimes in tents which were subjected like other dwellings to purification enjoined by the Law. In the hut of an unbeliever the ceremonies of the Avesta would of course not be practised.

However, such could scarcely have been the case in more than a temporary way. Herdsmen who watched the cattle on their pasture-grounds may have lodged themselves in tents. It is also to be borne in mind that every dweller in a tent is not therefore a nomad. Many inhabitants of Afghānistān who pursue husbandry prefer the tent to a fixed habitation. This predilection appears to be a remnant of an earlier period, of a time in which the tent was indeed the sole homestead of the family.

What then was the usual form of settlement amongst the Avesta people?

As a rule the Mazdayasnān dwelt in *villages*. The village was composed of a certain number of dwellings, each of which harboured a family[2].

Thus it is said in a certain prayer : '*Into my house* may there come the contentment, blessing, guilelessness and appreciation of the pious men. May there now arise *for*

---

[1] Elphinstone, *Kabul*, II, 90–91, 97, 212 seqq. ; Spiegel, *E.A.* I, 309–310, 324.

[2] *Vīs* 'village '; *nmāna* 'a single habitation, farm.'

our village, piety and power, blessing and magnificence and happiness, and long-lasting dominion of the faith, which originates from Ahura and from Zarathushtra. Soon may there issue from our village cattle and corn (?) and the strength and adherence to Ahura, of the faithful men [1] !'

Into these villages the wolves secretly steal to seize their prey. The villagers stand under the special protection of the *manes*. The spirits of the departed ones also return to them annually at the season of *Hamaspatamaidhaya* [2].

By the last name are frequently designated the villages of the Mazdayasnân. They are visited by the hordes of hostile plundering tribes, who suddenly rush upon them to murder men, to drive away their cattle and to carry away into cruel imprisonment their wives and children [3]. They therefore pray to the good spirits that the villages may be lasting, good and peaceful settlements, chiefly that there may not befall them any scarcity of water and failure of crops, which might compel the inhabitant to quit his beloved homestead and to search for new dwellings [4].

Along with the village-system, there, however, also existed the *farm-like settlement.*

The reasons for different forms of habitations spring entirely from the natural conditions of the land, to which man adapts himself at all times and places with an instinct peculiar to himself for choosing that which is necessary and wholesome.

Extensive plains, be they low-lying grounds and deserts, or high plateaus, do not favour the foundation of fixed settlements. They are essentially the territory adapted to wandering tribes. Thus the nomadic mode of life and extensive cattle-breeding must have always prevailed on

---

[1] Ys. LX, 2–3. 'Corn ' = *ashem.*

[2] Vd. XIII, 11 and 40; Yt. XIII, 49.

[3] Vd. XVIII, 12 ; cf. p. 28 ; cf. *kulha · nasu*sh · *apayasānē · hacha · avanha*t · *vīsa*t · *ya*t · *mazdayasnōi*t, Vd. XIX, 12.

[4] Ys. LXVIII, 14 : *hushkiti rāmō-*sh*kiti* besides *dareghō-*sh*kiti.* Ys. XII, 2–3 : *us · māzdayęsninām · vīsam · zyānayaęchā · vīvā-patcha* (mod. Pers. *biyāb*) . . . *nōi*t · *ahmā*t · *āzyāonim · nōi*t · *vīvāpem khsh*l*ā māzdayasnī*sh *avi vīsō.*

the rather sterile elevated plains in the south of Afghānistān and on the steppes of the Caspian and Aral Seas.

Mountains, which of themselves render the free movement of larger masses of men and animals difficult, are usually the first cause of permanent dwellings. Even wild rugged mountain-districts appear at a very early period to have been inhabited by settled populations to as great a height as the climate would allow men to dwell in, the higher parts, however, being still available for pasture [1].

The expansion of the settlement is of course entirely dependent upon the condition of the soil. Larger settlements can spring up only where continuous pieces of fertile land are found. If the cultivable soil consists on the contrary of broken and isolated pieces of smaller extent, interrupted by steppes or barriers of rock incapable of cultivation, the tendency to separate and establish independent farms and hamlets will predominate [2].

Finally, another consideration has likewise a mighty influence upon the security of life and property.

In an open country which is exposed to hostile inroads, people are always obliged to unite in one large community in order to enable themselves to make a successful resistance against their enemies. This is particularly the case where a nation of agriculturists have as near neighbours nomadic tribes who are indeed their natural and most dangerous enemies [3].

In mountainous countries, where nature itself offers the means of protection, the settler enjoys greater freedom. Here he can separate himself from his relatives and companions, and look for pasture and arable land according to his own taste. He can live as a free lord upon his farm independent of neighbours, unhampered by the restrictions necessary in a large community.

---

[1] Andrian, ' *Ueber den Einfluss der verticalen Gliederung der Erdoberfläche auf menschliche Ansiedlungen,*' in the transactions of the Anthropological Society of Vienna, vol. vi, 1876, pp. 2–6.

[2] Inama-Sternegg, *Untersuchungen über das Hofsystem im Mittelalter,* p. 7 seqq.; Roscher, *Nationalökonomik,* § 75.

[3] Andrian, l. c. p. 12.

These universal laws affect the most diverse nations of all ages and countries, and may be likewise applied to the condition of settlement of the Avesta people.

Under what circumstances larger communities are found is clearly seen when we fix our eyes upon the present boroughs of Eastern Irān. These are generally situated on the banks of rivers, where they pass from the projecting mountains into the plains or from fertile *oases* into the flat land. Here are combined the two requisites which chiefly render possible the rise of larger settlements.

On the one hand, the best arable land is really found at the foot of the mountains near the rivers and of sufficient extent to maintain a very large number of people. On the other hand, the edge of the plains is naturally most exposed to the pillaging inroads of the nomads. In fact, the large river valleys serve as roads through which to penetrate deeper into the mountains.

Andkhūi, Shibarghān, and more particularly Merv are towns which owe their existence to *oases*. The tracts between the flat land and the mountains are held by Kunduz, Khulm, Balkh and Sarakhsh. Siripūl, Maimane and Herāt lie in broad and easily accessible river-valleys, and indeed just in the parts where the valleys begin to narrow.

In the south, Farā, Girishk, Kandahār exhibit quite the same natural features. The last-mentioned town especially is founded with an exceedingly skilful adaptation to the nature of the ground. It lies on a plateau which is formed by the last projections of the mountain-range. On the west and the east it is sheltered by the Arghandāb and Tarnak, which unite below the town. The plain is thus on all sides naturally protected by these rivers, while the mountains rise in its rear.

Gazni and Kabul were probably built partly for strategical reasons and partly on account of the richness of the surrounding country in arable and pasture land.

In all these places native legends maintain the high antiquity of the towns.

Balkh is regarded as a populous and fortified town even

in the legends of Ninos and Semiramis, and is called the 'mother of towns' by the natives [1]. The foundation of Merv is ascribed to Tahmūrāth, the *Takhma-Urupish* of the Avesta [2]. Kandahār is said to have been built under Lohrāsp, called Arvat-aspa in the Avesta [3]. On both sides of Girishk, ruins of great antiquity are found on either bank of the Hilmend. These are the remnants of an important town, which, according to the belief of the native inhabitants, flourished in the time of Alexander [4]. To the pre-Macedonian period must also belong the golden age of the ancient Farā; however, we do not know how far back in ancient times we are entitled to place it [5].

In conclusion, I have yet to mention the numerous and extensive ruins scattered over the plains of Seïstan. They contain the remains of towns, castles and other buildings, whose erection is ascribed by native tradition to the sovereigns of the legendary dynasty of the Kayānians. The want of security against the pillaging Baluchees even now forces the inhabitants on the delta of the Hilmend to unite themselves into larger settlements.

On the rugged and rocky heights of the Hindukush and in the Alpine regions on the upper Oxus regular towns could not be erected. Here the natural circumstances are favourable to the establishment of smaller villages and hamlets, and even of single farms. Arable land is here found only in small fragments, which do not allow a large number of people to live together. The variegated character of the soil furthered the segregation of the inhabitants. The natural security of the country permitted the separation into small groups or into single families.

The existence of the farm-settlement along with the village-settlement can be proved also from the Avesta.

---

[1] Burnes, *Bokhara*, II, 204; Ferrier, *Voyages*, I, 389 seqq.; Vámbéry, *Reise in Mittelasien*, 206.

[2] Burnes, *Bokhara*, III, 30 seqq.

[3] Ferrier, *Voyages*, II, 132, note 1.

[4] Ibid. II, 120.

[5] Ibid. II, 278—279.

The Vendidād, referring to the provisional places for the disposal of the dead body called *Kata*, contains the definite command that such *Katas* should be built *in each village* and *in each house*[1]. Certainly it cannot be meant thereby that the whole community, and moreover each individual family, should have *Katas* of their own. That would be palpably absurd. The commandment is only intelligible if we take into consideration the co-existing forms of settlement.

Where people dwell there must be *Katas*, even in each separate farm-house, where it may prove necessary in the event of death taking place. For a village the building of one set of *Katas* is, however, sufficient. There they are evidently the property of the community, ready for use whenever a death occurs in a family residing in the village.

The Avesta people were not without enemies. Their exposed settlements were subject to sudden inroads of the nomads of the steppes, without taking into consideration that in threatened districts, where a larger number of people united themselves, measures had to be taken to ward off such dangers.

On convenient sites were built castles, which in time of war gave shelter to the women, children and herds, or else the village was surrounded with a wall and entrenchments. The way in which people secure themselves to this day in Khorāsān against the attacks of the Turkomans is similarly characteristic. Everywhere, even in the immediate neigh-

---

[1] Vd. V, 10; cf. p. 94. Also in Vd. VIII, 103 I recognize an allusion to the system of villages and farms; in that passage the last two words of *nazdishtem · avi · nmānemcha · visemcha · zaṅtumcha · dahyūmcha* are to be erased as glossarial additions; for it is non-sense to say that a man who has become impure, should run to the next district, or even to the next province and ask, with a loud voice, for the performance of the purificatory rite; whereas it is proper that this should be done at the first village or farm where he arrives. The wish to place together those four current expressions caused the awkward interpolation. Analogous passages are Ys. IX, 28 and Yt. X, 75; but I believe that, on a particular examination, still more passages would be found.

bourhood of the villages, towers are built on the fields. When the dreaded horsemen appear, the people who are on the open fields escape into the nearest tower, and maintain themselves there until either help arrives or the Turkomans withdraw.

As in the Avesta we have no direct evidence of any of the modes of defence mentioned above, we must confine ourselves to general observations [1].

Fortified places that stand vacant in time of peace and are occupied on the outbreak of a war, only fulfil their object to a certain extent. They are suitable where a regular war occurs, the outbreak of which may be calculated on with some certainty. Near the edge of a desert where war is more or less incessant, and where people have to be on their guard against sudden attacks every day and every hour, such fortified places serve no purpose. How could it have been possible on the alarm of a very sudden and wholly unforeseen invasion actually to convey women and children into the castles, and to collect the herds and drive them behind protecting walls?

Against such dangers there is indeed no absolute security. In addition to the union of a large number of warlike men, which inspired the barbarians with respect, the practice of always maintaining permanent dwellings in a fit state for defensive warfare offered the best protection. Whoever was surprised in the open country by robbers was infallibly lost. Only the lives and property of those who were sheltered behind walls were safe.

It is my opinion, therefore, that even in the most remote period *fortified* places were founded where the present Eastern Irānian towns are situated. The development of the town from the fortified village is quite normal.

---

[1] Very difficult is the passage Yt. V, 130, and therefore little fit for proving the fact; one might possibly thus translate it : ' I will set up a fence (*vāreman*) in the plains (*upa staremaęshu*), which protects all that belongs to livelihood (*hujyāitīm*), and makes to increase the power when it is necessary to withdraw' (*sazāitē*, dat. sg. of the pres. part. of rt. *sā* ?).

I might even consider it as by no means improbable that
the beginnings of the town-like settlements go back even
to the age of the Avesta.

The point to be most considered here is, what we should
understand by a 'town.' Towns where houses are ranged
one close to the other in regular streets, where the profession
of the tradesman is held in the same honour as that of
the agriculturists, yea, even surpasses the latter, and where
commerce and mercantile pursuits flourish; such were
unknown to the Avesta people.

In the case of the Avesta people the characteristics of
the village and of the town are so fundamentally different,
that a particular name for the latter could not but be
wanting in the Avesta language. Trade, besides, does not
play in the Avesta nearly such an important part as
cattle-breeding and agriculture. The entire life, as it is
pictured to us, is the life of herdsmen and peasants. Commerce seems to have been completely unknown, and the
conditions of intercourse, the exchange of products, purchase
and sale, were evidently quite primitive.

If, on the other hand, we define the town as an enclosed
and fortified settlement, constantly inhabited in all its parts,
of larger extent and with more numerous inhabitants, the
existence of town-like settlements amongst the Avesta people
is at least probable. In that case the fortified village and
the town properly so-called differ only with respect to their
dimensions.

The large village ranks just below the town. Through
the accession of fresh communities and the constant growth
of population, circumstances are generally brought about,
under which a real town life first develops itself.

The preliminary conditions for the formation of town-like
settlements were offered, if anywhere, in Eastern Irān. The
economical possibility of maintaining a larger number of
people is limited to certain countries. But just where it
exists, the insecurity of life and property combines to make
the union into extensive communities necessary.

Here I refer also to the condition of settlements amongst
the kindred tribes.

The practice of dwelling in open villages and boroughs was by no means so exclusively an Indo-Germanic custom as it is generally supposed to be. In every place where historical circumstances or the special aspect of the soil are conducive to it, people even at very early periods are led to the foundation of enclosed and fortified towns [1].

The Italici had already passed the stage of village life, while they still dwelt in the valley of the Po. Their settlements discovered there are without exception surrounded by trenches and walls of earth. They exhibit a systematical design in the form of a rectangle, and cover an area of three or four, nay, even of ten hectares [2].

The Germans, too, who still manifest in general a distinct inclination towards independence and separation into their settlements, abandoned the farm or village settlement even where the external condition made it desirable. The large settlements of the Quades on the March and the Danube are, therefore, characteristic. For instance, the village in the province of Braunsberg, which is surrounded with a large circular wall, covers an area of thirteen hectares, the space occupied by dwellings, the place of arms in Stillfried on the March, even extend over twenty-five hectares.

Such places, however, did not merely serve for refuge during war. On the contrary, discoveries made in them prove that they were also fully and constantly inhabited in times of peace [3].

The Gorodists of Southern Russia may also not have been mere castles to be used in case of war. The discoveries made within the circuit of the walls compel us rather to assume that those were constantly inhabited [4].

---

[1] With the following cf. Pöhlmann, *Die Anfänge Roms*, p. 29 seq.,

[2] Helbig, *Beitrag zur altitalischen Kultur- und Kunstgeschichte*, *I*, *Die Italiker in der Poebene.*

[3] Much, *Transactions of the Anthropological Society of Vienna*, V, 39 seq. ; cf. Inama-Sternegg, *Deutsche Wirthschaftsgeschichte*, I, 6–7.

[4] *Revue des deux mondes* of 1874, p. 795; Pöhlmann, *Die Anfänge Roms*, pp. 35–36; but see Zimmer, *AIL.* pp. 146–147.

As regards their dimension, it is true, they are considerably inferior to the enclosed villages of the plains of the Po, or to the settlements of the Jurades.

Finally, I come to the nation which is most closely akin to the Irānians—to the Vedic Indians. Here we have a very clear instance of how the geographical and historical conditions severally affect the form of settlement. I place myself without any hesitation on the side of Zimmer, who denies the existence of urban settlements among the Arians of the Rig-veda.

'Nowhere do we meet with any certainty with the name of a town in the hymns of the Rig-veda. The people dwelt rather in villages, hamlets (*grāma*), which were mostly completely open. . . . The *pur* served as a defence against the attacks of enemies as well as against inundations; they were, as far as we can perceive, situated on elevated points, and were protected by mounds and entrenchments, within which people took refuge with their wives and chattels in the time of danger. They may have been particularly abundant on the shores of rivers, for there the most obstinate battles were fought, according to the testimony of the Vedic hymns[1].'

Now nothing would be more improper than to transfer such conditions from the old Indians to the Irānians. Even subdivisions of the same people often display according to circumstances a great difference in their settlements. The Slavi lived, partly in entirely unfortified abodes, partly in regular and enclosed settlements[2]. The testimony of Tacitus regarding the division of the Germans into single farms and unfortified hamlets is by no means applicable to all tribes and districts. Italican peasants in the Apennines lived, even in the Imperial age, in small boroughs, whilst the Italici of the prehistoric period had already become builders of towns.

---

[1] Zimmer, *AIL.* pp. 147–148.

[2] Thus, according to Prokop's descriptions, the advancing and therefore nearly nomadizing Slavi on the Danube. *Vide* Pöhlmann, *Die Anfänge Roms*, p. 35.

Thus the Vedic Indians and the Irānians of the Avesta, owing to the great difference in the nature of the countries in which they lived and of the historical circumstances which influenced them, may have and must have gone different ways.

We know how the nature of their soil must of itself have led the Irānians to the building of larger and enclosed settlements.   To a great extent this was not the case with the Indians.   The Indus valley and the Panjāb display, by far, greater uniformity in the aspect of the soil.   It is a flat and open land which, of itself, conduces more to the splitting up and scattering of the people.

The chief point of difference is, however, quite another one.   An urban settlement certainly presupposes a longer establishment in the land.   This is applicable to the Avesta nation who, so far as our information goes, dwelt in the districts north and south of Paropamisus.

With the Indians the case was entirely otherwise.   The Rig-veda does not at all represent them to us permanently settled.   The Arian people of that age are, on the contrary, continually moving.   They advance slowly, from west to east, drawing near to the banks of the Ganges.   One river-line after another of the Panjāb becomes occupied ; the aborigines are more and more forced backward or driven into the mountains.

Under such circumstances a town-like settlement could evidently not develop itself.   For the security of property the building of castles was sufficient.   A circumvallation of the village was required only in isolated localities.

The troops marching at the head of the migrating Arian nations were engaged in constant and bloody wars with the Dāsa, and lived probably in a sort of military camp.   The tribes living further back enjoyed a relative security, which was only disturbed by actual feuds between the Arians themselves.

Of such sudden invasions as the Irānians had to expect, the Rig-veda says nothing, to my knowledge.   They were certainly not so common and not the usual form in which war was waged.   The preparations which people made against the impending dangers from enemies, must consequently have been entirely different in India from what they were in Irān.

Indeed, the settlements of the Arians of the Avesta and of the Rig-veda developed under totally different conditions. Accordingly the result must have been entirely different with the respective nations in spite of their close relationship, and notwithstanding all other uniformity of custom and culture.

In conclusion, I come to the question whether the founders and inhabitants of a village were bound together by relationship, or whether they had united themselves in settlements for any other causes, that is, whether the Eastern Irānian village was the village of kindred races or not.

The following explanation respecting the development of a village would appear to be the most probable one. Every individual man selected at pleasure his piece of ground, on which he settled himself with his family. The sons, when they were grown up and established their own homesteads, built their dwellings near that of their father. Around their farms followed afterwards those of grandsons and great-grandsons. The field was cultivated as a common property and its revenue divided [1].

Moreover, I consider this primitive development of the village of a family out of the single farmhouse as in many cases possible. That farm-like settlements were known amongst the Avesta people is not to be doubted. That the descendants of a head of a family settled in the immediate neighbourhood of the family mansion, rather than remove

---

[1] In that manner the Bohemian village is said, by Palacky, to be originated: 'According to him (Palacky), the Bohemian built his house in the midst of his landed property. His descendants managed the paternal estate, often during several generations, in common, and without dividing it; if the paternal house was not more capable of holding their increased number, other houses were built in the proximity, and this was the origin of the most ancient Bohemian villages that were as many in number as small in extent, since all their inhabitants originally formed but one only family.' Pöhlmann, *Die Anfänge Roms*, p. 51.

themselves to a distance from it, altogether corresponds with the old Irānian spirit.

Amongst the Parsees in Bombay a most highly remarkable custom exists even at the present day, in which the inclination towards the closest possible union of the respective families is strikingly manifest. Here the sons are not wont, even when they are grown up and married, to set up really independent households. So long as there is any room, they dwell, together with the other relatives of their father's family, in the house of their parents. Even if a man has six or seven sons, they all live, with their wives and children, with the head of their family[1]. We may also add that when any scarcity of room occurs and a new dwelling has to be occupied, the latter is looked for in the closest possible vicinity of the father's house.

The Tājiks also in Badakhshān live together in kindred families, and we may imagine that such is the case with the rest of the Galchas, of whose manner of life and customs we do not, unfortunately, possess any account.

In the whole of Badakhshān the villages, called *Kishlak*, exhibit the same design[2]. They are divided into several

---

[1] Dosabhoy Framjee, *The Parsees*, p. 87.

[2] I give here a very interesting passage of Wood's *Journey to the Source of the River Oxus;* it is a very clear description of a Tājīk village in Jerm; the description may also be regarded as a kind of addition to p. 52:

'It is customary in these countries for relations to live in the same hamlet, often to the number of six or eight families. An outer wall surrounds this little knot of friends, within which each family has its separate dwelling-house, stable, and cattle-shed; and a number of such hamlets form a kishlak, or village. . . . The style of building does not differ throughout the country, and our quarters at Term may be taken as a fair specimen of them all. The site is the slope of a hill, and a rivulet is usually not many paces from the door. Its course is here and there impeded by large whitened boulders, glassy-smooth from the constant action of running water; while its banks are shaded by a few gnarled walnut-trees, and the lawn adjoining planted in regular lines with the mulberry. Down in the bottom of the valley, where the rivulet falls into the larger

quarters or hamlets, each of which is surrounded by a wall. In such a hamlet dwell families connected by blood, often six to eight in number. Each of them has its separate division, enclosed again by a wall within the hamlet itself, with its own dwelling and rooms for the household.

---

stream, lie the scanty corn-lands of the little community. The mountains rise immediately behind the village, and their distant summits retain their snowy coverings throughout the greater portion of the year. An enclosure is formed by running a dry-stone wall round a space proportioned to the size and wealth of the family. The space thus enclosed is divided into compartments, the best of which form the dwelling-houses, whilst the others hold the stock. These latter compartments are usually sunk two feet under-ground, while the floors of the rooms for the family are elevated a foot or more above it : flat roofs extend over the whole. In the dwelling-house the smoke escapes by a hole in the middle of the roof, to which is fitted a wooden frame, to stop up the aperture when snow is falling. The rafters are lathed above and then covered with a thick coat of mud. If the room be large, its roof is supported by four stout pillars, forming a square, in the middle of the apartment, within which the floor is considerably lower than in the other parts, and the benches thus formed are either strewed with straw or carpeted with felts, and form the seats and bed-places of the family. The walls of the house are of considerable thickness : they are smoothly plastered inside with mud, and have a similar though rougher coating without. Where the slope of the hill is considerable, the enclosing wall is omitted and the upper row of houses are then over the roofs of the lower. Niches are left in the sides of the wall, and in these are placed many of the household utensils. The custom of relations grouping together has its advantages, but they are not unmixed. Many of the sorrows of the poor are thus alleviated by the kindness of friends : the closeness of their intercourse adds to their mutual sympathy; and when death occurs, the consolation which the afflicted survivors receive from those near around them is great indeed. But to the newly married couple the benefits derived from this arrangement are frequently very dearly purchased; and the temper of the poor bride, it is to be feared, is often permanently damaged by the trials she has to undergo at the hands of a cross-grained mother-in-law. . . . Small as is the population in many of the valleys or narrow mountain glens, it is yet too great for the limited extent of their cornlands.'

Anyhow, in my opinion, the foundation of single farms was at least an exception.   As a *primitive* form of settlement they occurred in Eastern Irān, at all events, as seldom as in other countries and with other peoples ; and especially for this reason, that the settlers, at least as I believe, had first to conquer the land from hostile aborigines, against whom they could naturally defend themselves only when in sufficient number.   Indeed, in low stages of civilization the dwelling together in a village offers eminent advantages. With the first seizing of a country the settlement is, therefore, everywhere by far more frequent than farm-like dwellings[1].

Eastern Irān was, without doubt, partly at least, already conquered by the Indo-Irānian tribes.   The first settlements go back to the Arian period, and cannot therefore be conveniently designated as properly Irānian.   But again, after the secession of the tribes, afterwards known as Indian, the Irānians, who remained, were by no means in a settled state. The battles with the aborigines continued also down to the Irānian period.   In the spread of civilization there was no standing still.   In the West particularly, cultivation was pushed more and more forward, and fresh soil was won.   It is also certain that special Irānian families, as first settlers, often took considerable quantities of land into their possession, and a large number of primitive settlements owed them their origin.

When we have thus traced the rise of village communities from one another, the following question suggests itself as to the character of the Eastern Irānian village : Did the Irānians migrate in search of land in miscellaneous crowds and thus found settlements? or, had they already grouped themselves according to relationship and in tribes ?

That the latter was the case is proved to a certainty. The word *vis*[2] does not designate the village locally only,

---

[1] Roscher, *Nationalökonomik*, p. 252 seq. ; Pöhlmann, *Die Anfänge Roms*, p. 52.

[2] To the Av. *vis* corresponds Skr. *viç* ; here it is important for the relation between the Irānian and Indian settlements that

but at the same time also genealogically the race composed of several families. It is only in the original actual combination of both these ideas, when every race built and inhabited their own village, that the double meaning of the single word *vis* is intelligible.

Often enough, indeed, this state of things was only the ideal and not the actual one. The principle of relationship was obscured by purely accidental or local circumstances. It also happened that smaller tribes, not originally related, united themselves into a common settlement, or that neighbouring, though not kindred clans, were formed into a large community for practical reasons.

But even such communities were evidently organized very much according to the old bonds of tribe [1]. The village of a clan formed the model according to which the new settlement was arranged and managed. The inhabitants of a village, founded by two or more families, then form only a single clan, under common direction, under *one* head. If such were not the case, it would be impossible that the two-fold signification of *vis* could have been preserved fresh throughout the entire literature of the Avesta.

The conditions of settlement of the Avesta people are therefore very various; they are altogether adapted to the nature of the land in which those people dwelt. The village and farm systems existed side by side. Single farms were more rare and were found chiefly in mountain-valleys.

Villages were founded more frequently, and, indeed

---

viç signifies in the Rig-veda ' house, family, race,' whilst ' village ' is designated by *grāma*. Obviously the Indian village was principally a local bond, or at least, the identity of village and family is not more so manifest as among the Avesta people.

[1] It seems to follow from the inscription of Behistan, I, 65, that also in Western Irān the village of a clan was ordinary; there we must translate *gaithāmchā · mānijāmchā · v'ithibishchā* apparently by 'the settlements and houses according to the races.' The Medes and Persians had, therefore, settled according to races or clans; several related families formed the community of the village. Cf. Spiegel, *Altpersische Keilinschriften*, pp. 8–9.

naturally, in more open and more fruitful districts. As such places were particularly found on the *transition rocks* in the deserts, and exposed to the pillaging incursions of the nomadic tribes, the villages were surrounded with walls and trenches.

In the positions where the Afghān towns are now situated, the conditions favourable to the rise of more extensive settlements exist to a certain extent. Here there were probably already in the Avesta epoch, fortified villages of such a dimension, that we may justly speak of them as the first step towards the formation of urban settlements.

As a primitive form of settlement the village was more common than the single farm. The villages were villages of races ; their inhabitants were bound together by ties of relationship. But it must be admitted that from the original single farm-house also, sometimes through the gradual growth of the family, the race-village has been developed.

END OF VOL. I.